Behind Closed Doors

The Boardroom

How to Get In, Get On and Make A Difference

Reviews

Baroness (Virginia) Bottomley, Chair of Board Practice at Odgers Berndtson;

"It is high time an accessible comprehensive volume on being a Board Director was published, particularly from the UK plc perspective. 'Behind Closed Doors' is a tremendous achievement and a first rate guide to the boardroom. Simon Laffin has over 25 years' experience on UK company boards, as an executive director, non-executive director and chairman. In that time, he has seen the good, the bad and the ugly in terms of board dynamics and effectiveness. His experience, warts and all, is now condensed in his book, 'Behind Closed Doors', which I am delighted to recommend.

Simon's book addresses some of the technical elements of the board of directors' role – for example, how to evaluate and mitigate risk, told in an accessible and easy-to-understand manner. But equally, he addresses some of the 'soft' factors that are central to whether a board succeeds or fails. Ultimately, boards of directors are teams of people. Board behaviours, culture and ethos are subtle to grasp and vary with businesses. This book provides an excellent means to navigate some of the subtleties and threats to a cohesive board. Bringing that group together, smoothing individual idiosyncrasies and managing egos, so that the board is truly more powerful than the sum of its parts is ultimately more art than science. Simon, a practitioner with years' of experience, explores those arts in detail.

'Behind Closed Doors' is an invaluable companion for both those embarking on their own board journey, and indeed those like me who are well down the path."

Bob Cowell, Co-founder Makinson Cowell;

"Simon has certainly blown the Boardroom door wide open with a book that combines great storytelling with unique perspectives on key protocols that make for an effective Board. This is not some theoretical treatise written by an academic or management consultant, but a book full of practical advice from someone with many years of listed company experience [and scars to prove it]. Both existing and aspirant directors will learn from this book [with Simon's observations on risk management the standout chapter for me]."

Michael Jary, former Managing Partner OC&C Strategy Consultants. Chair Duchy Originals, Chair Fairtrade Foundation, and non-executive director Barclays Bank UK plc;

"A desperately important book for anyone who's wondered what boards actually do. Behind Closed Doors is written from Laffin's broad experience as a board director and chair, and with deep insight and reflection on the challenges of the role. Throughout, tips are practical and the author's personal anecdotes are relevant and even entertaining. I would recommend this book to anyone interested in serving on a company board – or indeed for anyone currently in that role and wondering how they can do better!"

Dr Maria Z Kempinska MBE, founder of Jongleurs;

"I never thought I would pick up a business book at 6.30am and be so engrossed that I would not be able to put it down. But Behind Closed Doors is the book every woman and everyone in business must read. It is the territory to a destination many people want to reach."

Liz McMeiken, FTSE 250 senior independent director and RemCo chair;

"I most definitely recommend 'Behind Closed Doors'. It's a must read for those embarking on a journey into this new and somewhat *opaque world of the boardroom. It's interesting, useful and, moreover, an enjoyable read, as well as being practical and accessible. It will appeal not only to aspiring directors, but also to experienced ones like me. I learned a lot reading it, and only wish that it had been available in my early days on a board."*

William Rucker, Chairman Lazard UK;

"For a new board director or somebody thinking *about a board seat, Simon's book provides a really practical and insightful guide to what really matters. A must read for any first time board member"*

Roland Rudd, Chairman Finsbury Glover Hering;

"Simon brings his formidable experience to bear in this must-read for anyone interested in how boardrooms have worked and how they should work."

David Webster, former Chairman of Intercontinental Hotels Group and Safeway;

"Few directors can have had such wide ranging and testing challenges as Simon Laffin both at Chairman level as well as non-executive director. His book draws fully on those rich and often uncomfortable experiences which gives the book a welcome degree of authenticity. Simon has written a highly readable, well-constructed and thoughtful guide for all prospective as well as existing board directors. As someone who first became a non-exec almost thirty years ago, in 1992, and still serving, I only wish that its equivalent had been available to me back then. It will I believe attract an appreciative readership."

Mark Young, Joint Head of Corporate Broking, Stifel Nicolaus Europe;

"This well-crafted book is as enjoyable to read as it is informative. If you sit on a Board, read it. If you hope to sit on a Board, read it. If you advise Boards, read it."

Dedication

For Diana, Beth, Ed & Will,
who supported me through all of this learning.

This book is dedicated to all those who serve on boards or who aspire
to join a board. It is a great privilege and honour to be a director.

In spite of the difficult times,
serving should also be a source of great pleasure and satisfaction.

Acknowledgements

I would like to thank my daughter, Beth Laffin, for her patient reading, wise advice, tough editing and great encouragement, as this book transformed from an idea into a finished manuscript. Thanks also to my wife, Diana, and my family. Finally, Taryn Johnston, of FCM Publishing, who believed in the book and gave great support and advice.

There are too many people to list everyone who has helped me over the years, but I thank you all, from the teachers who encouraged me, to the colleagues who educated and put up with me, to the friends and commentators who pointed out my many mistakes.

Table of Contents

Introduction

I gave a nervous laugh. The head-hunter had just suggested that I could start my non-executive director (non-exec) career by joining Northern Rock. Why would I want to join the board of the first British bank for over a hundred years to suffer a run? It was October 2007, a few weeks after Northern Rock had suffered the first run on a UK bank for 150 years. Struck by an uncharacteristic sense of adventure, I agreed to the offer, and became chairman of the audit committee. In the next year, we handled a number of bids for the company, got sued by angry shareholders, took a government bail-out, got nationalised and then gradually rebuilt a business model. I had indeed been blooded in my new life as a non-executive director.

I'd been an executive director for the previous sixteen years, but becoming a non-executive was a revelation, as it put me on the other side of the boardroom table. I realised how little I really knew about the whole picture of being a board director. There is little training to be a company director, even though it is one of the most complex, finely balanced and fascinating jobs there is.

My executive career included being Finance Director of FTSE100 retailer, Safeway, through ten adventurous years; a failed merger with ASDA, four competition and merger inquiries, two chairmen and two CEOs, several strategic reviews, and a completed merger with Morrisons in 2004. I had also taken four months away from the boardroom to be a store manager. On the other side of corporate life, I then worked with CVC Capital Partners in private equity, on bids for companies from USA to China to Australia, via most European countries.

Seizing my first opportunity to branch into being a non-exec director, I suddenly found myself on the Northern Rock board, less than a month after the global banking crisis led to its much publicised downfall. At that moment, in spite of all my experience, I was in a different position, one for which I was initially ill equipped. Non-executive directors particularly seem to be expected to pick it up as they go along. Since then, I have gone on to be chairman of Assura plc and Flybe Group plc, as well as a non-executive at four other UK companies, and one Japanese-listed global media group. My boards have often found themselves in controversial situations; three completed take-overs, one successful defence, one IPO, two major public shareholder battles, several boardroom disputes, one nationalisation, and numerous other company crises.

I am not claiming to be an exemplar, or even a particularly good, company director (that is for others to judge, not me). Many of the errors and mistakes I have made appear in this book. However, I am passionate about passing on the lessons that I have learnt, and others have taught me, over my board career. It is now more urgent than ever that directors, and indeed anybody who is interested in boards, understand more about what happens behind the closed doors of a boardroom. Companies have a huge responsibility to society, and directors have that responsibility in their hands. Outsiders, however, also ought to try to understand what is happening inside boardrooms, so that they can study, analyse, commentate on, and regulate what is happening behind those closed doors.

And the business world is changing fast.

Boards are being held to ever higher standards and can be judged instantaneously

The rules of running a business have changed almost unrecognisably in the last 30 years, and I'm not just talking about the introduction of the Corporate Governance Code in 1992. Where once the board was a remote set of besuited grey-haired wise men (remember the bank board in Mary Poppins?), now a board can be held up to the highest public scrutiny by investors. Directors can be mercilessly mocked and shamed by social media, grilled by Parliamentary Select Committees, boardroom disputes laid bare, and even their private lives becoming the subject of gossip and leaked mass internal apology emails. All this at literally the speed of light. Boardroom meetings are being interrupted by breaking news on social media[1].

There is no place on boards to hide anymore

The demand for higher standards is overdue. A business is better for being run transparently by CEOs, boards, executive and non-executive directors, who are openly accountable to investors, customers, employees, and social media. The day that Tony Hayward, boss of BP, reacted to the media storm over the Gulf oil spill in 2010 by telling Reuters "*I want my life back*" was a turning point in corporate relations. Jeff Fairburn's job as CEO at Persimmon was doomed the day that he not only accepted a £75m bonus in 2018, but then walked out of a TV interview telling the journalist that it was "*really unfortunate*" that he'd been asked about it.

---

[1] For example, the fastest source of information for an airline about a problem in an aircraft is social media. A video showing a fire in an engine – even inflight – is likely to be on Twitter before the pilot has spoken to the operations team and they have communicated this to the directors. When Flybe had an undercarriage failure at Schiphol, the first message I had, as chairman, was that we had had a problem and I should look on Twitter, as the best source of information at that time was a video, which showed the landing and subsequent collapse.

Businesses and boards now live in a greenhouse, and when the sun illuminates the interior, it can get very bright and very hot in there.

The demands on board directors are higher than ever

This means that it is more important than ever that directors understand how to react to challenging situations, how to understand what is being presented, how to use the board and committees to make good decisions and how to evaluate and make good decisions.

The rules of the game are changing all the time. The environmental, social and governance agenda (ESG) may be being pushed by regulators and lobbyists, but increasingly, the enforcement of these new rules is being driven by social media, journalists and politicians, using public pressure and shaming. Tesco felt it had to 'voluntarily' return over £500m pandemic business rates relief in 2020, following a media storm about (perfectly legally) taking government money despite actually trading better through the lockdown.

Directors need more help and more training

Directors need both ability and experience. If someone doesn't have an open and flexible mind, capable of understanding complex issues, they will not make a good board director. It's not a job for everybody. But directors also need a good understanding of their company, the market, the governance and workings of a board, and of their fiduciary responsibilities. Much of this comes from experience and learning from colleagues. There are development programmes available, but they often focus on law and governance, and are often not taught by practising directors.

This book captures my 30 years of experience of serving on boards and facing real situations and crises, precisely to give the reader a crash course in the issues and how to tackle them.

One of the themes of this book is that we need to go beyond governance. Basic rules are very important, and the Corporate Governance Code is actually a pretty good set of standards. But raising the bar for boards needs much more than this. Personal relationships and communication are more important than box-ticking compliance. Directors who keep asking questions, and don't give up, are a better mainstay of successful boards than all the boilerplate disclosures in annual reports.

Boards are still dominated by white men

This entry-requirement for *earned* experience holds back underrepresented sections, females and ethnic minorities, as, by definition, they have less experience. This is one reason why boards are still predominantly pale, male and, sometimes, stale. This book will greatly help those who as yet lack actual director experience, to understand board issues and how boards work. This volume should give you the confidence to face an interview with a nomination committee, secure in the knowledge that you may not yet have experienced sitting on a board, but you will have a good idea of what to expect. In that sense, you, the reader can get some *learned* experience.

Good practice for boards goes beyond good corporate governance

It is no longer enough to learn about the Corporate Governance Code, the Companies Act 2006, the latest dry, nannying and worthy FRC pronouncement, or yet another board governance textbook. It's about understanding how things actually work, learning how to avoid the many pitfalls and knowing what questions to ask when. There isn't any hiding place anymore for directors, even for non-execs. Directors need to understand not just the rules, but how to participate in and use boards and committees to make good decisions. It's like seamanship[2], skills, techniques and knowledge needed to navigate the sea. This book

---

[2]The term 'seamanship' goes back a long way, so it refers to man. 'Seapersonship' would be more politically correct, but would be a mouthful and sounds confusing. It is for these reasons that I have avoided trying to coin the words 'boardmanship' or 'boardpersonship', though the concept is a good one.

is about the skills, techniques and knowledge needed to steer a company from the boardroom. I want to open the boardroom door, so that people understand what happens in there, believe that they can enter that room and take a place at the table, especially if you are female or from an ethnic minority.

We need more effective boards. Some business scandals (such as Northern Rock, Royal Bank of Scotland & Arcadia) may have been precipitated by external events, but there is no doubt that the boards weren't as effective as they could have been. This is even more so in some cases, such as Carillion, where the strategy was faulty and the company response inadequate. Boards almost always, play some part in their own downfall.

Regulation is failing and more regulation is not the answer

Politicians, regulators and media commentators all think that the answer to business failure is more regulation. The government (exemplified by the 2021 White Paper on audit and corporate governance) feels it has to *do something*. It's less important what that *something* is, and after all, the regulating classes rarely feel the need to base new rules on something as mundane as evidence. The old lie is still a lie: '*The answer to bad regulation is more regulation*'. The answer to things going wrong is to assess what's happened, learn lessons, develop strategies, pilot some new rules and methods, test them and then roll them out if they prove successful. But in most situations now, governments look for board scapegoats to blame, consult the great and the good on ideas about what to do, and then impose them, without evidence, testing, or piloting.

Boards cannot guarantee success

Businesses fail in a capitalist economy. That's part of the system. Even having better boards doesn't guarantee business success. Businesses generally make money by taking risks. Sometimes those risks go wrong. This is inevitable. A good board takes measured risks and applies logic and judgement to make appropriate decisions, in the light of what directors know at the time.

Many media commentators, and pretty much all politicians, make little attempt to distinguish between well-run companies that fail due to circumstances beyond their control (such as retailers hit by competition from online) and companies that fail due to strategic errors or poor management (such as Carillion).

Any board of a struggling company is written off as incompetent, hapless or greedy, and sometimes all three.

I have seen good boards running struggling[3] companies, and bad boards running winning companies. Occasionally, I've had the great joy of seeing a good board run a winning company.

A well-run, quality board is no guarantee of corporate success. It will take rational decisions based on the evidence available to it. It is the quality of those decisions that marks a quality board, not necessarily the profitability of the company or 20:20 hindsight judging the outcome of a decision[4]. However, a good board is more likely to make a business successful as it will provide clear, well-judged leadership.

---

[3] Defining a 'struggling' company, for simplicity, as one that is struggling to make an adequate return. This maybe because either it is in a very tough competitive market with an inherent competitive disadvantage (such as a small player in an oligopolistic market) or it is in a declining market or being disintermediated. It is not necessarily a company that is badly managed. On the other hand, a 'winning' company is delivering a good return, perhaps because it is in an expanding market, or has a structural competitive edge (such as relative scale or technological innovation). It is not necessarily well-managed. For example, a monopolist doesn't usually need to be well managed to be successful.

[4] It is an important distinction to assess the quality of decision-making by the assessment of evidence and risk *available at the time*, rather than – as media and politicians love to – assess it purely on whether the subsequent outcome is seen as good. Annie Duke's 'How to Decide: Simple Tools for Making Better Choices' has a great discussion about what makes for good decisions and the importance of avoiding outcome-bias.

Summary

More and more is being asked of boards. They are being held to ever higher standards and ever tougher (and not necessarily better) regulations. There is now no place to hide for any director, executive or non-exec, as social and traditional media and investors are more demanding and faster to condemn. Directors need more help and advice, more knowledge and more experience. Meanwhile, this raising of the bar makes it more difficult for new directors, and those with less senior business experience, to get onto boards, further exacerbating the problem of lack of diversity at the top[5].

There is a lot that needs doing to make boards more diverse and effective. The sort of things that will make a big difference are better education, wider experience, and more rigorous challenge. You won't find the answer to these in corporate governance or government regulation, but you will find some pointers in this book.

---

[5] I generally use 'they' to avoid using he or she, but in any case, all references in this book to he or she are for literary convenience, not to draw any distinction between sexes. All should be read as referring to either sex.

How to use the book

The book can be read through cover to cover, or equally it can be dipped into, or referred to, as particular issues and committees arise. There are some sections that get quite technical, and these can be more referred to as necessary. Some parts will be particularly useful to new or aspirant directors and others will have more meaning to directors with existing experience.

Certain explanations may help current directors who haven't wanted to admit they don't understand some of their board's discussions.

Many of the tips and techniques would be useful to anyone serving on any committee, public sector or charitable board. The vast majority of the book applies to boards in any country, although some of the governance points may be specific to the UK.

If you have any feedback, please do contact me via my website:

www.simonlaffin.com

Chapter 1 - Executives, Non-Executives and Cashiers

There are two types of directors; executive and non-executive. The former are the most senior managers who have been appointed onto the board. Increasingly these may be just the chief executive (CEO) and the finance director (CFO). Non-executives are directors who don't work in the business and whose main role is to sit on the board and its committees, providing an outside and, hopefully, independent viewpoint.

Not all boards have non-executive directors. Sir Ken Morrison, founder and former Chairman of the eponymous grocery chain, didn't think they needed any. *"What do you want a non-exec for?"* he often asked[6] and suggested that a cashier might be more useful. I met Sir Ken several times when Morrisons was taking over Safeway (where I was the Finance Director) and liked and respected him. However, he was a man of his times[7]. Historically, non-execs would have been contacts of the chairman and chosen for being clubbable. 20 years ago, I would have had a sneaking respect for Sir Ken's view. Too many non-execs were executives phasing out their career or retired executives looking for a top-up to their pension. Too many wanted an easy life and saw

---

[6] The Telegraph 8/9/2003 https://www.telegraph.co.uk/finance/2862582/Wm-Morrison-goes-in-search-of-non-execs.html

[7] That failure to have non-execs on his board at Morrisons contributed to the botched acquisition of Safeway in 2004. This is discussed in chapter 10.

their role as just supporting management. There is still some of this around now, but growing public and regulatory interest in boards, as well as the role of head-hunters, has helped to make non-exec life more professional and accountable.

Board Directors

We have to start with a bit of the law here (and almost the only bit of law in this book), as government and regulators broaden the responsibilities of board directors to things other than making shareholders rich. There is an important point that all directors are equally responsible under UK law.

There is no distinction between executives and non-execs, all of whose duties are set out in the Companies Act 2006: section 172 (1)[8]. Directors hear the ominous words "*Section 172*" rather a lot these days, so, I've added it for you to review (see next page).

In other words, directors need to work for the benefit of all shareholders (i.e. members), but also take account of the interests of other stakeholders. This is a lot easier to write than it is to do.

How can directors balance up the respective interests of stakeholders that are often competing or mutually exclusive? For example, if the board believes that it needs to cut costs to protect profit, it is likely to make redundancies and put price pressure on suppliers. You have to argue that the company's long-term success will be in the best interests of both suppliers and remaining employees, so the short-term pain is justified.

The point of section 172 is not to put other stakeholders' interests above that of shareholders. It is to ensure that directors at least *think*

---

[8] https://www.legislation.gov.uk/ukpga/2006/46/section/172

about the interests of other stakeholders when they take difficult decisions. All directors are equally liable for this. Non-execs cannot hide behind the executives.

Companies Act 2006, Section 172 (1): Duty to promote the success of the company

(1) A director of a company must act in the way he[9] considers, in good faith, would be most likely to promote the success of the company for the benefit of its members as a whole, and in doing so have regard (amongst other matters) to:-

(a) the likely consequences of any decision in the long term,

(b) the interests of the company's employees,

(c) the need to foster the company's business relationships with suppliers, customers and others,

(d) the impact of the company's operations on the community and the environment,

(e) the desirability of the company maintaining a reputation for high standards of business conduct, and

(f) the need to act fairly as between members of the company.

---

[9] The Companies Act is indeed sexist, assuming that company directors are male.

Non-Exec Directors

Executive directors live and breathe their jobs five, or maybe seven, days a week. Non-executive directors are full board directors, but usually have other roles elsewhere and come and go into the affairs of one company, according to the annual cycle of board meetings, interspersed with corporate crises. The defining feature of a non-executive director is that they are not full-time, they're not managers, and have a working life outside the company and its board.

Sir Alastair Grant, the former Chairman of Safeway, Scottish & Newcastle and Governor of the Bank of Scotland, used to delight in mad job titles. His favourite was a beleaguered retail manager, whose job title was 'Buyer of Root Vegetables, not Potatoes'. How can you take seriously a job title defined as *not* being something else? Yet, that is exactly what the title non-executive is. They are defined by *not* being executives. Some other countries have a more positive job description - 'Outside Director'. This is indeed right, the non-exec is in many ways an outsider, or stranger, on the board.

The sociologist Georg Simmel argued that a stranger's position in a group is '*determined by the fact that he has not belonged to it from the beginning, that he imports qualities into it, which do not and cannot stem from the group itself.*[10]

He could have been writing about what it feels like to be a non-executive on a board, but also about how powerful that role can be.

A modern non-exec should be promoting the best interests of the company as a whole, not just a cheerleader for management. A non-exec is often described as a critical friend to management – encouraging and supportive, but also candid about weaknesses and problems. The non-exec also has to have enough independence to make impartial decisions about executives' careers and remuneration. At times, the non-exec has to 'do what's right', even if it hurts executives and short-term company reputation or performance, for example when the audit committee may have to override management on an issue where the auditors point out an irregularity.

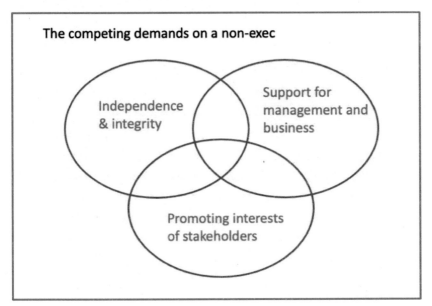

The competing demands on a non-exec

Independence & integrity

Support for management and business

Promoting interests of stakeholders

---

[10] 'The Stranger' by Georg Simmel, from 'Soziologie' 1908

The non-exec should be committed to the company and to furthering the interests of its stakeholders. They need to be close to the mission and strategy of the company, and support management in promoting the business. They must maintain independence and integrity at a distance from management and the execution of strategy. They need that distance to allow themselves to make difficult decisions about management's pet projects, personnel appointments and departures, remuneration and bonuses, even about selling the business. The trick is to balance these three competing demands.

This is very similar to Simmel's vision of a stranger, who is:

'not radically committed to the unique ingredients and peculiar tendencies of the group, and therefore approached them with the specific attitude of "objectivity". But objectivity does not simply imply passivity and detachment: it is a particular structure composed of distance and nearness, indifference and involvement.'

In other words;

- Not part of the group-think of management
- Regarding independence and objectivity as a key badge of office
- Actively involved in strategic development and decision-making
- Championing the interests of all shareholders, whilst taking into account of the interests of other stakeholders

The UK Corporate Governance Code[11] puts it succinctly, if a little dryly: *"They (non-execs) should provide constructive challenge, strategic guidance, offer specialist advice and hold management to account."*

---

[11] UK Corporate Governance Code is required reading for all board directors, and fortunately an easy read. https://www.frc.org.uk/directors/corporate-governance-and-stewardship/uk-corporate-governance-code

Different forms of non-executive

There are a number of different forms of non-exec:

1. **The independent non-exec.** This is the most common type in listed companies and is the purest of the 'stranger' directors.

2. **The representative non-exec.** They can be nominated or forced on the board either by a group of shareholders or by bankers (if the business is heavily indebted). This is more common in private companies or those in serious financial difficulties.

3. **The shareholder non-exec.** These are the shareholders themselves sitting on the board, rather than a third party representing them. This is more common in private companies, but activist shareholders may demand a board seat even in public companies. You would normally expect them to hold over 20% of the stock to be given one, but some activist shareholders will try it on even with much fewer shares.

Whether these non-independent, non-executives are helpful or difficult depends on the situation and their character. Shareholder representative directors can be particularly problematic. All directors have the same responsibilities, whether they are independent or not, to promote the interests of the company and to maintain the confidentiality of the board. This is particularly important when the board has price-sensitive material. A shareholder-representative director must not discuss any of this with their shareholder, unless the board agrees in advance to make the shareholder an insider. This can put the shareholder-representative director in a very difficult position.

My own experience has shown the good and the bad of non-independent non-execs. I had a good experience with a bank-nominated non-exec at Hozelock in 2011, despite my initial reservations. The non-exec shared a common interest with us in keeping the business solvent, liaising with and reassuring the bank, leading to a successful outcome[12].

Shareholder representative directors are often much more challenging colleagues around the boardroom table, feeling the pressure of their shareholders behind them. I was a shareholder-representative director, representing CVC funds, as chairman of a portfolio business. This is quite common in private equity.

On the other hand, Mitchells & Butlers had two large shareholders in 2009, who each nominated two representative directors to the Mitchells & Butlers board. The Board subsequently felt that it could not operate effectively in the interests of all shareholders (according to a company statement) with these four directors, who *"appeared to have a consistent view on a variety of business issues and that those views differed from that of the rest of the Board"* and then subsequently they refused to sign off the accounts (according to the statement[13]).

Tip

Conduct very thorough due diligence before joining a board with *non-independent* non-execs. You will want to satisfy yourself that they are all aligned with the rest of the board on future strategy and will promote the interests of all shareholders equally. Be sure to meet them before agreeing to join the board.

---

[12] A lesson well learnt that good people can still come up trumps in difficult situations.

[13] Mitchells & Butlers Letter to Shareholders 17 Dec 2009. https://www.mbplc.com/infocentre/article/lettertoshareholdersfromtheboardofdirectorsdec09/ The full letter is reproduced in the appendix, as it is a fascinating case-study in the ruthless exercise of shareholder power.

Chairmen are usually non-executive these days. However, they are in a quite different position to the other non-execs, situated somewhere in between executive and non-exec, giving much more time to the business and getting closer to management than other non-execs. I shall discuss the chair role in more detail in chapter 13.

The active non-executive director

"Objectivity does not simply imply passivity and detachment" – Georg Simmel[14]

This is, I think, the acid test of a good non-exec. There is an easy path for a non-exec, that tends to follow the executives' lead. Agreeing to proposals, no matter how barmy, is a lot easier than disagreeing with them. Holding someone to account is a difficult task and tempting to avoid. It isn't helped by executives having far more information and understanding about the company than the non-execs. You would expect them to be right more often than the peripatetic non-exec. However, non-execs should not assume that all execs agree, and sometimes they are waiting for an opportunity to give an alternative view to that of the CEO.

As a CFO once, I was doing a final rehearsal for a Results Announcement the following morning, when the audit partner phoned me up. There was something wrong with the accounts, and it looked as if a fellow director had signed off on a number that wasn't right. I revised the numbers late into the night, but I was leant on very heavily by colleagues not to make a fuss and to describe it as an innocent mistake in the subsequent emergency audit committee. I didn't believe that it was, but, put in an impossible position, I decided to play a straight bat. I

---

[14] 'The Stranger' by Georg Simmel, from 'Soziologie' 1908

described the event in an objective, dispassionate way to the committee, but left enough pointers that anyone who wanted to find the truth would have asked the right questions. Feeling unable to *volunteer* my real opinion, I hoped that someone would put me on the spot and ask my opinion as to whether misconduct had taken place. However, no-one asked my view.

The committee listened and then moved on. I was speechless.

I wasn't proud of myself that night and knew that in the future, I wouldn't keep quiet when something major wasn't right. But what of the role of the non-execs that day? Time and time again, a non-exec will find that they have a choice – sit back and go with the flow, or stand up for what they believe is right and make trouble. And this might mean that they stand alone. I believe that this willingness to stand up for what they think is right, as opposed to letting things go, is the greatest differentiation among non-execs.

Tip

To get the full story as a non-exec, you need to ask questions, including asking executives for their personal opinion. If you really want the whole truth, you may well need to ask the executives outside of a board meeting or committee. A quick phone call to ascertain some information privately before a formal meeting is one of the non-exec's most powerful weapons.

The Select Ccommittee report[15] on the collapse of Carillion quoted Philip Green, the chairman, about the role of his non-execs: *"Some people challenged by sending questions in advance by email; some people challenged in the meeting. I would say that it was a board that constructively challenged management."*

However, the Select committee concluded:

"Non-executives are there to scrutinise executive management. They have a particularly vital role in challenging risk management and strategy and should act as a bulwark against reckless executives. Carillion's NEDs were, however, unable to provide any remotely convincing evidence of their effective impact."

In reality, there's no way for an outsider to know whether this constituted enough challenge or whether it was done in the right way. In the end, having non-execs is not a panacea nor a guarantee of business success. All you can say is that a high level of involvement and challenge by non-execs can be an important contribution to the running of an organisation.

Tip

Board minutes can be very dry and tedious, but they are important. Always assume that they may get used by an inquiry or even a court. Make sure that they are accurate, sufficiently detailed and reflect challenges and differences of opinion.

---

[15] House of Commons Business, Energy and Industrial Strategy and Work and Pensions Committees Second Joint Report 2018 on Carillion https://www.parliament.uk/business/committees/committees-a-z/commons-select/work-and-pensions-committee/inquiries/parliament-2017/carillion-inquiry-17-19/publications/

No hiding place for non-executives

"All animals are equal, but some animals are more equal than others."
– George Orwell[16]

The Select Committee inquiry into the collapse of Northern Rock concluded:

"The non-executive members of the Board, and in particular the chairman of the Board, the chairman of the Risk committee and the senior non-executive director, failed in the case of Northern Rock to ensure that it remained liquid as well as solvent, to provide against the risks that it was taking and to act as an effective restraining force on the strategy of the executive members." [17]

The non-execs were held responsible not only for having failed to restrain management, but for failing to *ensure* that the business remained solvent. Michael Queen, the then Chairman of the audit committee was particularly castigated in the Select Committee Hearing itself. Ridiculously, it appeared that MPs believed that he must have been actually directing operations himself.

As we have noted, UK law does not distinguish between executive and non-executive directors. All are equally liable for their actions and those of the board. Executives live and breathe their company and have vast knowledge. Even the best non-execs attend meetings every month or so and read papers provided for them by executives, supplemented by occasional site visits and background reading.

[16] "Animal Farm" by George Orwell

[17] The Run on the Rock, House of Commons Treasury Select committee 24 January 2008 https://publications.parliament.uk/pa/cm200708/cmselect/cmtreasy/56/56i.pdf

There is huge information asymmetry between executive and non-exec directors. This doesn't necessarily mean, of course, that executives make better decisions or judgements, just that they know much more. Sometimes, in fact, a good decision can benefit from a little distance and impartiality.

Although UK law means that non-execs are equally liable as executives when things go wrong, in fact, as Northern Rock and Carillion show, non-execs can be *more* exposed in public judgement. If the directors ever get sued for the actions of the board, the non-execs will be there on exactly the same terms as the execs.

Being a non-exec confers significant responsibility that goes beyond reading papers and attending meetings. Increasingly directors are being held to account – fairly or unfairly – for the actions of their board and the performance of their company. Being a non-exec involves putting your reputation on the line and taking responsibility with much less information and knowledge than executive colleagues… and for a lot lower remuneration!

Executive Directors

This chapter has focused so far on non-executive directors, but executive directors also need to realise that they are not just senior executives, they too are full board members. Too often, executive directors sit silent in board meetings as the CEO, for example, puts a heavy spin on performance or promotes a project that the other executives know is faulty, yet they maintain a code of omerta (i.e. silence). It takes courage to contradict your boss in a meeting, but an executive director has even more responsibility than a non-exec to promote the interests of shareholders above organisational sensitivity.

Mind you, it takes pluck and can be career ending.

Summary

Being a non-exec is about balancing different and sometimes competing interests; management, shareholders and other stakeholders, whilst being enough of a stranger or outsider that they can retain impartial judgement and integrity. The role carries a lot of responsibility, requiring all these qualities, together with business knowledge and judgement. All of those will get questioned if things go wrong, and non-execs can be publicly named and shamed. They must play their part in avoiding this, by seeking information, challenging management and not being a passive cheerleader.

You could argue that a non-exec role is a bit like a cashier in a shop. The cashier should be supportive and helpful to a customer, but they must also ensure that the bill is correct, and that the customer doesn't forget to scan that whisky bottle hidden under the newspaper. Maybe Sir Ken Morrison was indeed on to something all those years ago in comparing non-execs to cashiers.

Chapter 2 - Getting on the Right Long-List

The phone call that started my non-exec career at Northern Rock came out of the blue, but this is fairly typical of how many people get such a role. It wasn't in truth, completely out of the blue. I had decided a few months beforehand that I wanted to start a portfolio of non-exec roles. To do that, I emailed and called head-hunters that I knew to remind them that I existed and was interested in non-exec roles. This laid the foundation for the call that came later.

The UK Corporate Governance Code says, "*Appointments to the board should be subject to a formal, rigorous and transparent procedure*" and "*Open advertising and/or an external search consultancy should generally be used for the appointment of the chair and non-executive directors.*" Most non-exec roles are nowadays appointed via an advertisement, head-hunter, banker, or other personal contact. The bigger the company, the more likely that it will be head-hunters that take the lead role.

The CV

You should start by writing your CV. There are plenty of guides available on the internet, so I won't repeat them here. A non-exec CV is not very different to an executive one, but the focus should be on board experience, especially other non-exec roles. Of course, if you haven't got board experience as yet, try to emphasise interactions with boards. For example, maybe you attend or support a board or board committee, and so have some experience of how they work. If you don't have this, think about why you might be recruited – perhaps a specialism or sector knowledge – and emphasise this.

It's worth putting a lot of effort into your CV. It is the thing that should get you in the door to start any process. Head-hunters sometimes simply copy and paste large parts of it into their report on you for nomination committees.

> **Tip**
>
> LinkedIn is very important for recruitment. Most head-hunters use it at some point, especially when searching for ideas for their long-list. Treat your profile on LinkedIn as being as important as your actual CV.

Am I ready?

The non-exec market is dominated by white men in their 50s and 60s. I was 48 when I got my first non-exec, but according to Spencer Stuart, the average age of new non-execs in 2019 was 57. The age profile reflects the level of experience that being a non-exec requires. It's just difficult to get that much experience earlier in your career. There are non-execs younger than this, especially in smaller or private companies. Younger candidates just have to work harder at showing how their experience equips them for the role.

In 2019, women were in a majority of new non-execs for the first time[18]. This reflects the drive for more sex diversity. There aren't enough women around with the 'required' board experience, because

---

[18] Quoted in CityAM 11/11/2019 https://www.cityam.com/women-make-up-bulk-of-new-non-exec-directors-for-first-time/

of the domination of men in executive roles. This is however, an opportunity for women, as recruiters increasingly realise that they need to demand less experience from women for non-exec roles, compared to men. Female candidates should be bold in putting themselves forward even if they lack some of the experience talked about here.

The same should be true of ethnic minority candidates. However, there are apparently, so few around that it is difficult to judge. There will be increasing pressure in the future on companies to have ethnic diversity on boards, so ethnic-minority candidates should also be putting themselves forward even if they have less experience.

Boards should be looking for the same fundamental talent, irrespective of sex and ethnicity, but will inevitably have to recruit underrepresented groups with less experience, simply because there are fewer of those candidates putting themselves forward.

"Kissing frogs"

The best place to start your quest for a non-exec job is to contact headhunters. A simple Google search will give the names of search firms, and a little research on their respective websites will identify the names of the Board Practice executives who specialise in non-exec appointments.

Some of the leading ones are (with apologies to the many I've omitted) are the next page:

Large Firms	Boutique Firms
Egon Zehnder	Clarity
Heidrick & Struggles	Independent Search Partnership
Korn Ferry	
Odgers Berndtson	The Inzito Partnership
Russell Reynolds Associates	Redgrave Partners
Spencer Stuart	Ridgeway Partners

The main difference between large and boutique head-hunters is just size. Even some large company boards opt to deal with boutiques, as they feel they get a more personal service.

There are a lot of head-hunters out there and you could spend many weeks visiting them all. However, as the saying goes, you have to kiss a lot of frogs to find a prince (this is just a saying; no offence meant to head-hunters, who are lovely people). You can't predict which head-hunter will have just the right role for you, so the more you know the better your chances.

No doubt you will know some individuals already. If so, it's probably worth calling those you know, even those ones who aren't in the Board Practice. You can ask them to pass your CV onto their colleagues who do handle non-execs. The trickiest part is getting the consultant to look at your CV or take your call. Personally, I found cold calling head-hunters to be very daunting, but sometimes you just have to do it. If you get fobbed off by a secretary, who just says send in your CV, you may need to find another route in. You could ask a respected colleague or contact whether they know the head-hunters and ask them whether they would call them and recommend you.

Do not assume that one consultant will tell all their colleagues about you. It does happen, but generally assume that the head-hunter you speak to is the one most likely to think about you for a role. Do not however, bombard head-hunting firms with multiple contacts. If you irritate them or appear too pushy or desperate, this will damage your chances. Non-exec appointments don't come along too often, so patience is needed.

Tips

1.   Try to speak to a consultant, preferably one you know, at a head-hunter, rather than just send in a CV.

2.   Find a reason to contact a head-hunter every six months or so, so they don't forget about you.

Investment bankers are also often aware of upcoming vacancies for non-execs, but this is only worth pursuing if you already know the banker. A cold call to a banker is unlikely to result in a lead on a non-exec appointment.

Promote yourself

It is helpful to network. Speak to old contacts and ask them for advice. Go to events staged by head-hunters and make sure that you speak to some of the consultants there. Just be seen at events and remind people that you are looking for a non-exec role. Post regular comments or articles on LinkedIn. Have a cup of tea with senior people you know. Ask other non-execs for their advice.

A job search is a project to promote yourself[19]. Like any marketing activity, you need to understand your strong and weak points, highlight what differentiates you from other candidates and try to encapsulate this in a few words.

Experience is probably the most important part of your positioning. If this would be your first board role, then you can only point to your previous executive roles, but for subsequent roles the non-exec experience is important. Many non-execs have got some board experience as execs, but as executive directors are increasingly limited to CEO and CFO, this proves difficult for many. If you have no board experience at all, you need to trade on specialist experience. For example, Human Resources executives are in demand to chair remuneration committees. Other specialisms that might get you past the lack of board experience include finance, IT and marketing. Some companies will look for legal experience or relevant sector experience or even just 'consumer' experience.

However, do not assume that a board will look for experience in the sector in which it operates. The last person many executives want is someone who knows as much about the sector as they do! I spent 14 years in retail, from store manager to main board, but have hardly ever been approached to join a retailer, or at least, a solvent one. Even when I did go for interview, I felt that my sector experience was treated with suspicion. After all, not every chair wants a non-exec who knows more than them. And, indeed, part of the purpose of non-execs is to bring in new experience, rather than to duplicate that already in the company. There are good reasons not to look for experience in the sector in which the company operates.

Some boards will adopt a status strategy and only interview candidates who have been on boards of companies of a similar size or bigger.

---

[19] A good book on marketing yourself is "Brand You: Turn Your Unique Talents into a Winning Formula" by John Purkis (Banahasta), himself a head-hunter.

FTSE 100 boards are prone to want FTSE 100 board experience, at least in a white male (there is likely to be more flexibility for female and ethnic minority candidates). It is as if the size of the market capitalisation alone is what makes a board uniquely challenging. In fact, the opposite may well be the case, as larger companies often have larger boards (with more places to hide) and more well-established processes and support.

Pretty much every board needs two non-execs to chair respectively the audit and remuneration committees. The former usually requires a trained accountant or MBA with finance experience, and the remuneration committee usually likes to have someone with HR or remuneration experience.

Choose the right board for you

Generally, non-exec recruitment is a buyer's market. You don't get to select one role from many on offer. It is important, however, to think hard about whether you would want to take a role that might be offered. Non-exec appointments may not be for life, but they are generally expected to last around six years (i.e. two terms of three years), and any less will leave you permanently having to explain why not. Join in haste; repent at leisure. You can't easily resign after a year or so. This means that you need to do your due diligence very carefully, looking hard at the existing board, the company, and its shareholders.

Companies come in all shapes and sizes. Some non-execs are also 'sizeist'. They only want to be involved in big companies. The biggest snobbery is the FTSE 100. However, larger companies tend to spend more time on governance matters. It can be more difficult for a non-exec to engage on business issues in large multinationals. If CV status really matters to you, then by all means aim for a FTSE 100 board. However, if it's cocktail party status you want, you will get that from working for any household name company or one in the public eye, irrespective of size. If you are on the board of a retail or well-known FMCG company, you will find that people want to talk about their experience of your brands. When I was at Safeway, everyone wanted to tell me about supermarket experience; at Flybe it was a particular flight; and at Northern Rock, it was how quickly they had got their money out.

In truth, 'smaller' companies are often more interesting, and the boards get more involved in business issues. The largest companies tend to have bigger boards and worry more about time-consuming compliance. There is usually a difference between FTSE 100 and FTSE 350 boards in size and governance workload. AIM listed and private companies are even more informal and focused on operational performance. Against this, the larger companies have bigger company secretarial departments that means that you have more people looking after the board and regulation, so you are less likely (theoretically) to get into trouble for forgetting to do something or not complying with some regulation.

The most important person in making a board successful is the chair. They set the tone of the board and generally have greatest influence over it. If you don't like or rate the chair, this is a major red flag warning against joining that board. Do they understand the business? Would you like working with them? Would you learn from them? Will they be strong enough to keep the board and CEO in check?

The most important person for the success of the business is, however, the CEO. You need to ask the other directors and form your own assessment as to how good they are. Joining a board with a successful CEO is very different to joining one with a CEO under pressure. Key to this will also be your assessment of how the chair and CEO get on together. The chair needs to keep a certain distance from the CEO, but if the two are fighting, then one of them will eventually have to go.

The role of the Senior Independent Director (SID) is usually important only when the board is itself having difficulties. You should satisfy yourself that they are truly independent of the chair, and not their buddy.

The SID needs to be strong enough to take the most independent and lonely stand, if necessary. On the other hand, a SID who is clearly ambitious to be the chair is a potential conflict for the future.

You may prefer a larger or smaller board, but beware that getting enough chance to speak and influence a board is inversely related to the number sitting round the table. Size does have a major impact on the workings and culture of the board.

You should meet all of the non-execs and the executive directors before agreeing to join a board. Look hard for what the politics are. I was quite keen on a role once, but was then interviewed by the SID. He told me that he didn't think the chairman was very good and that he thought he, the SID, might replace him soon. I made my excuses and left, as they say. Stepping into a catfight, and choosing sides, on a new board was not my idea of fun. It was the fact that the SID was so open about it at an initial interview that told me this was trouble[20].

It is a good idea to ask the non-execs, when you meet them, what they think of the board and ask whether it works well. You are much more likely to get a straight answer to a direct question, rather than relying on someone to volunteer the information.

If two directors interview you at once, watch the interaction and body language between them, especially when you ask difficult questions. If they look at each other before answering, or one develops a sudden interest in the carpet, beware. Better that you discover any difficult board issues now rather than after you've signed on.

Ask questions and assess the state of the board. It may be in a steady state and your appointment could be a direct replacement for a time-served non-exec. Alternatively, the chair, perhaps newly-appointed,

---

[20] My only regret here was that I didn't explain this to the head-hunter, as I felt that I had been told this in confidence. The head-hunter was irritated at my sudden withdrawal from the process without a good explanation, and no doubt was less inclined to approach me about other roles.

could be renewing the board with wholesale changes. Both situations have their advantages and disadvantages, although expect more challenge in the latter one. If your predecessor is not obviously time-served (i.e. six years plus), ask why they are leaving.

Tip

It is always worth talking to your predecessor, if you are being recruited to replace an outgoing director. They may well feel able to tell you things that the other directors won't.

Look at the background and experience of your prospective fellow directors. This will tell you a lot about how the board works and what meetings will be like. An entirely male, single-culture directorate all in their 60s would send you a signal. Maybe you too are like that, and would feel comfortable, or maybe you are not and would be the 'diversity' director[21].

Think carefully about joining any board with little diversity. It raises issues about the culture of that board, as well as how effective the board might be.

Look at the other directors' CVs. Are these people that you will learn from and enjoy working with?

Remember that you might be locked in a boardroom with these people for six years, without time off for good behaviour.

---

[21] I joined the board of a Japanese company, where, despite being white, male and in my 60s, I was a diversity candidate as I was the only non-Japanese outside director. It's a funny old world.

Choose the right company

The great investor Warren Buffet said: "When a management with a reputation for brilliance tackles a business with a reputation for bad economics, it is the reputation of the business that remains intact." [22]

Sadly, Buffet could well have been talking about board directors as much as management. He also said: "It takes 20 years to build a reputation and five minutes to ruin it." [23]

Choosing the right company to join is crucial to a non-exec. I had a reputation as a director for running into burning buildings, so I understand that you might relish the challenge of a 'difficult' company. However, the key is to be prepared and know what you are getting yourself into.

There are a few questions that a candidate non-exec should ask about the company:

1. **Is the market, in which the company operates, growing?** It is difficult to consistently increase market share in a stagnant or declining market, so if you want to be involved in a growing business, this is pretty important.

2. **Does the company have a sustainable competitive position in its market?** This is not only about growth, but also about sustaining a company's current position. Most people want to join a company that can develop and outperform. If you join a company in decline, the non-exec role is likely to be much harder and there will be many tough decisions to make.

---

[22]   https://www.quotetab.com/quote/by-warren-buffett/when-a-management-with-a-reputation-for-brilliance-tackles-a-business-with-a-repu

[23]   https://www.forbes.com/sites/jamesberman/2014/04/20/the-three-essential-warren-buffett-quotes-to-live-by/

3. **Are you interested in the product?** Although you would not be involved in day-to-day operations, board meetings can be terribly dull if you have no affinity with the product. I found it difficult to get excited about banking, but find consumer-facing and aviation sectors particularly fascinating. If you are a consumer person, then a heavy manufacturing board would probably be very tedious to you. If you are very interested in digital and IT, then perhaps a mining business wouldn't be right for you. This is a good place to be honest with yourself about what really interests you.

4. **Is the business at risk of cash problems?** Companies don't go bust when they make a loss, it's when they run out of cash. They can get liquidity problems even while making a paper profit. Have they got enough cash or debt facilities? This should be an easy question for a financially trained candidate, but everyone must ask it. The simplest markers are: is profit projected to rise or fall? What is the level of gearing (debt/net assets and debt to debt plus market capitalisation)? Is the business using cash (i.e. is net debt rising)? What do analyst reports say (a good head-hunter will send you some)? If a company is in financial difficulty, the non-exec role will be much busier, and you will bear some risk. Personal financial liability is potentially uncapped for all directors when their company trades on whilst insolvent. I forgot that when I agreed to join the Northern Rock board with £100bn of liabilities[24]!

5. **Do you like the philosophy/culture of the business?** You might not approve of gambling, tobacco or arms manufacturing, so this would be an immediate red flag for you. It may be that you get the impression that the business puts profit before people, or has a poor compliance record in some areas. This may be more subjective, but it's worth asking around in both the market in which it operates, and also bankers and other head-hunters. You'll normally get a good feel from their immediate response, particularly if it's a short silence while they work out how to say something tactfully. Googling the

---

[24] I regretted not transferring all my assets into my wife's name before joining the board. Once you're there, it's too late.

company or looking at Twitter will uncover critical comments about the company.

You might say that in joining Northern Rock, I ignored some of my own rules. Even I had spotted that the business was in financial problems, as constant TV news reports showed queues outside branches. I also discovered that I had limited appetite for banking. However, it was only because they had a financial crisis, and so most experienced non-execs wouldn't go near the company, that I got offered my first non-exec role.

If you want to be someone who puts out fires, first you need to find a burning building.

Check out the shareholders

I'm often asked if I prefer being on the boards of public, private or private equity companies. The big difference is not the ownership structure however, but the shareholder make-up. Any shareholder, or grouping of shareholders, with more than 25% of the stock, can exercise enormous influence on the board. If they are activist in some form (all private equity investors should be classed as activist), then the chances are that they will exercise that power at some point. Shareholders come in all shapes and sizes, whether the company is private or public. Large investment houses (such as Scottish Widows or Abrdn for example) will generally be rational, innately supportive to the board and act predictably. Private shareholders and family trusts may be the same but are slightly more prone to be unpredictable and fixated on non-value issues.

Shareholders own the company. The board merely manages it. However, this does not mean that all shareholders are necessarily rational and only interested in maximising their wealth. In one turnaround that I ran, the largest shareholder (a family investment house) became ever keener to remove me every time the share price went up. Their investment manager seemed to want to run the company more than he wanted to make the family richer. In another case, a very wealthy investor became fixated on removing the board to put his own men in place. Given that he had a few friends with other large stakes, he was able to do that, and he celebrated ultimately by firing one of the smartest CEOs I've ever worked with.

It's not always about money.

Tip

If there is a shareholder (especially one that is not an institutional investor) owning more than 25% of the business, ask to speak to them before joining the board. You want them to be favourably disposed to you and if you find that they are not, you could be storing up trouble for the future.

Any shareholder is more likely to be activist if the company isn't doing well. Remember that performance ebbs and flows, so, irrespective of current performance, think about how it might play out if things got difficult. The shareholders can always fire the board. The board can't fire the shareholders.

Make the decision to apply

In choosing a board to join, you should look at the company, the board and the shareholders. If the company is in a weak market position, being disintermediated or its market is disappearing, accept that the role is going to be difficult and probably thankless. If the company is basically a good one, in your opinion, but needing a turnaround, ask yourself whether the board has the right people on it to deliver this, or is the chair remaking the board so that it can.

If you are offered a 'difficult' board role, you can gain fantastic experience. But don't believe everything you are told by the existing board and the head-hunters. Gather as much information as possible from different sources and go into it with your eyes wide open. A good, supportive board however, with universally high-quality directors, will always be a good place to work. Even in adversity, you will feel supported as part of the team. A divided or poor-quality board will be no fun, even in good years.

Non-execs don't usually do the job because they need the money to survive. Most do it, or choose a particular role, because they think they will enjoy it and learn something. Do not go for one job because it pays a higher fee, or the company is bigger or more prestigious. In fact, if the role pays an unusually high fee, there's likely to be a reason for it. Treat this as an amber flag.

The most important thing is to decide if you think you would enjoy the role and the company. If you go into one that you don't really enjoy, you may well be stuck there for several years.

That would give you plenty of time for regret, whereas a fun job will always be a fun job.

The acrimonious dispute between the Mitchells and Butlers board and its largest shareholder, the wealthy Joe Lewis, in 2010 centred on a battle for control of the board[25].

It was a very unpleasant experience, and I wouldn't want to repeat it. However, the saving grace was that the board was united, supportive and firm in the interests of all shareholders.

[25] See the appendix for more details

As I said at the time:

"This could be a John Grisham novel. It has got billionaire tax exiles, faraway places, horseracing connections and a glamorous location. And those forces are ranged against me and a plucky board in Birmingham." [26]

Give me a plucky board anytime.

---

[26] The Observer 24 January 2010 https://www.theguardian.com/business/2010/jan/24/laffin-mitch-ells-butlers-departure

Chapter 3 - Getting Appointed

Being interviewed

Are interviews a good way to select non-execs? Probably not, but I struggle to see how you can do it better. I've not yet discovered the secret to identifying the ideal non-exec. Nor have I, on the other side of the table, discovered the secret to always getting selected myself. An interview at this level is about personal chemistry on the day. Are the interviewers in a good mood? Does the interviewee say the right things?

I was interviewed once for the board of a prestigious television company. Going in, I had imposter syndrome. I was just not convinced that I was the type of non-exec they would want. One of the board directors had been on the board of a financial regulator and just wanted to take the opportunity to explain to me where Northern Rock had gone wrong. There are two lessons here. Firstly, as an interviewer, don't use an interview to lecture a candidate, especially not about something they know more about than you do. And secondly, if you are a candidate, don't point that out to them. My TV career did not take off.

The focus is not generally whether you can do the job. That is vouchsafed in your CV and the head-hunter's write-up that actually got you the interview. The interview is more likely to be on whether you will 'fit in' to the board and whether you will 'add value'. There's not much you can do about whether you would fit. Be yourself and hope that is what they want. Also look at it the other way - as Groucho Marx didn't say: *"I don't care to belong to any club that wouldn't have me as a member."*

Looking at how you would add value, start by thinking: Why are you being approached for this role? Is it for your sector expertise, your financial or remuneration background? Some chairs like sector knowledge, as it gives the board more weight in dealing with the CEO, but others may not want it as they feel that it may cause conflict with executive management. They may want indirect sector experience. I was asked to join the Northern Rock board, without any financial services knowledge, as my private equity background was thought to be helpful in case of a bid.

If you can't see why they have chosen you for interview, then, as in my TV interview, there's a good chance that you are a 'left field' or 'marker' candidate. The directors may just be interested in meeting you, or think that you have an interesting background, or just be 'window shopping' a completely different sort of candidate. You don't generally lose anything by going in as a marker candidate. You will earn goodwill from the head-hunter and gain interview experience. Just accept that the 'marker' candidate generally helps the board to decide which of the other candidates to appoint!

Interview tips

1. **Research the company beforehand.** Most interviewers will want a candidate to have done research on their company. The question: "What do you know about our company?" is a classic. There is little excuse these days for candidates not to have done some basic research. Do read the last Annual Report.

2. **Research the directors beforehand.** Again, this is very easy using Google, LinkedIn and perhaps Twitter. It is very flattering for an interviewer to hear that you know about their background. Alternatively, it can be fatal to say the wrong thing if you haven't researched. I interviewed a candidate who seemed fine, until he started making

silly and ignorant remarks about supermarkets. I asked him if he knew that I had been on the board of the grocer, Safeway. His face went the colour of frozen cod.

3. **Ask the head-hunter in advance for any pointers.** You may be able to get some guidance as to what the interviewer will be looking for, but often the head-hunters themselves won't really know.

4. **Try not to talk too much about any specialism you have.** You will want to show that you can make a broad contribution to the board.

5. **Let the interviewer guide you.** Don't try to impose yourself on the meeting and don't keep coming back to a subject just because you want to talk about it.

6. **But try to push the conversation into an area that you think is helpful.** If you can, especially if it highlights your expertise or experience.

7. **Avoid commenting on the company's strategy.** This is a trap, that I have, I'm afraid, used myself as an interviewer, and frequently fallen into as an interviewee. You won't know enough to take on a board director and you are likely to show how much you don't understand. It is much safer to make it clear that you have read quite a bit about the company, demonstrate that briefly by replaying the company's stated strategy and then ask the interviewer for their view.

8. **Don't overclaim about your past board contribution.** It is much easier to reference check a non-exec, where the candidacy is not generally regarded as commercially sensitive. The head-hunter is likely to know your previous chairs and would be expected to speak to them.

If the board is all or largely male, especially on a listed company, the chances are that they will want to appoint a woman. This is unfortunate if you are male, but it is still a good idea to continue going to the interview, because withdrawing would look churlish, harm your relationship with the head-hunter and you may still get the job after all. The nomination committee may start out looking for a particular type or sex of candidate but might change its mind if none is available, or another candidate is otherwise perfect.

A non-exec appointment is not a meritocratic process. A board is unlikely to be looking solely for the most skilled person to play the role, more likely a 'square peg for a square hole'. If the board, for example, has already got some very forthright individuals, it may be looking for a quieter, more thoughtful person, or vice-versa. A board that is rather 'cosy' may not want an individual who asks difficult questions.

In this case, they are likely to give the 'not the right fit' feedback. This type of feedback is, of course, no help as guidance for you, and even the head-hunter may look embarrassed at it. However, it may also be the truth.

The candidate is more likely to get honest feedback if the interviewer felt that they are too inexperienced or quiet, as this is relatively easy to say. Most feedback will be along the lines of 'they enjoyed meeting you and were impressed by your CV, but they preferred another candidate as they had more relevant experience.'

Sometimes, a candidate emerges who is perfect for the role, usually because the board wants something very specific. The unsuccessful candidates will often be told that the board 'fell in love with another candidate'. You should not worry about this. It's the golfers' equivalent of birdying a par 3 only to find your opponent scores a hole in one[27].

Your final due diligence

If you are happy with what you have seen of the company, its board and shareholders, it is worth doing a final due diligence check.

---

[27] Golf is still a very popular sport for directors, along with shooting for the wealthier ones. I however wouldn't recommend talking golf in an interview. Shooting is safer as a topic only if the chair is a shooter.

Ask to speak to the company's broker or investment banker and the audit partner. You will have to ask the questions. If there is a possible problem, company advisers are unlikely to offer it up, but equally are likely to give straight answers, or, if they don't, you can draw your own conclusions.

Do not simply assume that things must be fine because it is a household name or a listed entity.

Do not assume that things must be OK, because they are continuing to recruit a new non-exec. Carillion recruited two new non-execs onto its audit committee in the couple of months before going bust in 2018.

Although full of guff and regulatory waffle, the Annual Report may tip you off to issues. It was only when I was doing final due diligence on the Assura and Mitchell & Butlers annual reports that I noticed that both had major derivative problems (see Chapter 5). Probably unwisely in the latter case anyway, I chose to continue to join both, and those issues caused many subsequent sleepless nights.

The toxic derivatives were indeed listed in the Annual Reports, but were so surrounded by reassuring jargon, that it took me several interrogations of the respective CFOs to confirm their real nature. In fact, the words in the Annual Report are very unlikely to warn you.

Despite the regulators attempts to ensure that reports are balanced and fair, they are still largely promotional documents.

Areas to look out for[28]:

1. **Apply scepticism.** Annual Reports will naturally enough always accentuate the positive about the business.

2. **Question whether numbers are unconditional.** Future revenue and pipeline numbers sound impressive, but are unlikely to be guaranteed. Banking facilities should be judged on whether they are fully unconditional, not how big they are (you will probably need to ask the CFO to find this out).

3. **Watch out for specialised accounting, such as long-term contracts.** Some rules require profit to be booked before it becomes unconditional. Do not assume that the accounting rules are designed to protect the investor (and definitely not the non-exec).

4. **Take a close look at non-underlying costs.** They may well be genuinely one-off or technical, but they are still important.

5. **Cash is king.** Businesses don't go bust because they make a loss, but because they run out of cash or facilities, sometimes even when profitable. Look very hard at cash flow, covenants and debt facilities.

6. **Study working capital seriously.** It is the most likely source of cash problems in a profitable business. If the company is making strenuous efforts to manage working capital, it may be under strain. Year-end quoted cash numbers are of limited value. Focus on the average balances and try to find out the peak numbers too.

7. **Segmental profitability matters**. But, you will probably need to look at the numbers rather than rely on the commentary. Try to understand revenue trend, net margins, net capital employed and cash flows by segment. Check that it is the higher margin/return segments that are growing the fastest.

---

[28] Don't be daunted by some of the things in this list. Chapters 4 and 5 will look at some of the financial issues in more detail.

8. **Underperforming acquisitions are an amber light.** Businesses under pressure may seek to alleviate this by acquiring other companies.

You may find a question that you would like answers to, and you should indeed inquire further. If you don't understand the issue, ask to speak to the CFO. If they can't explain anything here in a way that you can understand, there may be a problem.

Your engagement terms

You've done your due diligence, you're happy with the company and you've received a Letter of Appointment to become a non-exec. After you've had a brief celebration, sit down and look carefully at what's in the detail of the Offer before you accept it.

What to look for in the offer letter

1. **Time commitment:** The letter will say to which committees you will be appointed and the fee payable. Most public companies will pay a fee for chairing a committee. You should expect such a fee, as chairing does involve significantly more work. It may also name a number of days it expects you to be able to commit, but expect to give as much time as is needed. The number and scheduled length of the board and committee meetings gives you as good a guess of time commitment as anything else. Don't just believe the number of meetings that the head-hunter tells you, as this might exclude unscheduled meetings. Look at the Annual Report to see how many meetings they actually held in a year and then assume a half to a whole day's preparation for each, in addition to the meetings themselves.

2. **Notice period:** Executives may fight for 6 or 12-month notice periods, but non-execs are lucky to get 3 months. Some non-exec contracts have zero notice periods. Others say that in particular circum-

stances the contract can be terminated immediately. This often includes when a director is not re-elected by the shareholders. The offer may be ambiguous on this point, and may be unclear as to whether immediate termination would still pay out a notice period. offer letters are often poorly worded in this area, because Company Secretaries have historically not thought such events were very likely. However, annual elections for directors now should raise everyone's awareness.

3. **Length of service:** The Letter may talk about one period of three years and a review at the end, or two periods of three years. I don't think this makes much practical difference in the end. It seems to be just different drafting or history. Take a good look at it however, just to make sure you are clear what it says.

4. **Insurance cover:** Firstly, ensure that directors have appropriate directors' and officers' (D&O) liability insurance cover. Depending upon the industry and size of company, the cover could be £20m or even much more. Is that the right number? Speak to the Company Secretary. Not only should they be able to explain the cover to you, but they should also be able to explain the rationale for the size of cover chosen.

5. **Next, ensure that the D&O cover has full 'run-off' protection.** This means cover that would still protect you if a claim emerged after you had stepped down from the board. This has occasionally become a real issue, for example, when a company was taken over, but the acquirer tried subsequently to call foul and claimed misrepresentation by the old board.

6. **Check that the cover protects you in all circumstances in which you might leave the board.** One (nameless, but leading UK) insurance company tried retrospectively to limit its liability to the Northern Rock board by pointing to the wording that the policy covered a director 'retiring' from the board, which it now decided meant a full retirement from all active employment. It claimed its cover would not extend to directors who just stepped down or resigned from the

board, but continued to work anywhere else. Fortunately, the insurance company did eventually back down from this skulduggery, but do not assume the obvious when you look at an insurance policy!

7. **Good/Bad leavers:** For private or private equity portfolio companies, the letter of appointment should be scrutinised for good leaver/bad leaver provisions. This is especially important if you are expected to co-invest or have an incentive agreement beyond a basic fee.

8. **Lawyer:** You could pay a lawyer to review the contract, but in my experience, they can worry about the fine wording, but miss key commercial points. They tend to have a lot of experience on executive contracts, but non-exec offer letters are a little different. However, you certainly could ask a lawyer to look at it, and you could even try to get the company to pay for your legal advice. However, don't be surprised if they politely say no to that!

Summary

For any board interview, do your research on both the company and the interviewers. Ask questions and get answers to areas that might raise red flags to you. Do due diligence as joining a board should be regarded as a long-term commitment, and your reputation (and sleep at night) is dependent on this. Look hard at the engagement letter and make sure that you are happy with it. Finally, good luck with the process.

Chapter 4 - The First 100 Days

"And indeed, here's what I have learned from all of my 'first days' at work and in business: being an outsider to an organization is a gift, for them and for you." - Tim Leberecht[29]

You may be feeling nervous about your first 100 days on a new board. It's important to have a good start to a new role, so this chapter looks at ways to smooth the rite of passage into a new board. Starting with an induction programme, it will talk about formal meetings and one-to-one discussions, working out your own role on the board and ways to smooth relationships with others. There is a lot to learn as a new-comer, or stranger, on a board, but also much valuable insight you can offer coming from outside. There is also the opportunity to lay the groundwork for a long and successful board career. The chapter will focus on a non-executive joining a board, but many of the lessons are also appropriate for new executive directors.

Induction programme

Any new director should have some form of induction programme. However, rather than leave it to the Company Secretary, it will be a better and more comprehensive one if you take control of it. Unless

---

[29] Tim Leberecht, Psychology Today, February 2015 http://timleberecht.com/article/first-100-days-stranger-long-can/

you've already met them in your induction programme, you should meet the following:

The executive/operating board members. The chances are that they will all be very upbeat and positive to you (whatever their private views), but you should get a sense of the strength of the team. If one or more are at all reserved in their comments, then this should be a warning sign. If you sense this, ask more questions. Now, while you're a stranger or 'naïve outsider', you can get away with asking these questions. Once you're inside the board, the same questions may be perceived to be slightly threatening or pointed.

The audit partner. Ask them about their view of the quality of the CFO, their senior staff, the control environment, any large provisions, and whether they have had any disagreements with management over accounting. The audit partner may well be a good source of independent views on the company. Nowadays, the audit firms take a good look at the quality of the board, the control environment and corporate culture as part of their risk assessments for each audit. Ask them about this. Do they, for example, regard the company as a low or high-risk client?

The broker. They should be positive about the company. However, ask them about who the significant shareholders are and what they say about the company. Ask for their latest written feedback to the company about shareholders' views (typically produced following a results announcement). If there are brokers' notes, and you haven't read them yet, ask for them all, not just the favourable ones. Don't however, believe that just because they have the company on a 'Buy' rating that everything is fine. It's difficult for a broker to have a really insightful hard-hitting critique of its own client.

Others. There may well be others, especially if you are to chair a committee. For example, a remuneration committee chair may want to meet the remuneration advisers and the audit committee chair will want to meet some of the finance executives.

The business: It is worth at least one site visit if the business has different locations. You gain a much better feel for the business outside the boardroom than in. Try to get a local manager to escort you, rather than an executive director. You will learn more that way.

The product: If possible, buy and use the product yourself. If it's a consumer product, ask retail store staff what they think of the product. One business told me it had great product reliability, but a knowledgeable sales assistant in a shop complained to me how many faulty returns he got.

Meet with the chair

There is merit in speaking again to the company chair after the appointment has been finalised. The chances are that they will be much more open with you now that you are on board. Talking to the chair should enable you to establish a good starting relationship with them, and it is worth asking them if there are any particular things or sensitivities to watch out for. For example, you might want to know if some key people don't get on well, or whether there has been some conflict in the past. You don't want to put your foot in it at your first board meeting or inadvertently raise a highly sensitive issue.

On my first day joining one board, I was invited to lunch with the chairman. I was expecting just some nice food and a convivial chat. However, it became clear that the chairman wanted to tell me that the CEO was having an affair with one of the executives. Now you might argue that the fact that the chairman waited until this stage to tell me, says as much about the chairman, as it did about the CEO's love life. Actually, these sorts of affairs are not as uncommon as you might think, and are usually corrosive to the team, so it is now one of my due diligence questions before I join a board.

Your first board meeting

A wise non-exec will approach their first board meeting with care. There will be unwritten codes of etiquette that vary from company to company, so you will need to learn them individually. It helps if you have identified a kindred spirit on the board, who can tip you off to them.

Directors, especially non-execs, may arrive up to half an hour before the start. This gives them a great chance to chat to colleagues in a relaxed format. You should find out where the chairperson sits, usually in the middle or at the end, so that you don't sit in their seat. They may want the CEO or Company Secretary next to him as well. Don't feel shy about asking: 'Where should I sit?' It's a small point but it will smooth things along.

It is probably wise not to say too much in that first meeting as you gauge how the board runs. Some boards like lively discussion and some are more sedate. Some tend to let the executive directors speak for most of the time, and the NEDs may hold their fire until after the meeting. If you observe the meeting carefully, you will soon understand how things work. This doesn't mean that later you can't rebel against these unwritten rules, if you think that they impair the board's decision-making. It's just that you need to learn the rules first before challenging them.

No one will expect you to know the business, so this is your chance to ask 'stupid' questions. Incidentally I've asked hundreds of 'stupid' questions, and rarely has anyone complained (to my face anyway). However quite a few times it has proven to be a better question than I realised.

Shortly after the first board, it may be an idea to speak to the chair and ask how they felt the board went and ask if they were happy with your contribution. It shows that you are thinking about the team dynamics and your own part in it and respect the chair's views. If you feel nervous about doing this, for example, if you feel that this suggests that you are insecure, then turn it round and ask if there is anything more that the chair would like you to do. A good relationship with the chair is absolutely crucial for a new director.

Tips

Enjoy being a new director. It's great fun and an opportunity to learn so many new things, whilst contributing to a company at the highest level.

Make contact with the chair to check in and get feedback after your first few meetings.

Working out your role

Every director has a role. The executive ones are usually fairly obvious. A non-exec may be asked immediately to chair a committee and that helps to define what role they play. It may be that the board employed you as it needed more challenge or, perhaps, softer people skills. Perhaps you were identified as an expert in consumers, strategy, law or a particular sector. All of those may define what your colleagues will expect you to offer.

But remember that you alone should define the role that you want to play. It may be only after a few meetings that you see that something is missing from the board dynamics and that you can supply that. However, you should always be yourself, even if others are expecting something a little different.

We recruited a non-exec once, with a view to chairing a committee. I'd liked her from the off, as she was intelligent, interested and had done her homework. When she joined the board, it soon became clear that she had a very independent perspective and was unafraid not only to express it, but also to stick to it for a long time. She had a habit of waiting until the discussion had nearly finished in apparent consensus and then ask a bombshell question. This could be a little irritating, more so as she was often right and had seen something the rest of us hadn't. It might have been painful at the time, but she made the board make much better decisions.

The board as a team

The board is at once one team and three teams. The executive directors are a team, as they work together every day and have common objectives and incentive programmes. The non-execs have a common role as outsiders, they meet together and have to make some decisions together. Yet the board has to also function as one team as well to be successful. Non-execs are not supervisors, but directors with full board responsibility. The best boards have a common purpose. I've been on boards that worked fine, but when they face a crisis suddenly the camaraderie and unity come to the surface and they move to a new level. Great teams are sometimes forged out of adversity. A good chair is very important as they can help to bridge the divide between the executive insiders and the non-executive outsiders.

Tip

If you feel that the board is not gelling as a team, then have a quiet word with the chair and ask their opinion. If this doesn't work, then raise the issue as part of the board annual appraisal (assuming there is one. If not, suggest that there should be one).

Joining and chairing committees

A non-exec is likely to be asked to join one or more committees straight away, perhaps even to chair one. Committees tend to be dominated by the non-execs. Indeed, this is where much of the non-exec work is done. Committees are discussed in more detail in later chapters, but note here that, whereas the board should be one team, the committees with their non-exec strength, are acting more in judgement or supervision of the execs. For example, the audit committee is expected to review the quality of published numbers and the company control framework, and the remuneration committee decides on all aspects of executive remuneration and bonuses.

Speaking offline

It is always helpful for non-execs to have off-line (i.e. outside formal meeting) contacts with both execs and other non-execs. This is particularly important before the first few meetings. I have never regretted speaking to colleagues before a particular meeting, but I have often regretted not having done so. Of course, some directors don't want to be bothered or are difficult to get hold of and phone you back late or not at all.

One non-exec seemed to be on the golf course every time I phoned, he explained that he played all day and there was a dinner afterwards, so he couldn't return any call until the following morning (presumably on his way back to the golf course). Others are easy to get hold of and happy to chat. You will soon find out who's who. Incidentally, I have found that difficulty getting hold of directors is an indicator of trouble. They are either too busy or not interested in the board. The perpetual golfer eventually had to be asked to step down from the board.

Why execs resent non-execs

It won't be long before non-execs may start to feel that the executives resent them. It's okay. You haven't become paranoid. They really do resent you.

Being an executive director is a tough job. They work all the hours that the Working Time directive allows, then they opt out and work some more. The market is very tough and competitive, and they end up making numerous difficult decisions. They do this for a couple of months and try to summarise what's happened and why for the Board. Then a few part-time directors waft in, criticise the papers, ask stupid questions and then waft out.

But being a non-executive director is also a tough role. You are invited to join the board of a company about which you probably know little and possibly in a sector of which you know nothing. You may get a cursory induction programme and then it's straight into a board meeting. The performance information may be either perfunctory or so detailed that you can't get any sort of meaningful overview. Management may be defensive, resentful and resistant to questions. You ask yourself, *"how can I add value to this board?"*

Executives often complain that non-execs come to board meetings '*to mark their homework*'. This is very difficult to avoid. Execs usually work very hard and in their heart of hearts, really want the non-execs to turn up and just applaud them. It's only natural. When I stepped from non-exec to executive, becoming executive chairman following the departure of the CEO, I couldn't stop myself resenting the same questions that I would have been asking myself only a month before.

There are few things more irritating for an exec than having a non-exec appear and come up with a good idea or question they hadn't thought of. Even if it's helpful, human nature means that they may resent it.

In the spirit of support[30], here are some tips. Many times, I reflect on a meeting that didn't go well, and wish that I'd taken my own advice:

Tips for non-execs to smooth relationships

1. **Avoid stating the obvious.** Or asking a question implying that executives don't know their job.

2. **If you see errors or omissions in the papers, try to point them out privately outside meetings**. Preferably in advance, rather than in board discussions.

3. **Try to ask questions that arise from reading advance paperwork directly before the day of the meeting, in person, by telephone or email.** This may of course be difficult if papers come out just before the meeting.

4. **Try then to ask questions in board meetings only when they have just occurred to you or will elicit an answer that you would like everyone to hear.** If the latter, you could also warn executives in advance that you intend to ask the question and give them time to prepare a good response. This will make them much less defensive as they won't feel that you are trying to catch them out.

---

[30] You can find a wealth of ideas on how to build personal relationships and trust in "The Trusted Advisor" by Maister, Green and Galford. Although it is aimed at professional advisers to boards and executives, most of the advice is equally applicable to non-execs seeking to build stronger board relationships with both execs and fellow non-execs.

5. **Keep interventions and questions short.** The longer you go on, the more pent-up anger may build in others.

6. **Don't confuse asking a question with making a speech.** There's a time for both, but not at the same time.

7. **Try to put important questions or points early in the discussion.** Rather than dropping them in like a depth charge, just as the chair is drawing the discussion to a close.

8. **Use cautious language, with plenty of conditional tenses and get-outs.** ("I was wondering if…"; "Perhaps this might be an issue…")

9. **Offer to meet separately (offline).** Particularly if the discussion goes on for a long time or has generated some unwelcome heat.

10. **Remember that when you leave this meeting, you can go onto other things.** But, the executives are stuck dealing with the same issues full time until the next board meeting.

Board meetings can be very sensitive affairs. A good one informs all participants and pools knowledge and experience to come up with good decisions. A poor meeting stokes resentment between the various participants. Directors should remind themselves that it's not an oral exam and board papers are intended to be the genesis for a two-way discussion. There is no marking of papers required!

Summary

Your first hundred days on a new board can be daunting. Fight any imposter syndrome that may creep in. If the nomination committee chose you, it's because they believed that you would bring something new and valuable to the board. Don't waste that sense of newness that you will have as a stranger and outsider, and don't forget any sense you develop that things could be done differently. Your first impression may be a valuable insight before you become assimilated into the way the board works.

If this isn't your first non-exec role, a new board is also a chance to start off on a new footing. You can leave behind you all the mistakes you made on another board. Being a stranger works both ways.

Chapter 5 - What's the Risk?

I've seen grown men weep at the prospect of a half-day board review of the Risk Register. Many an eyelid droops at an audit committee discussion on risk prioritisation. I've yet to meet anyone who actually reads the risk section in the Annual Report, even probably the regulators who insist on it. Does risk really need to be so dull and boring? And what is the board's role on risk?

Any business discussion about business needs to encompass risk. But because risk is often presented in a dry, superficial form, directors can be bored into submission. Here are some ways to rescue a risk discussion and turn it into a vital debate about the business.

Risk is the heart of any commercial decision

Let's start from the basics. Businesses create value by taking risks, and the bigger the risk, the higher the return should be expected. In fact, this is summarised by a very famous and well-used equation. I promise you that this is the only equation in this book[31]! Some people, such as some bankers and consultants love to bamboozle boards with these concepts and terms. But it is really not complicated, and it will help if you understand it. Don't be put off!

---

[31] Well, almost the only one.

The Capital Asset Pricing Model (CAPM)

Rate of return = Risk-free rate + beta (market - risk free rate) + alpha.

This means that the rate of return on a company is the sum of the rate of return that you would get taking no risk (e.g. lending to a major government),

plus;

The additional rate of return achieved by the overall market above that of the risk-free rate (i.e. the market premium, as achieved by some market benchmark, such as the FTSE 100)

multiplied by;

How volatile that company's share price is compared to the benchmark (beta)

plus;

The additional return the individual company achieves above that of the market benchmark

The important thing to note is that rates of return should be linked to the risks taken. Theoretically, you can look at a company's return by building up what the market expects a typical company to deliver and adjust this by how volatile (i.e. risky) that company's share price is. The remaining return is the unique value that the company generates from its particular skills or assets. A market-average level of volatility would have a beta of 1.0. A company in a low-risk sector (such as infrastructure, say a water company) would be expected to be less risky than others, i.e. have a beta less than 1.0. So, its benchmark (risk-adjusted) rate of return would be lower than other companies. It is judged against a lower benchmark because it is able to take fewer risks in day-to-day operations. A water company for example, doesn't have competitors, and everyone needs water.

The CAPM is a theoretical concept aimed primarily at investors, identifying whether the return a company makes adequately compensates for the risks implied by investing in that stock. An investor will buy a passive indexed (benchmark) fund in the expectation that they will get a return better than investing in, say, government stocks. Long-term total returns on shares are usually about 7%, whereas long-term government gilts yield (at the time of writing) are around 4%. This implies an 'equity risk premium' of 3%. But if an individual business is more volatile than average (like an airline), investors would expect to get a higher return than 7%, to compensate them for that additional risk. This is the *beta* factor. If a company delivers a return higher than this risk-adjusted benchmark, it is then achieving positive *alpha*. You will sometimes see active funds boasting about their 'search for *alpha*'. This just means they are looking for companies that do better than a risk-adjusted benchmark.

Tip

Two terms to remember are;

Beta – a ratio, often around 0.8 to 1.2, that represents how volatile a company's share price is compared to others, and;

Alpha – A company's individual rate of return against a benchmark, adjusted for the implied relative risk of that company. For example, 2.0 would suggest a 2.0% points higher return.

Companies may adopt a similar approach. If a project is riskier than most, they will expect it to deliver a higher return. If, for example, a company were intending to buy an additional production machine, very similar to others it owned, to save costs, it might look for a return of 10%. However, for a riskier project to launch a completely new product, it might require a 15% or 20% return to make it worthwhile. You can see therefore how the evaluation of risk is crucial to business decisions.

Any risk implies a reward and a cost. If the reward exceeds the cost, the company creates value, i.e. delivers a return. If the cost exceeds reward, then it destroys value. But since the company almost certainly doesn't know in advance what the final reward and cost will be, it has to estimate them. The company is taking a risk that the reward and cost will be different to that planned. Risk must therefore be at the heart of any board decision.

Too often, risk is put in a silo and left to the risk and audit committees, and treated as a form-filling exercise, not as the heart of any business decision. The regulators don't help. Their well-meaning interventions require companies to lay out risk register forms for the Annual Report and demand disclosure of the 'risk appetite' without any real understanding of how companies really need to understand risk.

As the great aviator Ernest K. Gann wrote: *"Rule books are paper – they will not cushion a sudden meeting of stone and metal."* [32] The typical risk register is about as useful.

Why companies get safety risks right, and board risks wrong

The business model in commercial aviation is to have a thin tube of highly pressurised metal being propelled at 600 miles per hour by inflammable fuel at 35,000 feet in all weathers at temperatures of around

---

[32] Ernest K. Gann (1986) "Fate is the Hunter: A Pilot's Memoir"

-57 degrees. Now that sounds pretty risky, so have you ever wondered how aviation got to be one of the safest forms of transport?

High-risk industries, such as aviation, marine, chemicals and nuclear, have to get safety right. There is no risk appetite that tolerates a major accident. In aviation, for example, the feedback loop on an aircraft is very fast and exceptionally forceful. If bad decisions can suddenly kill the pilots and hundreds of passengers, then the company and the pilots will take risk management very seriously indeed.

In contrast, poor board decisions usually take months, if not years, to become evident, and tend to result in financial losses, rather than personal injury. A pilot may not survive a really bad decision, but a CEO does, and may even keep their job. Bad corporate risk management has a much slower and less lethal feedback mechanism than safety-critical functions. Boards therefore can get away with much less advanced and rigorous risk management. This is reflected in the differences between the regulators. For example, the UK Civil Aviation Authority (CAA)[33] mandates safety/risk management systems in a detailed and rigorous way, on a completely different level to the boiler-plate risk management requirements of corporate regulators.

Good risk management requires detailed and well thought through analysis of why risks happen, what barriers can be put in place to reduce the risks and to ameliorate their consequences. High-risk industries put in place rigorous and detailed step by step processes to ensure that this happens and to avoid the pitfalls of risk management. In contrast, too many corporate boards focus on writing bland risk registers for their annual reports.

---

[33] Well worth looking on the CAA website, as their tools are well-suited to corporate risk management. https://www.caa.co.uk/Safety-initiatives-and-resources/Working-with-industry/Safety-management-systems/Safety-management-systems/

Why risk management can fail

Let's start with the pitfalls of risk management. Why does risk management fail?

1. The risk wasn't considered

2. The risk was believed to be too unlikely to bother about

3. The risk turned out much worse than thought

4. Two or more risks were inter-related, and the effects multiplied

5. The risks were known, but no-one made effective plans to counter them

For example, not many boards had the risk of a global pandemic in their risk registers before the COVID-19 outbreak in 2020/21, because they either didn't think of it or believed that it would be a government problem. After all, the last really dangerous global pandemic was the flu in 1918, over a hundred years previously.

Even if people had thought of it, most had no idea how serious it could be, and the extent to which governments would lock down economies.

The pandemic is also a good example of interrelated risks. It didn't just cause increased absenteeism and overworked medical services, it forced people to stay in their homes, restricted them from shopping, eating out, and going to entertainment venues.

Offices were closed, which then devastated transport networks and city-centre hospitality businesses. Economies went into recession as a result of the pandemic.

Tips

1. Focus on events, not causes. For example, companies may not add pandemics to their risk registers, as there are so many different aspects of a pandemic that the exercise will be too broad ranging to be useful. Instead, try to get the board to focus on an event, such as having no access to head office for a long period. Then work back from there, to what might have caused it and what might be the consequences.

2. Force consideration of even very unlikely events. These are sometimes called 'black swan' events. They happen more frequently than is allowed for. The extreme credit crunch of the Global Financial Crisis (GFC) in 2007/8 was thought to be so unlikely that few companies – and no governments seemingly – had prepared for it, yet it happened. Even if something is judged as a 1 in 100-year event (and remember that we have had two world wars in just over 100 years), there is still an 80% chance that you will see it in your lifetime.

3. Always challenge the worst-case scenario. Time and time again, we see events unfurling that are worse than our worst-case scenarios. Before the GFC, companies thought that interest-rates couldn't possibly stay below 1% for any sustained period of time, yet since then they have, and even at times gone negative. This failure of imagination cost many businesses dear when their interest rate swaps turned toxic as a result. For example, Northern Rock's problem at heart was that no-one thought that a credit crunch would ever be so bad that even AA or AAA rated securities would be regarded as too risky.

Challenge for interrelationships. The biggest danger is often that one hazard triggers two or more risks at once, or that one mitigation stops another mitigation from working. Assura plc, when its interest-rate swap went toxic and its bank withdrew support, had two possible mitigations; an equity raise from shareholders and non-bank borrowing. However, shareholders wouldn't contribute more equity until it had got more borrowing secured, and debt providers wouldn't lend until there was more equity subscribed. It was a chicken and egg situation.

Also, bear in mind that when one or two things go wrong, others tend to follow.

Sometimes, a risk is foreseen, but nothing significant is done about it. The UK government has well-illustrated this in the COVID-19 era. As an insider remarked:

"We just watched. A pandemic was always at the top of our national risk register – always – but when it came, we just slowly watched."[34]

This is the 'deer in the headlights' syndrome.

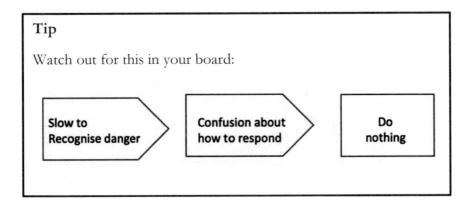

Tip

Watch out for this in your board:

Slow to Recognise danger → Confusion about how to respond → Do nothing

---

[34] Insight in Sunday Times 19 April 2020

The Bow-Tie Model: How high-risk industries manage risk, and so can your board

High-risk industries[35] put the emphasis on process, procedures and systems and very precise language. You need to understand their terminology to follow their models. They first identify a hazard, or general area of risk, say for example poor people management.

The event[36] is what happens when the risk crystallises, i.e. you lose control of the hazard. You then identify the threats that might cause the event, such as remuneration becoming uncompetitive and any preventative barriers that either alert you to the threat or allow you to ameliorate it.

The assumption is then made that the event has happened, so recovery barriers are identified that allow you to reduce the impact of the event happening. These might include interviewing leavers and making counter offers.

Escalation factors make barriers less likely to work, for example, financial constraints and work stress.

---

[35] An excellent analysis of risk in safety-critical industries is found in Charles Perrow 'Normal Accidents'.

[36] High risk industries call an 'event', rather quaintly, an 'abnormal condition', showing the process thinking behind this risk model.

The general area of risk

Threats   - A cause of the event

█ Preventative barriers – things that detect the threat and aim to reduce or eradicate it

Event   - the moment you lose control of the hazard
                     (ie a risk crystallises)

█   Recovery barriers – things that may reduce or eradicate the consequences

Escalation factors – things that make barriers less likely to work

Consequences - results of the event happening

High-risk systems accept that humans will make mistakes, and indeed, recognise that the higher the stress levels, the more mistakes will be made (an escalation factor). They emphasise the need for several barriers to any threat, i.e. multiple lines of defence[37], knowing that some will fail, so others are needed as back-up. These defences also need of course to detect a threat to prevent it.

There are four key principles:

1. **All systems have weaknesses**, and will fail at some point

2. **All humans make mistakes**, and you need to plan for this

3. **You need to detect** an event to manage it

4. **You need multiple lines** of defence against any risk

---

[37] Companies often talk about lines of defence in their financial controls, where level one might be the process itself and the employees running the operation; level two is management supervision; and level three internal or external audit. This is a different take on the basic need to have multiple layers of controls.

Given these principles, how do you prevent hazards triggering events? The analogy that is commonly used is Swiss cheese.

A general hazard creates a number of specific threats. You therefore have to create a number of barriers, as different lines of defence, like slices of cheese, to detect and prevent any threat from causing an event. However, every slice of Swiss cheese has some holes in it, as any line of defence will have some weaknesses and human operators will make mistakes. An event will occur only when the holes in the different slices line up, i.e. all the barriers or lines of defence fail in some way to stop a threat. For a pandemic hazard, lines of defence against mass spreading of infection (the event) will include taking temperatures, vaccines, washing hands, wearing a mask, and maintaining social distance. None of these are completely effective on their own, but together they provide a significant degree of protection. If all of them fail in enough cases, the hazard of a pandemic will become a real event.

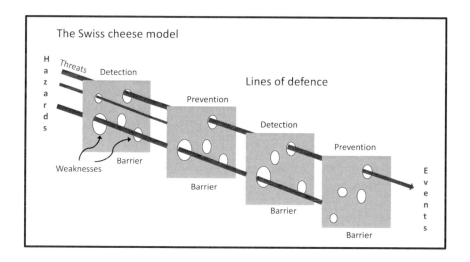

The Swiss cheese model demonstrates why any effective control of risk requires multiple lines of defence to maximise your chances of stopping a hazard becoming an event. It is also used to explain how you attempt to stop an event having bad consequences – by having multiple recovery barriers. Like prevention barriers, you need several levels of recovery barriers, as one barrier may not be enough on its own. In a pandemic, once there is a mass infection, recovery barriers would include mass testing, lockdown and isolation measures.

The Swiss Cheese model is the basis for a detailed risk methodology, called the Bow-Tie model. A simple business example of this model in action is set out below, using the example, touched on above, of the hazard of poor people management. You identify a specific event that might come from this hazard (resignations of key personnel). The methodology then identifies the threats that could cause resignations, and, importantly, what preventative barriers you put in place to stop them. In this case, the threat might be uncompetitive remuneration and the barriers would be benchmarking salaries (detecting the threat) and pay reviews (action to prevent the threat).

An example of a Bow-Tie model for a business risk is on the next page.

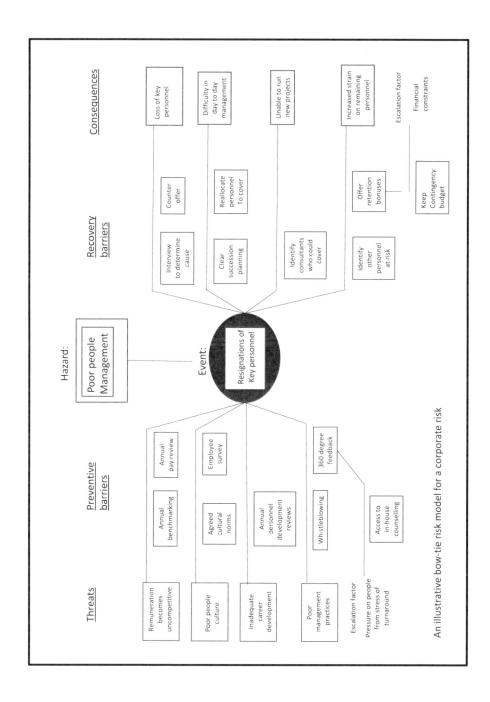

An illustrative bow-tie risk model for a corporate risk

This model always assumes that the event may happen, so it also high-lights the need to mitigate the effects of an event. Recovery barriers are designed to reduce the consequence of the event happening. In this example, it would include post-resignation interviews and counter-of-fers to staff who want to leave. If the recovery barriers don't work either, the model identifies the consequences. Escalation factors are also considered, being things that make the barriers less powerful or more difficult to work, such as work-place stress or financial con-straints.

This is the gold standard of risk management, but it won't necessarily be popular with management, because it requires a lot of work and thinking. But that precisely is the point of risk management. Corpo-rates spend lots of time trying to quantify risk, often at the expense of working out how they would stop the threat. An airline doesn't spend a lot of time working out the cost of a major aircraft accident. It knows that such an event is an existential threat. PanAm never really recov-ered from the bombing of Flight 103 over Lockerbie, even though it was not at fault. The airline industry focusses on working out how not just to avoid an accident, but also how to reduce the harm of an event. Hence there are safety systems to reduce a risk of an aircraft accident, but also safety systems that protect life in the event of an accident (such as strong seats and oxygen masks).

The Bow-Tie model forces you to consider how you would deal with an event happening. Too often corporates list out their mitigations and then decide that the event will never happen, so they don't need to worry about working out what to do if it did. I estimate that 90% of all corporate risk 'mitigations' are preventative barriers, and barely 10% are recovery ones.

Tips

1. Assume that a risk will crystallise into an event in risk management.

2. Ensure that there are recovery barriers. So-called 'mitigations' are actually almost always preventative, rather than recovery, barriers. Ask questions about what we would do if the event did happen, and don't accept that the mitigations are so good that it never will.

Using Swiss Cheese and Bow-Ties to challenge board risks

You may not be able to persuade management to adopt the Bow-Tie model, as it requires a lot of work[38], but you can still use the methodology to analyse the risks and to point you to the right questions to ask.

Take this example of corporate risk wording, taken randomly from a recent annual report of a leading UK company[39]:

The risk is "*Failure to deliver an effective, coherent and consistent strategy, to respond to our competitors and changes in market conditions in the operating environment, resulting in a loss of market share and failure to improve profitability.*"

This is a pretty fundamental and existential threat.

---

[38] I've had limited success as a non-exec in getting corporate executives to adopt the full model, but if I were management, I definitely would use it.

[39] This happens to be from Tesco plc Annual Report 2020, but it could be from almost any. In fact Tesco's report is better than many.

Here are some extracts from how the company describes its "key controls and mitigating factors", together with my analysis of each:

1. "We now have a consistent approach to building impactful customer propositions, offering high-quality and competitive value while improving the customer experience." ** *This should be a preventative barrier to try to avoid the risk happening, but it's not actually an action, just a gentle piece of reassurance.*

2. "Propositions are being developed across channels and geographies to ensure consistency in the engagement with customers. Group-wide customer insight management is undertaken to understand and leverage customer behaviour, expectations and experience across the different parts of the business to improve our propositions." ** *This could be described as a preventative barrier, but it's very vague.*

3. "We monitor the effectiveness of our processes by regularly tracking our business and competitors against measures that customers tell us are important to their shopping experience." ** *This is a preventative barrier aimed at detecting a threat.*

4. "We have well-established product development and quality management processes, which keep the needs of our customers central to our decision-making." ** *This is probably a preventative barrier, but it is not clear what it actually does as it is mainly just a piece of reassurance.*

The statement of this risk and its mitigations are typical of corporate risk registers. They are complacent and vague. Most of the 'mitigations' are in fact generalised reassurances that they wouldn't let the event actually happen. Even if they do reduce the risk of it happening, they don't say what they would do to reduce the harmful impact if the event happened. There is no clue, for example, what this company would do if its customer proposition did fall behind competitors and it lost market share and profitability.

Tips

1. Ensure that business risks have 'mitigations' for both preventing events and recovering from them.

2. Ask for more specificity and challenge warm words of reassurance: "What exactly would we do 5 minutes after the event occurred?"

3. 'What are the risks?' is a key question for any business proposal. Ensure that every business proposal has a thoughtful risk section, that identifies clear risks and quantifies them. It should also identify what might happen and how the company will avoid this event and how it would deal with the event if it did happen.

4. Could the company survive the worst that could possibly happen from a risk or a new business proposal? This should be asked time and time again.

What is your risk appetite?

Boards are required to state publicly their company risk appetite: "*determining the nature and extent of the principal risks faced and those risks which the organisation is willing to take in achieving its strategic objectives*"[40]. This means the amount of risk that a company is prepared to take to achieve its objectives. In simple terms, you might go to a casino and be prepared to lose up to £100. That would be your risk appetite.

Most businesses attempt to quantify risk on two levels. Unmitigated (sometimes called gross) risk is the likely consequence of the event

---

[40] Financial reporting Council 'Guidance on Risk Management, Internal Control and Related Financial and Business Reporting' 2014 https://www.frc.org.uk/document-library/corporate-governance/2014/guidance-on-risk-management,-internal-control-and

happening, if the company did nothing to stop it. Mitigated risk (sometimes called net) is the likely consequence after the company has applied its mitigations.

If you believe that there is a one in 10 year (i.e. 10%) chance of an event that would cost £50m, the unmitigated risk would normally be shown as a £5m (i.e. 10% of £50m) net consequence. If the mitigations mean that the board believes that the risk would now be only 1 in 50 years (i.e. 2%), the net consequence would be logged as £1m. This is of course just one number representing a range of possible outcomes. Remember that the probability of the event happening is just a guess and the consequence will have a range of possible costs. You might be given the mid-point of best and worst cases. Even a risk of 1 in 100 years may still happen, and it is little consolation that you were unlucky that it happened on your watch.

You can try to compare the forecast consequences of key risks against the board's stated risk appetite. This is demonstrated in this diagram:

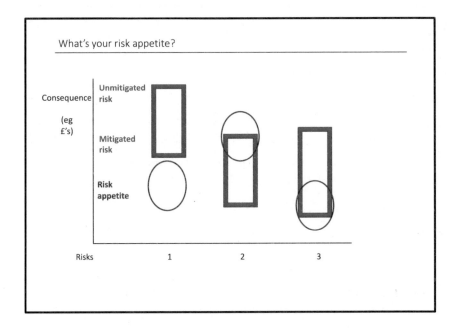

This shows, for each of the three risks, the quantification of the unmitigated risk (top of the blue bar) and the mitigated risk (bottom of the blue bar). The vertical size of the bar shows the 'effectiveness' of the measures taken to mitigate the risk. The red ovals represent the board's risk appetite.

In this example, you can see that the mitigations have the greatest effect on risk 3, whilst the impact on risks 1 and 2 is less.

For risk 1, the mitigations are powerful, but even the mitigated risk is still judged to be higher than the board is comfortable with.

In risk 2 however, the unmitigated risk is within the risk appetite, so you could ask whether there are potentially unnecessary mitigation measures, and perhaps money could be saved by having fewer.

Risk 3 shows a situation in which the unmitigated risk is high, but that there are very effective mitigations that reduce the mitigated risk within the board's risk appetite.

When assessing the corporate risk register and your board's risk appetite, this diagram demonstrates the size of each risk, the degree of mitigations and the risk appetite. It enables the board to discuss relative risk and whether there are sufficient mitigations in place.

Tips

1. **Are consequences mitigated or unmitigated amounts?**
   Make sure that you understand whether the consequence is
   the total cost, or whether it's the total cost weighted by
   (times by) the probability of it happening. They will be very
   different numbers! In the example above, the unmitigated
   risk might be shown as £5m, but if the event actually happened the cost would be £50m.

2. **Remember that probability is a theoretical exercise.** If
   an event happens, the fact that it was a low risk is no consolation.

3. **Probability based on frequency of occurrence can be
   misleading.** For a one-off risk, a 1 in 10 probability seems
   unlikely. However, think about an event that might happen
   once every ten years. If you serve on one board for nine
   years, then the chances are very strong that you will see it
   happen! For example, should the board be prepared to tolerate a risk that could bankrupt the company once every 30
   years?

4. **The consequence may not be the worst case.** If the expected cost were £50m, that could well be a mid-case estimate. Ask management what their worst case would be.

Are risks interdependent? This model implicitly assumes that risks
are independent, but we know that risks are often linked, interdependent or may suffer a cascade effect. This means that the ultimate consequence may be a multiple of the individual risks shown. For example,
the hazard of an economic downturn on a property company might
result in rental yields rising, and so the value of its properties would

fall. However, it might also trigger another risk, that rental defaults increase, reducing further the market value of its properties.

Upside risks

This chapter has concentrated on risks that have adverse consequences. Of course, some risks will bring good news; sales were higher than expected, a project was completed earlier or costs were lower than planned. The principles are all the same for upside and downside risks. The differences are simply that we end up caring more about downside risks than upside, and there just always seem to be so many more bits of bad news around than there are happy surprises. Not many people worry too much about planning for good news, but it is worth considering.

Summary

Understanding risks is a key part of any board's work. The Corporate Governance Code says: "The board should also establish a framework of prudent and effective controls, which enable risk to be assessed and managed." But risk shouldn't be a tedious boiler-plate compliance exercise. It should be what boards do every meeting – assess and manage risk in order to create value.

When a board evaluates a project, it needs to weigh up the potential value creation against the risks that things won't go to plan. You can think in terms of a project risk premium, depending on how risky you think it is, that you would expect to want the company to earn to compensate for investing in that project.

The reason many directors find risk management to be dull is that it is carried out at a superficial and glib level. Who wouldn't be frustrated by the sheer boredom of having to read that Annual Report extract on the risk of being beaten by competitors because the strategy isn't right? But what director wouldn't be fascinated by a discussion about why the company might lose market share and profitability, and what would they need to do about it?

There are techniques and tips here that would help you to understand, contribute to and challenge a board discussion on risk. There is no easy answer to any of the risks that you face. However, good quality discussion and challenge is exactly what all directors should bring to any board discussion.

Chapter 6 - Accounting Almost Killed Me

"I have to say accounting almost killed me. I'm telling you, it messed my vision up."

– Venus Williams

What if you have no finance background?

You can't avoid financial issues on a board. Venus Williams did a degree in business administration and still struggled with her accounts. Fortunately, a director doesn't necessarily need too much financial knowledge to play a full role on a board or even on an audit committee[41]. There are however some basic things that will help, such as understanding profit, profit adjustments, cash, working capital, financial planning, trends. There is a longer discussion here on derivatives, as this is a particular area where directors are usually very cautious in expressing an opinion, but their role in decision-making is actually more important given the risks that can be created.

---

[41] There are courses available to introduce finance for non-execs, which are worthwhile if you feel that your understanding of basic finance is poor and you want to really understand it. However, they are not necessary for you to play a full role even in an audit committee.

These explanations should be enough to give directors the confidence to ask questions of management and contribute to board decisions by:

- Holding management to account for the financial numbers, so that they are drawn up complying with all external regulatory requirements (see next chapter on audit committees)
- Understanding the accounts and forecasts enough so that they can challenge the direction of the business and the deliverability of plans
- Providing constructive challenge to management on significant financial decisions (such as on funding, dividend, capital spend and derivatives)

A non-exec has the advantage of distance, whereas management has more knowledge, but is inevitably caught up in the rush of operational issues. Being a stranger to these issues, gives the non-exec a different perspective free from too much detailed knowledge. A non-exec shouldn't apologise for this. It's why they're on the board.

Tip

Don't assume everyone knows more than you, or that the finance team has always got it right. If you ask apparently simple questions, you may be surprised at the answers. Finance people, like anyone else, have areas that they are unfamiliar with, get caught up in group thinking or get sweet talked by advisers. If you are worried about raising the questions in the full board, ask the questions privately first of either the CFO or the audit committee chair.

Profit

Profit is generally the No 1. financial metric that boards look at. It is calculated in the Income Statement, which used to be known as the profit and loss statement. There are different levels of profit and it's worth understanding them to start:

- **EBITDA** – earnings (i.e. profit) before interest, tax, depreciation and amortisation is used to show the cash profit (because it excludes depreciation and amortisation, which are not cash costs) generated from trading, before taking account the interest cost of debt and corporate taxation.

- **Operating profit** – profit before charging interest and corporate tax. It may also be called Earnings before interest and tax (EBIT). Profit is often quoted at this level when looking at divisional profit in a group.

- **Profit before tax (PBT)** – profit after interest costs, but before corporate tax. This is often used as the 'bottom line' profit.

- **Profit after tax (PAT)** – profit after deducting corporate tax.

- **Earnings per share (EPS)**– Profit after tax divided by the number of shares issued. This shows how much profit has been generated for each share. It takes account of whether the business has issued more shares and is often compared to the dividend paid per share.

There are also a number of potential adjustments to profit that a director should understand:

Underlying adjustments. Profit is often shown *before* non-underlying costs or income, including exceptional or extraordinary items. Most (but not all) non-underlying adjustments are losses or extra costs. Cynical commentators, with some justice, describe these measures as profit before bad news.

- Extraordinary items are amounts that arise from events outside normal business, such as the disposal of a large subsidiary or something completely extraneous, such as a natural disaster.
- Exceptional items are from events that are part of normal business, but are unusual in size and frequency, such as a redundancy programme, a major asset disposal or large one-off remuneration payments.

The main reason to show these one-off or unusual amounts separately is that they may otherwise distort the trend of profit and so mislead anybody reading the accounts.

Tips

1. Look hard at non-underlying costs. Labelling costs as non-underlying gives a higher underlying profit figure, which looks better to the board, investors and is usually used for management incentive calculations. Be particularly cautious about repeated non-underlying costs, as they begin to sound pretty underlying! On the other hand, one non-underlying event may trigger costs spread over two (or more) financial years.

2. Watch for too much focus on EBITDA. There is a role for EBITDA, as 'gross cash flow' from trading, often compared to the capital expenditure required, to show whether the business has the potential to generate net cash. As such, it is beloved of consultants and private equity. However, you can grow EBITDA while spending a lot on capital expenditure, leading to even higher depreciation and thus lower operating profit.

3. Treat profit before tax as the bottom-line number to look at. This is because it takes account of the extra interest cost of capital expenditure and other cash flow.

Goodwill: This generally arises when a company buys another and pays more for it than the value of its tangible (physical) assets, i.e. it has paid for something intangible, which is then put in the acquirer's balance sheet as goodwill. The value of a successful company being acquired is likely to be higher than its tangible assets, as it is probably delivering a higher-than-normal rate of return. So, an acquisition is very likely to generate goodwill in the acquirer's balance sheet.

Amortisation: This is the writing off over a period of previously capitalised intangible assets, such as customer information. Some companies may exclude it from PBT shown in management accounts, as they see it as just an accounting entry. This however tends to obscure the fact that an acquisition may be successfully generating profit, and this has been paid for.

Constant currency: In a multi-currency business, the board will want to know how that business is doing, free from distortions from movements in exchange rates through which foreign units are being reported. Constant currency therefore reports every unit at a set currency rate, probably the budget one. Boards will want to see the actual currency version as well, as this is ultimately what the value is in the home currency.

Cash

All boards should take cash very seriously. You pay employees, suppliers and shareholders in cash, not profit. Profit is just a theoretical concept. Cash is real. Companies differ very much in their attitude to the importance of cash. If a business is private equity owned, highly geared (i.e. has a lot of debt) or hasn't got much headroom against its overdraft or debt covenants, it is likely to be very focused on cash. Others, especially subsidiary boards, may look just at profit.

Tips

1. You should take particular notice when a profitable business is using cash. It may be because it is in an investment phase, and it is spending capital to expand. However, it may be that it is having to spend excessive capital, or acquire other businesses, to drive profit growth, in which case that growth may cause the business to run out of cash.

2. Be very cautious of sudden or large increases in working capital, which could be a tell-tale sign of a problem.

There are two different measures of cash; cash and cash equivalents; and net debt/cash. This is very important to understand.

Cash and cash equivalents

Cash and cash equivalents comprise cash in hand and demand deposits, together with short-term, highly liquid investments (that are readily convertible to a known amount of cash and are subject to an insignificant risk of changes in value[42]). In other words, this is ready money (liquidity) available to pay for day-to day needs: largely bank accounts, but can include deposits that are available at up to 3 months' notice. This is like the money in your current and savings accounts.

---

[42] I.e. the cash that you can get hold of within 3 months without having to accept a smaller amount just to get it that quickly.

Net debt

Net debt includes all other debt that a company has, as well as cash and cash equivalents. It is the commercial equivalent of a person adding up all their cash, bank and savings accounts, less any overdraft, mortgage and other loans they may have. Whereas cash and cash equivalents tell you how much money a company has to pay its immediate requirements, net debt sums up the money the company would need to pay off all its debts. If a company's cash exceeds its debts, then the company has net cash, rather than net debt.

Net debt is a vital indicator of how the business is faring. Its absolute level tells you how much of the business is being funded by borrowing, and movements in net debt tell you whether the business is generating or using cash.

Net debt and its movement should be reported in board papers. The standard (IAS7) Cash Flow Statement[43] required for published accounts is pretty useless to management (and if truth be told, to everyone else too), because:

- It adds down to movements in cash and cash equivalents. Whereas it is important that companies have sufficient liquid cash to pay for their next few months, that is not the point of a cash flow statement to a board. The board wants to know whether the company is generating cash funds as a whole, not just cash in its current bank account. If you looked at the cash flow and took comfort from an increase in cash and cash equivalents, you may well miss that the liquid cash has been generated solely by taking out a large long-term loan. It's a bit like saying that you've got more cash because you borrowed more: Technically true, but highly misleading.

---

[43] IAS7 Statement of Cash Flow is required in published financial statements. IAS stands for International Accounting Standards. It is a great example of the perils of letting professors and theoreticians loose on things they don't really understand.

- It mixes up different activities in a nonsensical and confusing way. Not many companies talk about 'investing activities' and include capital spend, interest and dividends received in the same box, or 'financing activities' including new share being issued with new debt and dividends paid as similar activities.

A board really needs to focus on the movement in net debt and its causes.

> **Tip**
>
> Ask management for a cash flow statement that starts with operating profit (or at least a number that you recognise from the Income Statement, such as EBITDA) and ends with movement in net debt. Explain that you understand that this is not compliant with IAS7, but that is because the standard is nonsense (It's OK, no-one will contradict you).

The rest of the balance sheet

Skeletons, if they exist, will be hiding in the balance sheet. If something untoward is put through the income statement – or something should have gone through the income statement but didn't – there has to be the equal and opposite entry sitting in the balance sheet. And like a real closet, they will stay there until someone opens the door and recognises them for what they are. The balance sheet can be a checklist for trouble.

If, for example, some stock becomes obsolete, the company should take a charge through the income statement, and the opposite entry, a provision, in the balance sheet then reduces the holding value of the stock. If that charge is too high or too low, the incorrect provision will sit in the balance sheet. In another example, a fraudulent invoice will incorrectly boost creditors in the balance sheet, until either it gets paid by a defrauded customer or written off by the company.

Directors are not usually looking for fraud in a balance sheet, but they should keep a degree of vigilance on balance sheet items. When discussion turns to provisions being created and used or auditors question the recoverability of balance sheet amounts, directors should listen carefully. Dull it can be, but don't let that cloud your vision.

Working capital

The three main constituents of working capital are stocks, creditors and debtors. Key indications that you may see from working capital are:

Stocks: A significant increase in stocks, in the absence of a similar increase in sales, should be something to look at carefully. It may indicate that the business has problems in its supply chain and demand forecasting, as it is producing stock that isn't selling, or worse, perhaps, is producing stock just to enhance profit (because some costs can be capitalised into stock, removing them from the income statement).

Tip

Ask management if overheads are being capitalised in (i.e. added to) the stock valuation, which may mean that costs are actually higher than stated in the Income Statement. If this is the case, also ask the external auditors what their view is. Watch for any change in accounting policy, where management decides to capitalise more costs. High amounts of cost capitalisation can inflate the value of stock, leading to future stock write-downs.

Creditors: Trade creditors are what the company owes its suppliers. An unexplained increase in such creditors may show that management is conserving cash by lengthening payment terms or just not paying suppliers to terms. Other creditors can include taxation, social security, and accruals/provisions. An unusual movement in deferred income and provisions is definitely worth querying. If a company wishes to hide profit for a while, increased provisions would be one place where that would show. Similarly, a rapidly reducing provisions line might show that the company is drawing on previous reserves.

Debtors: Trade debtors are amounts owed by customers to the company. Again, watch for any movement in this line that seems out of step with sales. A step-up may mean that management has lost focus on debt collecting or even that, in its desire to maintain sales, it is offering customers longer payment terms. It is worth asking if payment terms are changing and, if so, why.

Borrowings/cash: Confusingly. these may appear to be working capital as they are put in current assets and liabilities in a statutory balance sheet, but they are really cash, not working capital.

Ratios to help watch movements in working capital are:

- **Stock**: Days stock held (stock divided by daily production) or stock turnover (annual production divided by stock).

- **Debtors**: Debtor days (debtors divided by daily revenue) or debtor turnover (annual revenue divided by debtors).

- **Creditors**: Creditor days (creditors divided by daily total costs) or creditor turnover (annual total costs divided by creditors).

Provisions: These are liabilities kept in the balance sheet, for example if there is a major restructuring programme, the company will anticipate significant costs and so will make a provision against profit in the income statement with the opposite side in the balance sheet. This provision will reduce as the cash costs get paid in time.

Planning – The Budget, Reforecasts and Strategic Plans

Almost every business will have a budget or plan, probably an annual one. This is set at the beginning of the financial year and will be the benchmark for financial performance and bonuses. The executives will usually also provide reforecasts during the year.

It is difficult for a non-exec to get a view whether a budget is set at the right level. Too low and it makes it too easy. Too high and it will be unachievable and demotivating. One benchmark will be *'City expectations'* or *'consensus forecasts'*. You should expect the budget to be set, at least in profit terms, a little above City expectations. This gives room for life being a little tougher than expected and still meet shareholder expectations. How much of a 'cushion' is needed will vary from business to business. Beware that *'City expectations'* are not an objective demanding target set by experts, they are developed by analysts in discussion with management.

If there are several reforecasts during the year, don't lose sight of the original budget. It's an important anchor point, as reforecasts may go up and down during the year.

Tips

1. When you first join a board, ask what full year profit variances were against budget for the last few years. This will give you an idea of the historic accuracy of budget forecasts.

2. A budget may also have a 'discount' or 'cushion' already built in. This is sensible, as most budgets are set initially with a 'can do' mentality that ends up with an ambitious number. Discounting this back gives a more balanced target. Ask the CFO to compare the current budget discount to historic budget variances to get a sense of how adequate it is.

The core tool for anybody trying to understand movements in profit forecasts is the profit track. This is a schedule that starts with last year or the budget profit and ends with the latest forecast, showing why it has changed; for example, lower sales, higher raw material costs, higher productivity, disposals, interest costs. Sometimes, it is presented as a 'waterfall' chart, but the message is the same.

You need to understand the answer to the basic question – why has profit changed?

Performance information

One of the board's key roles is to 'ensure that the necessary resources are in place for the company to meet its objectives and measure performance against them'[44].

---

[44] Corporate Governance Code, Principle C

To do this effectively, you should ensure that your board identifies the key performance indicators that measure best company performance, going beyond the purely financial. For example, this might include; revenue, PBT, change in net debt, customer satisfaction, factory utilisation, pipeline of new business and employee retention. It is important that these are boiled down to perhaps seven to ten absolutely key ones, as the more you get, the more difficult it is to balance them all, like spinning many plates at once. These should then have targets set and reported regularly throughout the year.

It's strange but true that even today many boards struggle to generate adequate non-financial performance information. Boards need regular financial and non-financial performance information, and not just a periodic income statement. Performance information can be comparisons against last year, the budget, a reforecast, across competitors, across divisions or time-series trends.

Performance information needs to be comprehensive to be of use. For example, how much can you really understand about a football match from the score alone? Is that goal a result of dominance, or a lucky break? Are the teams well-matched or is one team a minnow? Which team is becoming stronger over time, and has one team lost key players to injury? You need multiple performance measures, financial and non-financial, to understand true performance.

"Time is the Wisest Counsellor of All" – Pericles

Businesses usually divide their lives into 12-month periods. Whilst convenient, this can also be a trap. Take a close look at the timing ('phasing') of profit. In many businesses a disproportionate amount of the profit is made in the final period before the year-end. There are usually good reasons for this, for example, Christmas may be a boom time at the end of a December year-end. But it could reflect management holding reserves or profit back so that they can manage the full year profit outturn. It adds to the uncertainty of any business to leave its profit late in the year and it makes it very difficult for a board to understand true performance during the year.

Boards tend to focus on the full year and so miss clues that a more detailed phasing can reveal. Running rate is a really useful concept to deploy in trying to assess how realistic or ambitious a forecast is. It's always a good idea to keep an eye on running rates.

The possible H1/H2 trap

Phasing of profit is often an indicator of the degree of difficulty of achieving a full year profit. This point is particularly important as a business moves from a first half to a second half and one year to a next.

I was reviewing[45] a reforecast a few years ago that showed that profit would be down by £30m in the first half (H1), but they would recover to increase profit by £10m for the full year. This was reassuring – okay they had had a bad first half, down 30%, but they were now reducing costs and revenue would get a bit better so they would be down only 7% full year. However, it was only when you looked at what this meant for the first and second half running rates that it became clear that the second half (H2) required a Herculean turn around.

Profit	H1	H2	Full Year
Last year actual	£100m	£60m	£160m
This year actual/forecast	£70m	£100m	£170m
Increase year-on-year	-£30m	+£40m	+£10m
% change year-on year	-30%	+67%	+7%

---

45 The numbers are fictional but the experience wasn't.

What looked like a respectable turnaround became a mountain to climb, when you looked at what this implied for the second half. Profit would need to go up by £40m, which as the second half was usually less profitable than the first half, would mean an 67% increase in profit. A swing of a 30% profit decline to a 67% increase wasn't believable and didn't happen.

Tip

The director's best friend on forecasts is the running rate. In this example, the final period of the first half would have had to be showing the turnaround already happening, and perhaps profit beginning to grow already, for you to begin to believe. Boards should look hard at running rates, especially for H1/H2 forecasts, and as a believability check on annual budgets.

A simple graph like this is very valuable to understand running rates. The moving annual average(maa) is an annual running rate, important when profit is uneven or seasonal, as it gives the de-seasonalised trend. Here it can be easily compared to the budget full year number (shown as the green bar on the left-hand side).

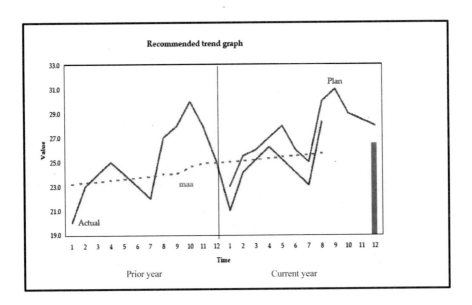

Recommended trend graph

Derivatives[46]

"Never in the field of company finances, has so much damage been done by so few contracts with such good intentions." – Simon Laffin[47]

If there's one topic that is almost guaranteed to quieten a board meeting, it's when the CFO starts proposing that the company takes out a hedge. This is a very complex area of financial management and almost no-one understands them, and even fewer want to admit it[48]. Typically, the proposal is couched in obscure technical language, usually inspired

---

[46] A major reason for the 2007/8 Great Financial Crash was that even the banks' management didn't understand their own derivatives, and certainly not the full risks that they were incurring.

[47] Apologies for quoting myself, but this is my book and the comment is painfully true.

[48] I am neither a banker nor an expert in derivatives. This is just some practical cautionary words based on my own unfortunately extensive experience of companies trying, and sometimes failing, to hedge risks.

by astute advisers, who outdo themselves to devise ever more complex devices and jargon.

However, directors should not be afraid to ask questions about proposals for hedging and should not assume that anyone else on the board understands it more than they do. In fact, there are a set of eight basic questions that every director should ask about a hedging proposal.

Companies put hedges into place to transfer a financial risk from themselves to someone else. This is like an insurance policy, which transfers the risk of something happening from the policy holder to the insurance company. Hedges are usually put in by using a derivative[49], which is simply a financial contract whose value depends upon the outcome of something else. The whole purpose is to reduce, or hedge, the risk for the person buying the hedge.

Most hedges are successful in achieving their objective to manage risk. However, when they go wrong, they can do so spectacularly. Here are four case studies[50], based on real events, but simplified and with some details changed for legal reasons.

A bit too much to drink

Manufacturer W was a large food and drink company that wanted to gear up its balance sheet. Its bank was delighted to lend this money but insisted that the company hedge the interest rate risk of the variable rate debt. After all, the company wouldn't want to risk its interest rate payments increasing dramatically if market rates went up. Fortunately,

---

[49] I focus on swaps here, as they are some of the most dangerous derivatives, but there are many different, complex and exotic derivatives available. You should distinguish however between derivatives that FORCE an outcome (such as a swap) and those that ALLOW, but don't force, you to do something (such as an option). The former are usually much more dangerous.

[50] These case-studies focus on when the hedges go wrong. Of course, sometimes a company can get lucky and a poorly designed hedge becomes profitable. That however is not the objective of a hedge.

the bank was able to write a derivative to do precisely this and would be delighted to sell it to the company.

The derivative was finalised and signed just a few days before the loan agreement was ready. But in between these events, the market worsened significantly. As a result, the loan agreement was never actually signed. However, with the market downturn, market interest rates suddenly fell heavily. When the company tried to cancel the hedge, it found that the derivative was already heavily in loss. Assured by advisers that the market situation was temporary, and interest rates would recover, management held onto the derivative as the loss grew. Eventually it sold 75% of the hedge at a cost of hundreds of millions of pounds. The Board couldn't face up to taking a bigger hit. It persuaded itself that since it would always need debt, and as interest rates[51] couldn't go any lower, the 25% holding was justified. Neither was true and eventually, it conceded to the inevitable and sold the remaining for a further loss of nearly £100m. Both the CFO and CEO resigned.

Nothing left on their plate

Mr & Mrs X ran a popular and profitable restaurant in South Wales. They took out a variable rate £200,000 25-year mortgage from their bank, who sent some sharp suited bankers to frighten them that interest rates could go up, making the mortgage unaffordable. The suits had the ideal product – a 25-year interest-rate swap (i.e. a derivative that swapped a fixed rate for a variable one, effectively fixing the interest rate), so that they need never worry about interest rates going up again. However, interest rates subsequently fell, so that as their mortgage payments reduced, this was offset by margin payments to the bank for the hedge. Five years later, they decided to sell the restaurant and move

---

[51] People tend to focus on the short-term LIBOR, but a long-term derivative is priced to the forward LIBOR. When short term rates are very low, as now, you would usually find that longer term rates are higher as markets expect interest rates will rise one day. If you get told that 3-month LIBOR is 0.5% and surely can't go any lower, ask to see the yield curve (i.e. future interest rates) and suggest that it could flatten.

on. There was no problem in redeeming the mortgage, but the bank explained that there was a big price to exit the hedge. Interest rates had gone down by 2% and so there were 20 years of 2% interest payments due, some £80,000. This wiped out the couple's equity on the restaurant and left them with nothing.

Property foundations sink

Company Y was a small listed property company. Pressurised by an activist shareholder, the company geared up and took a £200m 30-year variable-rate loan from its bank, which insisted also on the company taking out an interest-rate swap to fix that rate. Cash proved tight and so a couple of years later the company negotiated improved terms, for which the bank insisted that it get a break clause in the loan agreement at 5 years, giving the bank the right to unilaterally demand it be repaid at that point. The bank assured the company that this was just a technical measure to do with its capital ratios. Shortly after this, the bank announced that it would be withdrawing from commercial lending in a couple of years' time.

As Y's cash flow had improved in those intervening years, the loan had been gradually repaid, leaving £100m outstanding. The bank then informed Y that it would call in the loan at the first break clause, and by the way, the hedge would need to be cancelled at the same time. The mark-to-market loss on that derivative was now £40m. The company had to refinance the £100m loan while at the same time paying out £40m for the hedge. This £140m cash requirement was greater than Y's total market capitalisation. Both the CFO and CEO lost their jobs and Y, a good and successful property company, came within a few short hours of going bust.

Too little flying costs a lot

Company Z was a large airline. Like most airlines, it hedged the price of fuel, usually 90% of its annual requirements. Then the global COVID-19 pandemic suddenly devastated the market. Most flights were cancelled and the oil price slumped. Z was looking at a situation in which it would fly much less than half its planned number of sectors, and its fuel requirements were slashed. It was however, still committed to pay for the difference between the low market price of fuel and the higher hedge price for fuel, even on the fuel that it wouldn't actually be buying. The full loss was expected to be over £1bn.

What do we learn from these stories?

Hedges do not remove risk, they transfer it. A perfect hedge transfers a risk from the purchaser to the bank. Management focus tends to be directed on the 'rate' – whether the derivative is based on 0.5% or 0.7% interest rates, 3-month LIBOR, or $80 a barrel of oil, for example. However, there are other even more important elements that often don't get reviewed enough.

Directors should be particularly aware that:

1. **Hedges may actually increase risk.** At times hedges are liable to escalate risk and can quite easily become so big that they become an existential threat. It can be like trying to put a fire out with a petrol bomb.

2. **The tenor (i.e. length) of the derivative is important.** If a company signs up to a 30-year swap, in order to cancel it or sell it to another party earlier than 30 years, it will have to pay for any market loss (i.e. *the loss over the whole outstanding period of the derivative*) at that point. That could be 30 years of loss, that will add up to a lot of money, as the restaurant X and property company Y found out. Beware particularly that if a company takes out a long-term swap and the thing that it is trying to hedge (e.g. a loan) doesn't last that long, then it is exposing itself to interest rate risk that may well be much bigger than the original risk that was being hedged! A mismatched swap will *increase* risk, not reduce it.

3. **The 'size' of the derivative is crucial.** The size of the swap can be mismatched too. When property company Y reduced the size of its loan, the 'excess hedge' became an unmatched liability. It didn't bother to, or couldn't, face the loss that it would have to have crystallised in reducing the size of the swap. The airline couldn't conceive that it wouldn't need all that fuel, but it didn't in the end. Unless the size remains exactly in line with the underlying liability throughout the tenor of the swap, it will produce a new risk.

4. **A hedge may well introduce a new cash risk.** As Y found out, there may be a break clause in a derivative that is likely to require the settling of any market loss in cash now. The originator of the swap may well require that a company regularly pays any mark-to-market loss (i.e. make margin payments). If the swap is showing a loss (i.e. 'out of the money') a company may have to pay up the full loss immediately, whilst not receiving for many years the benefit of the lower interest rate, exchange rate or oil price. The small print of the swap documentation may well also require regular margin payments or may trigger them if the purchaser fails some covenant tests (i.e. their credit becomes less worthy).

5. **A hedge may introduce new P&L risk.** This seems counterintuitive. Why hedge something if it doesn't allow you to fix the risk at least in the income statement? The accounting rules (IFRS9) that allow a company to account for a hedge to match P&L impacts of the hedge to the underlying risk are complex and tightly written. If the hedge does not qualify as an 'effective' hedge, the derivative could be marked to market in each set of accounts, giving a lumpy profit or loss that does not match the underlying liability.

6. **There is no such thing as relationship banking in derivatives.** Companies W, X and Y all trusted their relationship banks and thought that there was a mutual interest in helping a customer. In fact, derivative trading is a tough numbers game,

with large profits and bonuses at stake. The bank that sells the derivative is quite likely to sell it on to another financial institution very quickly after it has issued it to a customer. In this way, a bank's profit and bonus can be locked in on day one, and the bank may have no further role or responsibility.

7. **You don't have to hedge every risk.** Boards need to decide how much risk they are willing to bear (their "risk appetite") and then model how much risk would there be if you didn't hedge. For example, say your annual profit is £100m, and you wouldn't want an increase in interest rates to hit you by more than 5%, i.e. £5m. You could therefore accept a 'value at risk' of £5m. If your floating rate debt is £150m, that means that you would accept a risk that interest rates would go up by 3.3% (i.e. 5/150). If you think it is very unlikely that rates would go up so much, then you may choose not to hedge at all.

8. **Swaps are potentially very dangerous.** They may well not be the most appropriate hedge. In the preceding example, if you think that there is a chance rates could go up by 3.3%, you could buy a derivative (a 'cap') that pays out only if interest rates increase by more than this. Options, by their nature, are less dangerous as you don't have to take them up. There are many different types of derivatives, but remember that the more complex and the more difficult to understand they are, the more risk this creates.

9. **Only agree to a hedge that is tightly and precisely related to a specific existing risk.** Hedges are not transferrable. A key reason why companies W and Y were willing to have an over-hedged position was that they persuaded themselves that they would always have some variable rate debt that they could ascribe the hedge to. It meant that they had to turn down attractive fixed rate debt, because they needed variable rate to justify the hedge. Y found that it just didn't need, and couldn't

afford, as much debt over time. You just can't hedge something that doesn't exist. It's like taking out an expensive car insurance policy just in case you ever buy a car.

Any derivative proposal needs to answer the following high-level questions for the board:

1. **If we don't purchase the derivative what's the worst that can happen?** You may want to tolerate some risk, for example, if the worst case still wouldn't have a serious impact on overall profit or cash. Companies may choose not to hedge an exposure or only a proportion.

2. **If we do purchase the derivative, what's the worst that can happen?** If the worst case with a derivative is not very different to that without, then maybe the instrument is not actually reducing risk. If the worst case with a derivative is worse than just living with the original risk, then you are not reducing risk.

3. **Is the derivative actually reducing our risk?** A hedge is designed to provide a cap or offset to a financial risk on another asset or liability. Where companies typically have got into trouble is when they have taken out a hedge that is not a mirror image of the target risk. Mitchells & Butlers took out an enormous interest rate swap to 'fix' the rate in 2008 on a number of debt instruments (i.e. loans). However, it did this before the loans were signed off and they were never actually taken out. It therefore had a massive swap exposure to interest rate movements on debt it didn't have.

On a more detailed level, these are the questions that should be asked of any specific derivative proposal:

Tip:

Eight questions a board should ask about a hedging proposal

1. Does the size and tenor of a proposed derivative exactly match that of a specific risk that already exists?

2. Do both the risk and the hedging derivative have the same break clauses?

3. Is the hedge treated as effective under IFRS9, and if not, why not?

4. Has the company had independent advice from a third party expert, and if so, what did it say?

5. What other forms of derivatives could the company take out, especially as an alternative to a swap?

6. What is the value at risk, i.e. what possible liability are they hedging? Is the value at risk bigger than we are comfortable with (if not, why hedge at all)?

7. Is the derivative effective as a cash flow as well as profit hedge? Are there circumstances where the company would need to make cash margin payments or terminate the derivative at a cost that exceeds any contemporaneous profit benefit?

8. If the risk goes away for any reason, what are the implications of getting out of the hedge?

Hedging is a very complex area, and I have barely touched the surface here. However, it is the complexity that usually hides the risks that many hedges introduce. At heart however, hedging is a simple activity – to reduce financial risk. If the CFO cannot answer these questions in a manner that is understandable to all directors, *do not approve* the proposal.

Summary

The basics of finance are not very complicated, although the detail can quickly become so. The trick for a director is to know enough to ask questions and then to judge the quality of the answers. There are people around to help a non-financially expert director; the CFO, the audit committee chair, and the external auditors, and you should not be afraid to ask them to explain things. Profit will still be the most important metric, but make sure that cash is a close second. Try to get good performance indicators, including non-financial ones, identified with targets set. Look at phasing as well as full year numbers and think about running rates. Be cautious when derivatives are proposed[52] and challenge them until you are satisfied that they will reduce financial risk.

The financials should be giving you a clear vision of company performance. If not, ask questions until they do.

---

[52] By no means are all toxic derivatives the result of mis-selling. However there have been many accusations of banks mis-selling derivatives, although few successful legal actions by companies. The courts have generally been unsympathetic in these situations as judges deem companies to be innately financially sophisticated and so should have understood what they were buying.

Chapter 7 - The Feared Audit Committee

The audit committee is in some ways the most powerful group of directors. It is certainly the most revealing one. So many areas of the business get discussed that it becomes an almost essential part of understanding a business. The company chair and CEO often attend the audit committee because they cannot risk missing hearing important information. Equally, it is a real disadvantage for directors who aren't on the audit committee, as they risk missing out on such intelligence.

Tip

If you, as a non-exec, are not on the audit committee, consider asking if you can attend as an observer, just so that you hear what is going on. This can be on a permanent basis, as part of your induction, or to hear particular subjects being discussed.

The audit committee is informative because it covers so many areas that are crucial to a successful business. This ranges from how the board describes its company performance in external announcements, to how internal controls are working or not, to how the external auditors view the business and to what the big variables are in financial performance.

This chapter looks at what audit committees do, and how both external and internal auditors work with the committee. Risk has already been covered in chapter 5, although it plays a large role in the audit committee too, especially if there is no separate risk committee.

Non-financial people may worry that the audit committee will be dominated by accountants and technical accounting arguments which they don't understand. There's good news and bad news here. The bad news is that financial people do tend to do much of the talking at the audit committee. The good news is that non-financial people are there too. The formal requirement is that at least one non-exec member is a 'financial expert', who has 'recent and relevant financial experience'[53]. Most audit committees are likely to have at least two or three 'lay' members. They are there precisely because many of the issues go beyond technical financial discussions and non-financial views are an important balance. The financial people don't always get everything right, and the ambit goes well beyond finance. The 'lay' viewpoint is important and valuable.

What does the audit committee do?

1. Ensure the integrity of financial statements: Reviewing significant accounting judgements and ensuring the integrity of published accounts and reports.

2. Review internal controls and risk management: This includes, but is much more than, the internal audit function (if there is one) and may share risk management with the risk committee (if there is one).

3. Manage external auditors: Appointing, reappointing, removing, evaluating and remunerating the external auditors, as well as ensuring their independence is maintained (subject to board ratification).

---

[53] The UK Corporate Governance Code

The integrity of financial statements

Generally, management will table a paper on accounting issues for an audit committee review of a results announcement. This should cover changes to accounting policies, significant financial judgements and estimates. The external auditors will also prepare a paper that covers these matters, plus how they have done the audit, and recommendations on how improvements can be made. It makes sense for the audit committee to review both papers together on a thematic basis, covering each issue one at a time. It is very wasteful - and tedious - to let management explain an issue in their report and then, a bit later, have the auditors give their view on the same issue.

In understanding the integrity of financials, the audit committee will usually rely on the views of management and the external auditors. If both agree, the committee is likely to assess that this is the right answer. However, occasionally, the non-execs may feel management is 'pushing' an issue or judgement, and that the external auditors are perhaps rolling over and agreeing too easily. Most committees will take their lead on this from the 'financial expert' on the committee, who is generally the committee chair. It is quite difficult to override the view of the external auditors, not least as they may refer to this in their published audit opinion.

One example happened at Northern Rock, when new management wanted to book large, exceptional restructuring costs. This is a common situation, with management perhaps looking to clear large costs out of the way at once, giving a subsequent improvement in performance. The audit committee believed that the amount being charged, went beyond the technically allowable amount (there are quite strict rules on accruing for future costs), but the external auditors accepted management's number. Stalemate followed, but the committee eventually accepted the accrual as the business had to continue and it felt that in the end, it had to give credence to a technical judgement from the auditors. However, the external auditors lost some credibility with the committee, as there was just a feeling that the auditors might have been trying too hard to get off to a good start with the new management.

It is when profit is tight, and management looks strained, that financial numbers and judgements also come under pressure.

As Warren Buffet said:

"Only when the tide goes out do you discover who's been swimming naked".

Tip

Be extra vigilant when financial performance is disappointing, especially if there are changes to accounting policies or large financial estimates are suddenly recalculated to give a better result.

Accounting Points to Watch

There are a number of ways in which financials can be changed when reviewed under pressure. I will confess to being a poacher turned gamekeeper in this section, having used all of these (perfectly legal) accounting methods as a CFO in my youth:

Changes to accounting policies: If profit is under pressure, there are typically a number of policies that can be reviewed to improve it[54]:

1. Asset lives can be extended, which reduces the depreciation charge. This should be carefully looked at to ensure that extended lives are justified.

---

[54] 'The Signs Were There' by Tim Steer is an excellent book on how accounting treatments can indicate problems in a company. It is well worth reading by any audit committee member.

a.   A particularly dangerous area is software life. Some software can be used for many years, perhaps a decade. However, expensive software can also be superseded and made redundant much earlier than planned.

b.   Be very cautious of extending any asset lives when times are tough, particularly as this is also often the time when assets are retired or no longer used as part of the inevitable reorganisation to cut costs.

2.   More costs can be capitalised, so that instead of charging their full amount to profit, they are spread over several years as depreciation. This often happens to project or software internal development costs.

Management can take a view that more costs are really directly ascribable to a capital project, and so can be capitalised. This should be challenged to ensure that it is really true.

3.   Interest can also be capitalised, but make sure that there is real debt costing interest to justify it being capitalised.

Accounting estimates and judgements: Look for a list of these in both the management and auditors reports to the audit committee. They are the heart of any discussion about whether the right numbers are being struck.

An accounting *judgement* is typically about which accounting policy to apply, such as; revenue recognition for long-term contracts; the discount rate to apply to value a liability; and the nature of a joint venture.

An accounting *estimate* however is focused on a particular number or amount, such as; how much to accrue for a liability; impairment of intangible assets (such as goodwill); and the cost of capital.

Some examples of potentially contentious discussions are:

1.   **Revenue can be brought forward**, although this is a lesser risk these days with the revenue recognition standard (IFRS15) being

much more prescriptive. Listen carefully to what the auditors say about this.

2. **Costs can be lumped together** as exceptional or non-underlying/non-recurring (these were discussed in the last chapter). However, non-execs boards need to watch out that management, naturally enough, usually wants to book all these exceptional items in one go as early as possible. Often the costs are actually spread over two or more years, but there is a temptation to try to book them all upfront. The accounting rules are pretty clear, so listen to the advice of the auditors. Effectively the costs need to be committed in the year in which they are booked, even if the cash impact is sometime in the future. This can be a little ambiguous, and the audit committee may agree to book the costs, even if the auditors are expressing some concerns. Non-execs just need to be sensitive to the point at which the auditors say that they really don't agree and will put their concerns in their audit report. This is certainly the point at which the audit committee must think very hard and be sure that it believes in its own decision.

3. **Costs can be 'kitchen sinked'**. There are times when management may want to put as much cost as possible into one year, to help the next. These might be to put them in an exceptional charge, or into the current because the outgoing year's profit, as it is already so good, or so bad, that the costs won't make any significant difference then.

4. **Goodwill**. This can be a very large number, yet is usually a rather academic one, as analysts and most investors will dismiss it as a theoretical construct. Generally, they, like boards, will look at profit before any goodwill write down. However, a large write off is usually picked up by media commentators, especially as they seize on it as it makes a very large hole in profit or forces the company into loss. Be careful if management dismiss it as non-cash, and so unimportant. Goodwill has been paid for in the past, so it is a write off of real money. The problem is that maintaining it on the balance sheet requires complex forecasts of future profitability and cash. A significant change in current profitability, such as in an economic downturn, can cause a major write down, as it can be effectively one year's

trading downturn being capitalised into many years future forecast poorer performance. This is why goodwill write downs are often very large numbers.

Tips

1. Remember that the question is how you apply the rules, not whether you think the accounting rules are right or sensible. In financial reporting, it doesn't matter what you think a number should be, based on your view of fairness or common-sense. As in a court of law, what matters is only how the facts fit with the rules.

2. Use the external auditors as a source of technical understanding on the accounting rules, as well as an independent judgement on the financials.

If you are the financial expert on the audit committee, speak to the auditors in advance to make sure that you understand the technical matters. The committee will look to you to give them a guide as to how to react where there is a difference of opinion.

In the end, financial statements are the responsibility of the company board, not the auditors. The auditors are advising the board what they think, and will report to shareholders if they don't agree, but the board makes the decision on what to report. If the committee suspects that the auditors are too pliable, then members should address this head on in the private session with the auditors. In the event that the concern remains, the committee can, in the last resort, institute a re-tender for external audit and prospectively change the firm used.

Internal controls

We have already argued in Chapter 5 that risk is not just an issue for an enterprise, it is what an enterprise does. A company aims to create value by taking risks, resulting in earning more revenue than costs. It therefore needs to manage its risks to maximise its chances of creating value. A company's internal controls are how a company manages its risks. Take a casino. It knows that the games all favour the house, so it can't lose. It can only fail by losing control of its risks; collusion between gamblers and croupiers, rigged tables or cards, card counters, poor accounting or fraud. Internal controls therefore are an integral key part of management, not just the pet topic of the CFO or head of risk.

There is increasing regulatory pressure on boards to take responsibility for internal controls. The Corporate Governance Code says: "*The board should establish procedures to manage risk, oversee the internal control framework, and determine the nature and extent of the principal risks the company is willing to take in order to achieve its long-term strategic objectives.*" In most companies, the board will delegate its initial review function to the audit committee for this, but the board must retain overall responsibility.

Tip

When reviewing the internal audit work programme, ask the team to explain how it links in coverage and prioritisation to the major risk areas (from the risk model and appetite) and already identified weaknesses in processes and controls. For example, if a critical risk has mitigations that greatly reduce its impact, you want to be sure that the mitigations actually work.

Since both risk management and internal controls are integral parts of executive management, they must be owned primarily by management.

The audit committee and board's roles are therefore to oversee management's controls. The first step should be to assess how good are the executives at actually managing risk, how good are their internal controls and how many control weaknesses and failures are there.

Basic questions that an audit committee should be asking of management;

(a) **Are the executives actively managing risk?**

1. Identifying key business risks, together with executive-owned actions that help avoid risks crystallising, and as well as identify and mitigate the impact of risk events occurring.

2. Identifying any trends or risks that are likely to emerge or become more critical in the future (you don't drive a car by looking only in the rear-view mirror).

3. Quantifying the business's risk appetite. How big a risk is the board comfortable with?

4. Undertaking a documented financial and fraud risk assessment.

(b) **How good are the internal controls?**

5. Agreeing and communicating a clear hierarchy of delegated authorities. Who can sign off decisions and expenditure? What decisions need to be approved by what level of management or the board?

6. Identifying & deploying clear, entity-level controls to ensure the right 'tone from the top', including Codes of Conduct, Anti-Bribery & Corruption, HR policies (especially recruitment, discrimination, and bullying), GDPR, Cyber security, disaster recovery and finance policies). This should include cultural issues too.

7. Preparing robust process documentation, with clear process owners for all business controls (including financial, HR, IT, media buying, customer management). You can't manage processes unless there is a clear agreement as to what happens and who is responsible.

8. Identifying key controls and monitoring their operation, reporting via first (line management), second (regional/central management) and third lines of control (internal audit). Processes need controls, and hazards need preventative and recovery barriers. Have the CEO and CFO confirmed the adequacy of controls?[55]

9. Ensuring that there are sufficient, high quality individuals operating first, second and third lines of defence, reporting deficiencies and possible future shortages at an early stage. This draws in manpower and succession planning, as many control weaknesses emanate from not having the right people at the right time.

10. Identifying and monitoring material IT controls, with precise ownership and adequate documentation. IT is absolutely crucial as a facilitator of most business processes and source of most hazard barriers, as well as a source of many risks (such as cybersecurity) itself.

11. Defining a robust process for the annual review of the effectiveness of business, financial and IT controls. This should be on every audit committee's annual agenda.

(c) How many control failures and weaknesses have there been?

12. Defining a significant control failure, or weakness, that would require detailed consideration, disclosure and remediation. Agree with management what defines a weakness or failure that must be brought to the audit committee.

13. Identifying any significant control failure or weakness, remediating and mitigating them. Taking appropriate process and control measures, as well as any required disciplinary action.

---

[55] This is required under US Sarbanes-Oxley (SOX) and Japanese JSOX law may well be mandated in the UK, following the Bryden review.

Tips

1. The 13 steps above can be turned into a comprehensive work programme for an audit committee. This will ensure that the committee is overseeing the company's risk management and internal controls framework.

2. Ask the CEO and CFO to sign off annually that the control framework is strong and that there are no significant control failures or weaknesses of which the audit committee is unaware.

Fraud

The board is responsible for preventing, detecting and investigating fraud. This is a very broad responsibility. The list above includes the need for a specific fraud risk assessment, and all measures to strengthen the control framework will of course help to manage fraud. However, you should assume that your company is being defrauded by someone. The fact that you haven't found any yet is not evidence that it is not happening, it is just that you haven't spotted it yet. Especially with cyber-based attacks, there are probably deceptions being attempted against you all the time.

Opportunity is one of the key drivers of fraud, as it leads to temptation. The better the internal controls, the less fraud will be attempted. According to KPMG, over 60% of frauds happen because of weak internal controls. 21% of fraudsters simply ignore the controls, and only 11% manage to circumvent good controls. [56]

The most common way of discovering fraud is following a tip off or a whistle-blower (44%). Management review and a suspicious superior

---

[56] Corporate Fraud, by Geraldine Lawlor of KPMG Forensic: October 2020

account for 32% of known fraud discovery, with only 14% by internal and 6% by external audit.

This emphasises how important the right culture is in a business and the value of a well-publicised whistleblowing service. People need to believe that wrongdoing will not be tolerated and that they will be listened to if they raise concerns. This culture absolutely has to come from the top, so the audit committee must be very sure that the CEO displays their commitment to the highest levels of integrity.

> **Tip**
>
> Beware the tendency to respond to an embarrassing whistle-blower report by trying to work out who the whistle-blower is. Some whistle-blowing is malicious, but most seems to be honestly intended, even if mistaken. As with fraud, whistleblowing is too valuable to risk being undermined.

[57]

The audit committee should check that the company policy is to report fraud to the police. This is an important sign of the company's commitment on zero tolerance of crime. The problem that often occurs however is that the lawyers argue that there is insufficient evidence to prosecute successfully, despite the company believing that fraud has been committed. More evidence often requires getting the police to investigate, as they have powers to seize computer equipment and search homes, but the police are often not interested in what they regard as minor white-collar crime. The company is left with removing the miscreant from the company without seeking a prosecution. This

---

[57] Barclays CEO was fined $15m by a US regulator in 2018 for trying to find out who a whistle-blower was.

is frustrating, but boards may need to accept it. The minimum should be to ensure that the fraudster leaves the business.

> **Tip**
> Personal expense claims are often a warning sign for other improper activities. Corrupt people are often unable to resist cheating on their expense claims, perhaps by inventing expenses, inflating them or charging for work on their private accommodation. If you get a report of an employee accused of excessive expense claims, it may be a good idea to look into their other work. You may also ironically find it easier to prove fraud in an expense claim than in the original questionable work conduct.

External auditors – friend or foe?

External auditors are appointed by the board to review financials and form an opinion on them. They work for the board, and ultimately shareholders, but have an overriding duty to apply accounting standards and ensure that financials represent a fair application of those rules. They provide a service to the board, but also independent regulation of the financials.

Regulators and politicians have become obsessed in recent years with the risk of auditors getting too close to management and failing to provide proper independent challenges. Some fail to distinguish the (non-executive) audit committee with executive management. Others, without evidence argue that non-execs are simply tools of management in signing off dodgy financials. As a result, new regulation forces regular rotation and retenders of auditors and even tighter rules are threatened.

The audit committee and executive management should regard auditors as a vital tool. If something isn't right, then most directors will want to know, and having an independent body looking at the numbers and how they are prepared is a vital source of intelligence for all directors. It's like having a surveyor look at your house. You may not like what they tell you, but you are much better off with an honest assessment of the structure and the fabric as well as the market value.

Auditors find themselves under increasing pressure from regulators, so are becoming very risk-averse. They have more tenders for work than they can cope with and are becoming choosy about only accepting 'low risk' clients. You may even find that they refuse to tender for your audit if they think that your sector is too risky, your controls weak or your governance not good enough.

Tips

1. The external auditor is your friend. Yes, like your other friends, they can also be annoying, picky and difficult, but they are still one of the board's best assurances that the numbers are right.

2. Ask your external auditor how risky they rate your company to be. They all have formal internal risk assessments, which they use when discussing an audit internally. This assessment is usually revealing and gives you a benchmark against other businesses.

[58]

Most reports to the audit committee from external auditors are lengthy. They have to give a lot of boiler plate disclosures. Most of their papers are explaining how they are going to do the next audit. It's as if your car mechanic gave you a long presentation about how he is going to dismantle the carburettor and grease the big end, when all you

---

[58] This tip may surprise and dismay certain politicians and regulators, who think that boards like to conspire with executive management to either ignore, bully or choose only weak and compliant auditors. On the other hand, these commentators may think that calling auditors friends just confirms this. You just can't win.

want to know is that they'll give it a service and tell you if anything is wrong.

As such, many of these reports are of limited interest to directors, but if you are worried about anything (maybe you've heard that stocks are ageing a bit, or you think bad debts might rise), then you should ask the auditors to look hard at that area, just as you might tell your mechanic that you are worried about a rattle from the engine. Auditors in general welcome such guidance from the board. Just like with your car, it is better to know what's going wrong long before the engine stops.

Materiality

There are two key concepts (and numbers) to watch:

1. **Performance materiality.** This is the amount of money that the auditor would regard as an 'error' that they couldn't live with. In other words, this is their red-line. It is usually calculated as a % of general materiality, i.e. an amount that would be likely to influence a user of the accounts. General materiality might well be set at, say, 5% of underlying profit before tax, and an auditor might decide that its performance materiality would be 75% of that amount. Setting a performance materiality lower than general materiality simply gives them some leeway.
2. **Audit differences.** This is the minimum amount of 'error' that they would bother to tell the audit committee about. It might well be about 5 - 10% of the size of the performance materiality.

Both numbers help the auditors to decide how much work to do. Most audit committees would not expect to have a dispute with the auditors that would go near the performance materiality level (though it can happen). The committee would typically be more interested in the audit differences number, as most debates will be about numbers that are larger than this, but well short of the performance materiality level.

Directors need to be aware that if an accounting error subsequently emerges, that is smaller than the audit differences, then the auditors will disclaim any responsibility. You have therefore, to be willing to accept that there is an increased risk of errors going undetected below that level. An audit committee can ask for a lower audit differences level, but as this will generate more work, the auditors are likely to ask to increase their fee to pay for this. Think hard about what size of error would be important to you in understanding performance?

Internal audit – policeman or value creators?

A company doesn't have to have an internal audit function if it is a small or simple business. However, for most companies, other than very small ones, internal audit is very beneficial. For an audit committee charged with ensuring financial integrity and effective internal controls, an internal audit function brings much-needed assurance.

Internal audit has come on a long way in its contribution to business over the years. Historically it would have been a compliance or policeman role, but now best practice looks for how it can add value. Internal controls are key to measured risk-taking and thus value creation. A good internal audit team will focus on processes and controls, understanding the need to balance control, risk and flexibility. It won't look for excessive controls or focus on compliance for its own sake.

Internal audit is the third line of defence, where operatives, first line managers and their processes (i.e. the doers) are the first line, regional and senior executives (i.e. the supervisory levels) the second line. Operational management sometimes looks at internal audit when a control weakness or failure happens and expects internal audit to come up with a better process or system. This should be resisted.

Internal audit should investigate and identify weaknesses, working with management to suggest improvements. However, making things happen is operational management's responsibility, not internal audit's.

Tips

1. Make sure that the messenger, internal audit, isn't shot for delivering the bad news.

2. If internal audit has a critical report, make sure that the relevant operational line management attend the audit committee. After hearing the report, ask operational management (not internal audit) to talk about how they are going to address the issue. It is often very salutary for line management to be put on the spot by the audit committee. Ask them to come back and report progress in a few months' time.

Internal audit can be staffed entirely by company employees, or outsourced, usually to an accounting firm, or a hybrid of both models. It doesn't really matter which model is used: it depends upon the circumstances of the company. Smaller companies may find outsourcing provides high quality support that they couldn't afford or justify in full-time employees. Whichever you use, make sure that the team understand your business and the need to use good controls to drive value.

Some argue that internal audit should report either to the CEO or the chair of audit committee. In my experience it is more practical for the reporting line to be to the CFO, but there must be direct personal and confidential contact between the head of internal audit and the chair of audit committee.

Summary

The audit committee is often the most interesting board committee because it can cover so many different aspects of the business. Admittedly, it is the place where the car mechanics are let loose to talk about what's under the company bonnet and this can become rather technical and detailed. On the other hand, if you wonder why the car keeps getting punctures, or why can't we go any faster, it's the place to find out.

Technical discussions will be dominated by the CFO, external auditors and the committee financial expert. However, they should be able to explain the financial aspects to lay members. In assessing the financial integrity of numbers, use the external auditors as they are there to provide advice as well as judgement. The committee should develop a good overview of the control framework, in all the 13 aspects covered here. This is a major piece of work so understand that it will take considerable time to cover them all.

Internal audit is also a key tool of the audit committee. Make sure that it is high quality and feel free to direct it to areas that you think are important. Remember however that line management is responsible for processes and controls, not internal audit.

Chapter 8 - The Rewarding Remuneration Committee

Now I'm going to take a wild guess here, that the least favourite part of many a non-exec role is setting executive remuneration. To the media and the government, it appears that non-execs love nothing more than awarding large pay increases, bonuses and pay-offs to executives. It often seems that investors share this perception, and believe that only institutional shareholder intervention can restrain the irrational generosity of the average non-exec. On the other hand, management is often pushing for higher pay and better bonuses and sometimes just can't understand why non-execs are so mean. The remuneration committee is pretty much a lose-lose game. Welcome to the world of today's non-exec!

This chapter looks at how you decide what to pay executives and how this reflects the market rate for that role. It covers remuneration advisers and performance metrics, asking whether executive pay is there to retain, incentivise or reward them. It then reviews both short and long-term incentive schemes, finishing with tips on avoiding being embarrassed by pay-outs and dealing with management on their pay.

What is the right remuneration for management?

How do you decide what to pay someone? It's difficult to see any rational justification other than market comparisons. Sometimes it's relatively simple. The head-hunter or the remuneration consultant tells you that the market for a role is around £200k pa, maybe with a range of £180-£220k. This fits with what you are currently paying an incumbent, or your new candidate is happy to accept that.

However, what do you do if you have undertaken a long and rigorous search for an executive and identified the perfect person? You had planned to pay £200k pa, but now you offer her the role, she says she won't accept less than £250k. The choice is simple; either pay her that or lose her. If you swallow your pride and increase the salary, you are effectively deciding that it is worth £50k[59] pa to secure her premium skills. You think that she's better than most, so she can command a premium. Alternatively, you may take the more pragmatic view that the premium is too high, but restarting the search will cost time and money, so it's worth paying extra just to get her in role and working, rather than waiting months to recruit another. The salary, in this case, is the result of a negotiation taking account of the market, rather than just the market rate.

The market rate is therefore the starting point for setting the right remuneration, but it has to be overlaid by pragmatism as to individual circumstances, and individual negotiation.

What is the market rate for a job?

The more you look into understanding the market rate, the more complex it becomes. Generally, a remuneration adviser will look at the job title, the specific metrics of the job (e.g. CEO, CFO, divisional direc-

---

[59] Beware that a £50k salary increase will cost the company a lot more than £50k. Employers' national insurance costs a further 13.8% (UK, at the time of writing). Pension costs might be another 5% - 25%. Annual bonus might be 100-150% and long-term incentives 100%-300% salary. That £50k salary increase could well cost the company nearly £250k pa.

tor, size of revenue and costs under management), and the market capitalisation[60] of the company. They will then come up with a market range for remuneration. However, they may not understand your business, especially if it is a particularly simple, complex or unusual one. For example, a metric based on revenue may not be very useful when you are running a property development company, which concentrates on assets and may have relatively small or lumpy revenue.

Tip

Do not assume that a remuneration adviser understands your business. Make sure that you challenge their comparative companies and ensure that they are truly relevant. This may seem like a rather obvious suggestion, but some directors treat any advisers' views as gospel. You shouldn't.

I had a constant problem with one company. The remuneration advisers kept coming up with a market range 30-50% above what we were paying, because they were comparing other companies with similar balance sheets. However, this business was a relatively simple one, with much lower risks – no trading risk, little transaction risk and minimal bad debts. The advisers simply could not understand that this was a very different scale of management difficulty to similar companies, and we should therefore pay less.

Equally, I've had an exceptional management team running a really difficult business in a tough market sector. Revenue, profit and share

---

[60] Market capitalisation is a very imperfect measure of a company's size, as it excludes the amount of debt that a company has. Enterprise value (equity plus debt) would be a better metric. For a private company or subsidiary, advisers will tend to look at other financial comparisons, such as revenue, profit or assets, or look to businesses in similar industry sectors.

price were all falling. The remuneration advisers wore long faces and recommended that we were overpaying. Whilst you couldn't reduce their salaries, it made any pay increases difficult and new recruitment pay levels unattractive. You wanted to pay the market rate, but the advisers were using basic measures of the market that didn't take account of non-standard circumstances.

Most remuneration committees want to pay the market average or above. Many want to be upper quartile, because they want the best executives, and they think their business is special. Very few non-execs want to pay their management *below* average. In the company discussed above, because the business was relatively simple, we wanted to pay lower quartile. The advisers never really understood this and explaining it to management was pretty tricky. After all, it's somewhat embarrassing to be paid in the lower quartile.

As a result, you have lots of boards looking to pay average or above market and very few indeed that want to pay below average. The result is that you get inbuilt inflation in executive pay. This is a real challenge to remuneration committees. The 'market' should be a tool to understanding, not a rationale to increase pay.

Tough Tip

If a company is relatively simple, or in a protected market position, or just lower risk, remuneration committees should be brave enough to conclude that they should pay below average remuneration.

Remuneration advisers

There are a number of sources for market comparatives. Specialist remuneration advisers, such as New Bridge Street, Deloittes, and PWC (to name but a few[61]), have good databases, broad understanding of legal and governance issues and are sensitive to investor feedback. However, some have a tendency to roll-out standardised remuneration advice, not necessarily sensitive enough to individual company circumstances.

They can also be very risk-averse when it comes to institutional investor – or more likely proxy agency[62] – reaction. It is damaging to the reputation of a remuneration adviser to be associated with a large AGM revolt.

Be aware that remuneration advisers have no incentive to keep salary costs low. They do not work for your shareholders and don't think about value for money from executives. However, these specialist advisers are essential to give remuneration committees some independent advice.

Head-hunters themselves are another source of market intelligence on pay and bonuses. They know what salaries are being offered and paid, including many that are not published in annual reports. Directors may be concerned that head-hunters have an incentive to suggest a high market salary for new recruits, as it makes their jobs easier. Make sure that the head-hunter really does have good experience of recruiting for the role for your type and size of company, so that their view of market

---

[61] But you cannot use any firm that is also your external auditor for remuneration advice. That would be a conflict of interest.

[62] Proxy agencies are discussed more in chapter 10

salaries is a well-informed and appropriate one. Usually, you would expect to get a head-hunter's salary advice for free as part of a recruitment or as a favour for a long-standing relationship.

Directors could of course, do their own research. For board positions, a quick look at online annual reports of companies that you consider are comparable, will soon produce a good idea of the market. Although cheap and effective, this approach might be considered a little ad hoc by institutional shareholders, especially if they believe that the resulting salary is high. Many committees will want the cover of getting independent advice to justify salaries, in case they ever get challenged.

Tips

1. If you are even a little uncertain on the level of pay or the attitude of your shareholders, it makes sense to get an independent view from a remuneration adviser. However, this is always only advisory and will only be as good as the input you give about your business and your unique jobs.

2. In the end, if you want to employ or retain a certain executive, then you will end up in a negotiation.

3. You should think about talking to a few of your large shareholders to get their view and hopefully their support, especially if a remuneration scheme could be controversial.

4. Don't bother trying to consult or influence the proxy agencies. They may consult you to check facts, but they are not generally interested in the board's opinions.

Metrics

One of the tricky parts of setting a total compensation package is the metrics to be applied to bonus and long-term incentive plans (LTIPs). Common financial measures are operating profit (i.e. profit before interest), EBITDA, profit before tax, earnings per share or 'underlying' versions of those. There is no one right answer. Which one is most important to the board?

Operating profit is a good all-round measure but doesn't include interest. This may be necessary for a division or subsidiary that doesn't have a meaningful separate balance sheet[63]. Operating profit does not reflect the impact of cash flow. For example, a growing business might have large capital expenditure, or be acquiring other companies, so it uses cash and increases its debt. A growing operating profit may be coming directly from expenditure that would be reflected in higher interest costs. I worked with one company that emphatically agreed that cash was really important. It was spending large amounts of capital, yet it still insisted on using operating profit as the main metric. Remuneration schemes need to reflect the business strategy and key metrics.

Some companies argue that low interest rates mean that interest costs are very low and can therefore be ignored in executive remuneration. But what happens when interest rates rise? By then the company might have already run up large debts, which are excluded from bonus calculations, that would be severely impacting profit before tax (PBT) and dividends.

---

[63] This could be because the division sits within a larger legal company or if the group moves cash around for other purposes, such as tax planning.

EBITDA, like operating profit excludes interest, but also depreciation as well. It suffers from the problem of ignoring cash flow, as well as the extra depreciation charge from capital investment. It is therefore relatively easy to grow EBITDA by spending on capital and acquisitions. Ironically, EBITDA is a beloved measure of private equity, even though they focus on cash in a much steelier way than most listed companies. They are so focused on cash that they regard depreciation as a theoretical irrelevance, as what matters is cash capital spend. Good cash flow is life or death to private equity-owned companies, and with management hugely incentivised by their highly geared equity ownership, the annual bonus can reflect EBITDA knowing that the cash position is still right next to management's heart (and wallet).

Profit before tax is the 'bottom-line', taking account of interest, but not corporate taxation. There is a good case to exclude tax as it is largely determined by government, not the company. For example, you wouldn't want to increase bonus pay-outs just because the government had reduced corporate tax rates, or vice versa.

Earnings per share (EPS) is a metric often used in LTIPs. This is profit after tax divided by the number of shares in issue. As such, it takes account of any new shares being issued or any issued shares being bought back by the company. It is also after tax, so represents most closely the earnings that could be ascribed to shareholders[64]. Some investors criticise EPS as being 'manipulable' by management, if they buy back shares[65]. Of course, this is only an issue if the company does buy back shares and a wise committee would retain some discretion to adjust for this.

Total shareholder return (TSR) is another key metric in many LTIPs. It is the real experience of shareholders who hold their shares throughout the time period. A three-year TSR would be the increase in market capitalisation together with the total dividends paid out over those years. The change in market capitalisation must exclude any new shares being issued or bought back, as these would distort TSR as a performance measure. The calculation can in fact be surprisingly complex.

I inherited one incentive scheme for a CEO that paid out based on growth in TSR, but did not adjust TSR for the increase in market capitalisation from new shares being issued. The individual was therefore entitled to a massive unintended pay-out just because there was a new equity investment by shareholders. Fortunately, the CEO saw sense and realised that it would be untenable for him to get such a windfall.

Tip

Make sure that the calculation of TSR is defined carefully, especially if you are not using an experienced adviser to write the scheme. Ensure that you understand it as it can be surprisingly complex. Do not just assume that the adviser will have got it right for you.

---

[64] Think about the EPS as the pot from which a company can pay its dividend. If a company has a dividend cover of 1.0, it pays out all its earnings per share as dividends per share (DPS). If the dividend policy is 2 x cover, then the EPS is double the dividend paid out.

[65] See more explanation of share buy backs in chapter 10

Non-financial performance metrics

There are other metrics that can be used, such as environmental, social and governance (ESG) targets, productivity, labour turnover, customer satisfaction or specific projects being completed. All of these will depend on the specific board priorities at the time. However, they may need to be limited by financial targets, as paying out, for example, for great customer service may not go down well with shareholders when profits are falling.

Reward, retain or incentivise?

The total compensation package for an individual is designed to reward, retain and incentivise them. However, it's never clear which bits do which.

This book won't attempt to review the literature on whether salary or bonuses actually incentivise[66] people, but there are a few key points to bear in mind:

1. **Monetary reward doesn't generally incentivise people.** Good employees want to do a good job. However, there are some people who are very focused on money and they will work harder if there is a sufficiently large monetary reward (the colloquial term is a manager who is 'coin-operated'). If you have one of these on the executive board, then the design of the bonus package is particularly crucial.

2. **Most executives however expect a reward for good performance** and a chance to share in profit that they help to create. I believe that this is the heart and the real justification of 'incentive'

---

[66] See, for example, a good summary of the thinking on incentives at work in a Harvard Business Review article: https://hbr.org/1993/09/why-incentive-plans-cannot-work

or bonus schemes. These executives will expect bonus plans in line with the market.

3. **One problem comes when times are tough** and bonus schemes look as if they are not going to pay out. This reduces the reward and removes any financial incentivisation at just the time when you need it most, especially if the downturn is not the direct fault of the executive team (e.g. if there is a recession or pandemic). This is where committees can pay extra attention to leaving some form of residual bonus available, perhaps by a low minimum pay-out threshold or using a Restricted Share Plan (see below) rather than a traditional LTIP.

4. **Retaining key executives can also be difficult in tough times** when little or no bonuses are paying out. The remuneration committee may need to be pragmatic, as, although shareholders may be calling for it to be tough with executives, the board has a greater need to ensure that it has the right management in place. No-one will thank the committee at the end of the day if the company loses key executives. This reiterates the need to pay market rates for remuneration and leave some hope of longer-term bonuses.

5. **However, the committee should avoid schemes that pay for failure**. The problem normally comes from long notice periods, although nowadays 12 months is usually the maximum. If the board decides that an underperforming executive has to go, it generally has to negotiate an exit settlement. This is because as poor performance in itself, is unlikely to constitute gross misconduct that could legally justify them being fired. Committees should look hard at the small print of incentive schemes to ensure that they allow discretion. As a last resort, boards can consider just terminating without any legal agreement and 'see the executive in court', but this is probably only appropriate when bad behaviour has also been involved. I have been involved on a few occasions, when the board decided not to pay out the theoretical full liability, as the individual had misbehaved (we have been threatened, but never as yet sued). There is however some reputational risk, especially from any possible court action, so this needs careful thought.

Annual bonus targeting

Most annual bonus schemes will have a mix of financial and non-financial targets. The financial ones (usually operating profit or PBT) tend to be the overriding ones, because it is uncomfortable to pay out big bonuses for great customer satisfaction or low labour turnover when profit is poor. The board would probably also be heavily criticised by investors and the media. The remuneration committee will have to decide what the maximum bonus will be set at as a percentage of salary (usually 100%-200% annual salary at board level), and how much of that will be paid for financial performance and how much for non-financial. Typically, the split is between 50:50 and 75:25 respectively.

Committees will typically design board director schemes with:

1. A financial threshold, below which no-one gets any bonus of any kind, including for non-financial elements.

2. A financial benchmark that corresponds to the annual budget, giving a target pay-out (perhaps 50-70% of the maximum financial element of the bonus).

3. A financial 'stretch' target that would trigger a full pay-out of the financial element of the bonus.

The remuneration committee can decide what level feels right for each and then calculate a straight-line pro-rata pay-out between these benchmarks. In the example below, the board felt that a stretch profit target of £120 was right, against a budget of £100, and that it would pay 70% of the financial bonus out for on-budget performance. A simple straight-line pay-out based on this however means that the minimum threshold would be very low, £53 profit in this case. To avoid this, the committee has two options:

1. Impose a minimum threshold (perhaps £80) and start the pay-out at whatever the straight-line dictates at that point (40% here); or
2. Decide what the minimum threshold should be (again say £80), and then straight line between the minimum and the budget, giving a 'kinked' scheme, shown on the right-hand side below.
3.

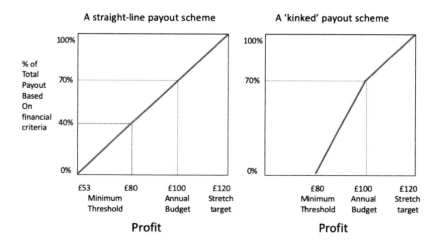

The straight-line methodology with the higher £80 threshold gives a cliff edge at this level, where management is suddenly going from 0 bonus to 40%, and this can give a big incentive to manage profit to at least that number. The 'kinked' scheme has the advantage that it is more highly geared around profit underperformance, as paying a bonus for missing profit targets can feel a little generous and you really want to incentivise every pound towards achieving budget profit.

Non-financial bonus elements

Non-financial targets can be purely personal objectives or broader non-financial metrics. Generally, remuneration committees will want to include an element of reward for individual contribution as well as broader company performance (for a CEO, their personal objectives may look very much like the company non-financial performance measures anyway). The problem then becomes how to weight the different non-financial performance metrics. How much should you pay out if some do well and some don't? There are three possible methods:

1. Treat all non-financial targets as the same and do a simple average.

2. Apportion different weightings to each measure and then do a weighted average (300,000 x 1.5 divided by 0.5).

3. Look at the non-financial measures as a whole and apply a judgement call as to how much bonus they deserve.

Tip

Because non-financial measures are so varied, I have generally found that applying judgement and discretion, rather than some arithmetic algorithm, can give the fairest and least controversial levels of bonus pay-outs.

Long-term incentive plans

These are the juggernauts of incentive schemes. Theoretically, LTIPs or performance share plans as they are sometimes called, align management incentives with the experience of shareholders, and try to ensure that the former reward long-term success rather than short-term. They generally work by allocating executives with a number of shares, calculated as some multiple of their annual salary. After a three or five-year period, a proportion of those shares, determined by the various performance measures, can be handed over ('vested') to the executive. The ultimate value to the executive is therefore the result of both the performance measurement and the increase in the total value of those shares (i.e. share price plus dividends paid on those shares).

The performance measures can be absolute or relative, i.e. the target could be a 10% increase in EPS or a 10% improvement in EPS above an external benchmark (typically a basket of comparable companies' performances).

The scheme basics:

X has a salary of £300k and an LTIP allocation of 1.5 years' salary, i.e. £450k.

The starting share price is 50p and therefore her maximum allocation is 900,000 shares. (i.e. 300,000 divided by 0.5 times by 1.5)

The performance conditions are 50% total shareholder return and 50% EPS.

The maximum performance targets for both are 15% compound growth pa and the minimum are 8% compound growth pa.

Performance outturn:

The business performs well with EPS rising by 40% over the three years (i.e. 12% pa).

The share price benefits from the 40% increase in EPS plus a 20% rerating (based on that performance), so the share price rises by 68% (i.e. 19% pa)

The dividend rises progressively with the share price, keeping the dividend yield at 4.0%.

Pay-out calculation:

EPS achieved 12% pa against a target of 15% pa, giving a pay-out of, say 70%.

TSR was 19% pa share price appreciation plus 4% from dividends makes 23% pa, above the cap of 15% pa, so a full 100% of this element is payable.

The pay-out is a 50:50 blend of EPS (75%) and TSR (100%) elements, i.e. 88%.

The reward:

X receives 88% of 900,000 shares, now worth 84p each, i.e. £665k plus dividends due on those shares of around £75k to give a total of £740k, nearly 2.5x the original salary (before tax).

Example of a 3-year LTIP in action[67]

As you can see, the growth in profitability has a geared effect on the final reward, not only in the increasing number of shares paid-out, but also in boosting the share price and dividends.

---

[67] This calculation can become extremely complex in different circumstances, so this is a simplified version that explains broadly how it works.

Tips

1. Do try and understand the proposed LTIP calculation. It may be complex, but you cannot assume that what is proposed is exactly what you want unless you do. I have found many issues in calculations from remuneration advisers.

2. When reviewing a new LTIP, ask for the above calculations, and triangulate expected profit/EPS growth and share price appreciation. Thinking about EPS growth and change in rating puts some logic behind viewing future share price increase and helps to categorise how challenging it is.

When a scheme is put in place, management tends to focus on the initial allocation of shares. This is where a lot of arguments happen. However, the subsequent performance of the business is a much bigger driver of the ultimate value of the scheme, not the initial multiple of salary. It is worth reminding management of this.

Don't move the goal posts

Make sure that you get the components of the LTIP scheme right at the start, but give some discretion to the remuneration committee. Any remuneration committee that tries retrospectively to rewrite key parts of the scheme is likely to get itself into trouble. This is particularly, and quite rightly, disliked by shareholders. Tesco's remuneration committee had agreed to judge its performance against a basket of other food retailers for its LTIP. However, when it came to pay out, in 2020, Tesco decided that one constituent company, Ocado, had performed so well that it was unfair to include it in the index. This sleight of hand turned a TSR underperformance of 4.2% into an outperformance of 3.3% and a TSR pay-out of zero to 33% of the maximum.

At the subsequent 2020 AGM, the remuneration committee report was rejected by 67% of the votes. Although the vote was advisory, Tesco said that, following the vote, the committee chairman would invite a number of the company's larger shareholders, who had voted against the resolution, to engage with him to fully understand their concerns. I bet they were fun meetings.

Tips

1. Talk to key shareholders before introducing a new pay scheme or before changing anything significant in an existing scheme, if it is unusual or potentially contentious.

2. Don't change any existing targets unless (a) you believe that it's absolutely essential and (b) you like a fight.

Don't fall into the share price trap

There's a particular trap in LTIPs when the share price falls considerably. Obviously, this hits existing LTIP pay-outs, but it can have a large impact on any new tranche being issued. The number of shares allocated to executives will increase as the share price falls. In the above example, X would get 900,000 shares based on 50p share price, a salary of £300k and 1.5 years allocation. But imagine that there is a sudden crisis, profit dips and the share price, which had been around 50p for a while, halves. If the remuneration committee followed its normal rules, X would now instead receive 1.8m shares.

If the profit and share price recover, over the next three years, to the same level as in the above example, the LTIP pay-out would reflect the EPS and TSR recoveries, subject to being capped at a 100% pay-out. X would receive her 1.8m shares valued at 84p, i.e. £1.5m plus the accrued dividends. Shareholders are no better off than in the first example, but the LTIP is paying executives over twice as much because the starting point was so low.

I had a situation like this when poor trading led to a dramatic fall in the share price. The committee decided to apply its discretion to calculate the allocation of shares based on the share price before the poor trading was announced to the market (i.e. give fewer shares than the standard calculation would give). This avoided management being seen to benefit from a low share price. This is yet another example of the value to the remuneration committee of discretion in applying its own rules.

Other types of LTIP

There are other types of long-term incentives around:

Restricted stock plans: These work by allocating an amount of stock to an individual, usually calculated as % of salary. This stock is then paid out after the vesting period, provided the executive is still employed. It is much less geared than the traditional LTIP, as the amount of stock is fixed and there may well be no performance conditions (other than employment). The executive of course, gets the benefit from any appreciation in the share price plus dividends that are paid on their stock. The gearing is much less on the downside as well. If the business under performs, there may still be the pay-out (subject to any performance condition applied) of the stock allocation, although its value will have fallen with the share price. Given the lower risk to the executive, investors generally expect that Restricted Stock Schemes award perhaps half the original value of stock that a traditional LTIP would. In the above example, X would get up to 9 months of salary in restricted stock, rather than the 18 months initial allocation in the LTIP.

Private equity rewards – the 'management strip'

Private equity (PE) tends to give management highly geared equity packages, known as the *'management strip'*, as well as annual bonuses. It's worth understanding how these PE equity schemes work, even if your company is not private equity-owned. This is because every so often a remuneration adviser starts touting schemes for listed companies that it claims replicate a private equity scheme.

The PE business model is to buy a business, load it with heavy debt, improve performance, generate cash to pay down the debt, and then sell the business delivering a 2x or 3x return on their investment. The management strip takes this even further, treating much of the original (small) slice of equity as high interest rate bearing debt owed to the PE investors. This leaves a much smaller *management strip* underneath. PE will probably ask management to pay for this strip equity, to ensure that they have plenty of *'skin in the game'*. As a result, management runs a highly geared business, with an equity stake that is even more highly geared again. Unless business performance is very good and the PE investor achieves their target return on investment, management will lose their money. However, once the target PE return has been surpassed, the value of management's equity rises dramatically, as it is so highly geared, and this is crystallised when the business is sold. Hence the headline multimillion pound pay-outs to PE company managers.

This is a very effective reward system, with no chance of reward for failure. If the business isn't sold, or sold for below the target return, management gets nothing. If the business is sold for a good return for the PE investors, they are only too pleased for management to benefit from sums that would have an institutional investor or voting agency apoplectic.

However, if an adviser suggests a PE style package to non-PE companies, remuneration committees should be aware that they are, rightly, not popular with shareholders. PE schemes work by having management at risk from losing their own money and ultimately requires a sale transaction that triggers the pay-out. This is unlikely to work with non-PE companies. Public company managers are not generally keen to put their own money into incentive schemes. A listed company board is also unlikely to have a strategy to build performance and then sell in a few years' time, let alone a pay scheme that advertises this publicly.

> **Tip**
>
> Don't listen to remuneration advisers promoting PE style schemes for other types of companies, unless it requires management to put money in and pays out depending on the success of a sale of the business.

A word on discretion and not being embarrassed

The ability to use discretion in any scheme is the remuneration committee's greatest friend. It is impossible to predict the future with any certainty, and unexpected events derail the best plans. A committee does not in these circumstances, want to be held immovably to a mechanically calculated outcome. Another prime example of the use of discretion is the definition and use of underlying profit to set the bonus. This enables the committee to exclude items that it thinks are not relevant; for example, a currency translation movement or goodwill amortisation[68].

> **Essential Tip**
>
> *Always* include the ability to apply discretion in remuneration schemes to avoid unjustly rewarding, or unfairly penalising, management for events over which they had no control or were just not foreseen. This doesn't mean that committees *have* to adjust for these, but a wise committee gives itself the *option* to do so.

---

[68] This is a good reason for the remuneration committee chair to attend audit committee meetings, so that they have a good understanding of any non-underlying adjustments.

The ability to use discretion is a major anti-embarrassment clause for both the remuneration committee and the company. Persimmon in 2007, had a bonus scheme for its CEO that entitled him to a £75m pay-out. The business had benefited enormously from the government help-to-buy programme, with half of its sales being eligible, so that the company had performed (presumably) far ahead of the committee's most optimistic expectations. Without a relevant cap on the award, an unacceptably high bonus was payable. The CEO was eventually asked to leave, and the company chairman resigned.

> **Essential Tip**
>
> *Always* include a maximum cap on any remuneration scheme. The chances are that, if the scheme is going to pay out spectacularly, it will be because of something outside the control of the company.

Bonuses, dividends and environmental, social and governance (ESG) concerns

To make life more complicated, many institutional shareholders are now holding executive remuneration schemes up to higher standards.

The COVID-19 pandemic threw this into sharp relief, as many companies that made redundancies or furloughed staff, took large subsidies and reliefs from the government and cancelled or delayed dividend payments. Not many – if any – committees will have included; not making major redundancies; not taking government money; and paying a dividend, as three of the conditions for paying out executive bonuses. Yet some institutional shareholders are demanding that boards apply this level of ESG rigour now.

Sacha Sedan, the well-respected then[69] Head of Governance at Legal & General said: *"If you've taken taxpayer money, cut your dividend and sacked people or furloughed them, then we wouldn't expect you to have a bonus this year. They might pay it back, but what if they've sacked half the workforce?"*

Most remuneration committees won't necessarily be affected by this. Mass redundancies, government bail-outs and missed dividends are usually the result of poor financial results that themselves, preclude any bonuses being paid. However, committees increasingly need to take ESG matters into account in bonus-setting, and importantly give themselves discretion to reflect unforeseen circumstances in any subsequent bonus pay-out.

Management and their remuneration

It goes without saying that human nature means that management is usually keen to maximise its pay. The remuneration committee tries to tread a careful line between keeping management onside, motivated, retained and happy, and more hawkish shareholders (or more likely their proxy agencies) onside and supportive, not to mention avoiding unhelpful media attention. There is also a conflict of interest, in that the remuneration advisers often do work directly for the executive management in setting pay below board level. I have, on a few occasions, thought that the advisers were rather too keen to keep on the right side of management, and that this could be influencing the advice that they were giving on board-level pay.

---

[69] Sacha Sedan subsequently moved to the Financial Conduct Authority as ESG director. Quoted in Financial Times 31 October 2020 https://www.thetimes.co.uk/article/dont-award-bonuses-if-you-cut-jobs-warns-legal-amp-general-investment-management-q5wlnxjcg?shareToken=db363bf6c13e81e6fe447f2e16a36db5

A wise CEO keeps close to the remuneration committee chair and doesn't propose new schemes or changes without agreeing them with the committee and company chairs beforehand. Similarly, the committee chair should discuss proposals with the CEO and company chair before presenting them at meetings.

Summary

There are many more complexities than I have been able to cover here, and these are increasing all the time. This chapter however has covered the basic knowledge that any remuneration committee member should have.

If the audit committee sometimes feels that it is mediating between management and the auditors, the remuneration committee definitely finds itself mediating between management and investors. Even more tricky is that remuneration committees practise a very imprecise art, as there is little proven evidence that incentive schemes actually incentivise most people.

Remuneration committees work best when they focus on pay schemes that attract, retain and reward the kind of executives that the board wants. They should try to keep the schemes as simple as possible, although they will find that complexity always creeps into even the simplest one. Always keep discretion in any scheme. Management may not like this, but it is vital to keep the ability to react to unforeseen circumstances. You may be surprised how often the unexpected happens.

If you want to avoid embarrassment, never agree to a package that doesn't have a cap. Non-execs need to understand that investors don't like embarrassment and increasingly are prone to seek revenge, particularly by voting against the re-election of a remuneration committee or company chair. You won't ever regret the power to avoid unforeseen outcomes and to do what you think is right.

Chapter 9 - People and the Nomination Committee

The audit committee doesn't just audit things, the remuneration committee doesn't just pay people and the nomination committee doesn't just nominate directors.

As with other committees, the responsibilities of the nomination committee have grown as governance has developed and the board has become more responsible for different aspects of the business. In many ways, however, the nomination committee is the little brother of the other ones. It meets less frequently and has less regular business, but is also often the most sensitive, as it deals with appointments and departures.

It is perhaps now rivalling the audit committee as the most powerful committee.

The nomination committee is increasingly becoming effectively a people committee. This is similar to the regulatory mission creep[70] that is pushing audit committee into general business controls and risk, and the remuneration committees into senior executive remuneration and general pay parities.

---

[70] This expansion of the role is being driven by regulators, government and investor governance demands, not by boards themselves. This is however, an example of helpful outside intervention in forcing these issues onto the agenda.

The nomination committee also now looks at senior executive development and recruitment and broader diversity issues.

The UK corporate governance requirement[71] for public companies, is that the majority of members are independent non-executives, although many will have the company chair[72] and possibly the CEO as members. A company with very large shareholders, who have a representative director on the board, may well have them also on the committee. It's fairly common for the company chair to chair the nomination committee, but it can be an independent non-exec.

Sometimes, the divide between a nomination meeting and a non-executive meeting can be blurred. If the CEO or other executive sit on the committee, the non-execs may feel that they want to discuss the executives privately, either by asking any executives to leave (itself a sensitive thing to do, as it tends to irritate and alarm those asked to leave) or in a separate discrete non-exec meeting.

The nomination committee has five responsibilities:

1. Overseeing succession planning for board and senior executives.

2. Managing recruitment for the board directors, both executive and non-exec.

3. Managing the board evaluation process.

4. Deciding if a director needs to leave involuntarily.[73]

---

[71] UK Corporate Governance Code, 2018

[72] The chair is not technically an independent director. They may have been independent at the point that they were made chair, but are deemed non-independent from then on.

[73] Curiously this is not in the Corporate Governance Code, which mandates individual performance reviews, but is silent on the possible consequence - the tricky business of actually getting rid of underperforming directors.

5. Overseeing the diversity and inclusion of the board and senior management.

Succession planning

Everybody enjoys a bit of succession planning, except when it comes to plotting your own replacement. It can feel like planning your own funeral – sensible, responsible, forward-looking, and yet a bit morbid. And let's face it, succession planning is hard.

There are three parts to succession planning:

1. Short-term contingency emergency planning

2. Medium-term planning

3. Career development

Short-term contingency planning

What happens if a key executive suddenly becomes unavailable? It's easy to dismiss this and think it will never happen. However, it can and does. You may not worry as, even if an executive resigns suddenly, she has a 12-month contract, so you know you've got a nice long handover period. Except that senior executives are rarely, in practice held to the full 12 months.

1. If she is going to a competitor, you might feel you have to escort a director from the building immediately.

2. People sometimes fall ill, or have accidents, and become unavailable. The COVID pandemic illustrated this when even the Prime Minister was rushed to hospital. I have sadly lost one of my CEOs who tragically died of cancer. This is, usually a long-term illness, but one that can take a person out of the office at short notice.

3. You may find that you have to dismiss an executive because of misconduct or poor performance, and again this can happen very quickly.

As a chair, I have overseen the departure of a number of CEOs, and especially if there is a significant performance issue, it tends to culminate in a crisis that demands immediate action.

The nomination committee, therefore, should always have a risk-management plan as to what it would do if each senior executive were to become suddenly unavailable. This can be filled by promoting someone, another executive covering across a wider brief, a boss covering a subordinate's role, or a combination of any of these.

Medium-term planning

This is what most people think of when you talk about succession planning. A board should always have a view, two or three years out, of who would do a role if an executive moves on, is promoted to another role, leaves, or otherwise becomes unavailable, or just needs to be replaced. Sometimes this can become a daisy chain, so what is initially one move causes a sequence of other moves to fill consequentially vacated roles. It is worth trying to identify at least two candidates for each medium-term role, so that you have some choice, or at least cover if something else happens.

The trick then, is to think about future promotions. If the committee decides that someone will be a good candidate for a more senior role in a few years, it should identify that person's development needs. It may be that they need more experience or maturity, more training, or different experience.

The succession planning process should, therefore, lead to a development programme for some executives to give them the best possible chance of taking on a more senior role in the future. It is worth reviewing this, as some CEOs can focus on short-term requirements to the detriment of long-term development. For example, sending executives on courses or moving them to different roles causes short-term disruption and so is a nuisance. It has been known for a CEO, perhaps a student of Machiavelli[74], not to be too keen on developing a promising subordinate as they fear that the executive may prove to be a rival in the future.

Tip

Always ask the question about an individual identified for future promotion: What is stopping them being ready now?

Diversity should also be factored in. This has to be consciously and deliberately fostered - that is why it isn't there already. Underrepresented groups tend to lack relevant experience (this is axiomatic if you think about it). You can't mandate talent or commitment or skills, but you can offer appropriate experience. Experience is one of the few things that a nomination committee can give people. Succession planning needs to be conducted with a strong override of how we encourage and develop underrepresented groups.

Tips

1. If you decide that you cannot see someone doing a role in two years' time because they lack experience, why not start to give it to them now?

2. Pay special attention to promoting diversity in succession planning.

---

[74] The Prince by Niccolo Machiavelli is not an ideal treatise on succession planning.

The committee may of course decide that it will need an external candidate for a role, either because it cannot see an internal successor, or it feels that the role needs a fresh eye from outside. In this case, the succession plan could involve head-hunters doing a confidential review of the market and likely outside candidates. Sometimes, if a good potential candidate is identified, you may be able to get an intermediary to persuade the individual to have a cup of coffee with you *"to get to know them with no agenda"*. I have seen this work well to initiate contact that can be built on later. Sometimes that individual suggests another good potential candidate instead and may even broker a further conversation with them.

Career development

There is a danger that succession planning focuses on the direct needs of the business to fill roles. However, executives have their own views on life and careers, and are generally marketable to other businesses. A key part of succession planning should therefore centre on individuals' career development, rather than just identifying round pegs for round holes, to suit a company's short-term convenience. The committee should look at key individuals. How big a role do you think they could do? Could they be CEO in ten years? What would we have to do for them to be a candidate? What do they aspire to, is it realistic and how can we help them? Such help could include moves to other roles, coaching, development courses or reading a book about serving on boards.

It isn't always a simple path. An executive may be great at his current job, and could even go a bit higher, but you might think that they are never likely to get the top job. Alternatively, you might need to recognise that with successful development, an executive might want to develop their career elsewhere. A good succession plan can take this into account, by motivating the individual to develop in their current role and perhaps higher, but equally understand that they may well move on after this. I employed a CEO who had been in a much bigger business and had left after a disagreement. He did a fabulous job for us, but we had an agreement that this was a way of him rebuilding his career, enhancing his reputation and then moving back to a bigger arena again. This suited both him and the business.

Board recruitment

This is the other side of the table to chapter 2, on recruiting directors. A nomination committee might be recruiting because the succession plan indicates a gap, an executive or non-executive might have left or indicated an intention to leave, or the committee might have decided that it needed to replace an incumbent.

The best place to start is with a job profile for the role you want to fill and then an initial person profile for a candidate. It is useful to begin with essential requirements and then desirable requirements. Personally, I would then move all the essential requirements to the desirable column. It is quite common for the 'perfect' candidate to emerge who doesn't have the 'essential' requirements on the brief. Even if you don't realise this, the head-hunter will, and so your initial long list will include candidates who lack one or more of your essentials. I've seen many a candidate specification for an audit committee chair that state that they must be a chartered accountant. They are mistaking the essential – that the individual is experienced in finance – with a technical qualification that would be helpful, but represents only one of a number of ways of getting that experience.

> **Tip**
>
> Keep the list of *essential* requirements to an absolute minimum, but think widely about *desirable* features, experiences, knowledge, characteristics or skills.

Having got the job profile, the committee moves to finding an initial long list of potential candidates. Most listed companies will use a head-hunter to work with them from now on.

Ways to choose a head-hunter

1. Hold a formal tender ('beauty parade'[75]) of three or four likely firms

2. Speak informally to a few firms

3. Use one that you have employed successfully before (often the company chair will have a favourite)

4. Seek recommendations from other experienced board directors

The formal 'beauty parade' is the most thorough method but takes time and effort. Whether the committee goes through this will often depend on the strength of existing relationships with the company or the preferences of individual influential directors. For example, if the company chair, who may also chair the nomination committee has a favourite head-hunter, they are likely to be very influential in proposing using that firm.

What to look for in a head-hunter

1. **Sector experience & knowledge.** If a firm has a strong track record in a particular sector, then that will suggest that they know the market and will be quicker to identify suitable candidates if your role requires sector experience. It is usually helpful to ask the head-hunter on initial contact, or for their pitch, to suggest some suitable names of potential candidates. You will

---

[75] Sorry, this is a sexist term, but it's the one I hear used most. We should call it a tender or pitch.

learn a lot by the quality and suitability of their initial suggestions.

2. **Role and functional experience**. Do they have a strong board practice for example? Are they renowned for recruiting CEOs or CFOs? You might find that a head-hunter will propose that their sector specialist will work with a functional specialist to give you the best service.

3. **Personal chemistry with the lead consultant**. You will want to feel confident with the lead person suggested by the head-hunter to run the search. Do they really understand your business and the role for which you are recruiting? Just be aware that the head-hunter may bring a top person along to get the business and you may never see them again (yes, this has happened to me). Make it clear that the lead must be attending every meeting with you.

4. **A good researcher.** Most of the work is done by the researcher, so note whether the head-hunter introduces them. We employed one firm because the researcher was so good, even though the lead consultant was not outstanding.

What to ask head-hunters

1. **Recent searches** that they have done to show their sector and functional experience. Make sure that you ask when each search was done, as several years ago is a lifetime in recruitment.

2. **What salary package** would they recommend? Do this even if you are using a remuneration adviser, as it is both a cross-check and evidence as to whether they truly know the market.

3. **What timetable** would they suggest? Most will give you a similar answer, but it may flush out if the consultant/researcher has a long holiday booked or other commitments at the crucial moment. Unless you really are not in any hurry, or the timetable they suggest is short, I would ask them how much faster they could do it. How responsive they are to this will tell you something about how customer-centric the head-hunter is, but equally if they are too cavalier and

look to be prepared to swop quality for speed, that may also influence your decision.

4. **What fee** will they charge? Expect the answer to be 30-40% of first year expected earnings, and don't be surprised if they all give similar answers. Head-hunting is a small world. However, expect to get a discount if you are a new business or they've just done a lot of work for you. Like selecting an auditor, I would recommend choosing the firm that you most want to use and then negotiate them down on price, rather than choose on the basis of price alone.

5. **What expenses** will they charge? This may seem a strange thing to have to ask, but the head-hunter may try to charge 30% of the candidate's expected earnings and then add on incremental expenses of the search (e.g. travel costs & advertising) and apportioned overheads (i.e. just a *'hidden'* charge). I would refuse the apportioned overheads, which can be 10-20% of the whole fee, and insist that they are included in the base fee.

6. **Will they offer a money-back guarantee?** If the successful candidate leaves within a year, then you should expect the head-hunter to offer a partial money-back guarantee. The smart ones will, however, simply offer you a free second search, or at least a heavy discount.

The long list of candidates

Whether you use head-hunters or some other means, it is useful to identify a long list of candidates. This should include any 'left-field' (i.e. slightly unusual) candidates that you have come across. The nomination committee can look at this list and try to identify if there are enough candidates and whether they seem to be the right quality, diversity and fit. You are not trying to spot the perfect candidate or select the short-list. The role of this is to decide if they are looking in the right areas and getting names with the right experience and level. This is very important feedback to your recruitment advisers, as sometimes a committee sets criteria that seem sensible, but when you look at actual people and experience this throws the criteria into sharp relicf.

You might, for example, start thinking that sector experience is vital, but when you see very few candidates with that, widen the brief to adjacent sectors. Equally, you might start thinking that prior board experience is essential, but soften when you see attractive CVs that don't quite have that.

To promote diversity, it is best to mandate that the long list includes a high proportion of ethnic minority and female candidates. A good head-hunter will offer this.

Tip

Candidates with diverse characteristics, almost by definition, tend to have less experience than the obvious 'white, male and pale' ones. When selecting new directors, balance any experience shortfall with the benefits to the board of having a diverse perspectives, experiences and outlook.

The short-list & interview

It is a good idea to formulate a short-list of two to six candidates. The higher number is better, but for some roles, there may simply not be enough suitable and willing candidates. Rather than interview 'possibles', it is more time efficient to start with the 'probables' and only turn to the former if you draw a blank with the latter.

Although it is tempting to try to interview a candidate with all the nomination committee together, my experience is that such panel interviews are clumsy. You can interview 1:1, although having two interviewers is often helpful, as it easier for one person to ask questions whilst the other observes. At a stretch, three interviewers can work, but more than that makes the interview too lop-sided.

I walked into a non-exec interview once having been told the two people I was going to meet and, had carefully researched them as preparation. However, when I walked into a room there were five interviewers, just finishing their lunch spread out on the table. I struggled to work out who was who. The interview felt like I was sitting in a bunker with various people taking pot shots at me from all sides. Needless to say, I didn't get the job, and, let's be honest, I didn't regret it either.

It is a good idea to work out what you want from the interview. Some people are believers in forms of structured interview (*"Tell me about a time that you faced this challenge…"*), others like to go through CVs, and some like just to have a chat. There is plenty of literature available on interview techniques, so there is no need to review them here. However, a non-exec interview is different to an executive one. You are generally not looking to check out technical expertise or management competence. Aside from specific experience and skills that you might want in a candidate, these are some things that you might look for in an interview (particularly a non-exec one):

1. **Sheep or goat?** Is the candidate someone who will stand up for what they believe, or will they tend to go along with the majority? If the latter, would they be, and do you need, a conciliating unifying team player? For example, I had a finance director once, whilst OK at her functional role, was fantastic at bringing a disparate and warring executive team together. She was the glue that kept the board together.

2. **Talker or doer?** If they are great talkers, is there substance behind the talk? Although a non-exec actually works only by influencing (as the executive are the doers on the board), they need to *work* to influence. For example, a good audit chair needs to keep up their technical knowledge, a good chair needs to be meeting people, and a good non-exec will often need to prepare a spreadsheet to check something or to challenge management. Make sure that it isn't all just talk.

3. **Peripatetic or retired?** Does the non-exec candidate want the role as pin-money in their retirement or will they treat it as a serious job?

If the candidate is a serving executive at another company, will they have the time to spend, and indeed the availability, especially at short notice, to be a non-exec? This isn't about age; it is about outlook and availability.

4. **Over-boarded or over the hill?** How many existing roles has the candidate got and how much time do they spend on them? Remember it is not just like filling a tank, you need their availability at specific times for meetings and ad hoc issues. Their 'tank' needs to have spare capacity all the time, not just on a Tuesday lunchtime. I would look carefully at any non-exec candidate who already has four or more other roles (fewer if one of these is a chair role), or a serving executive who already does a role other than their day job. On the other hand, a retired or out of work executive will have plenty of time, but may lack the drive to put the time in. If the golf course or a second home in the Caribbean calls, you need to be sure that they will sacrifice such pleasures when you need them.

5. **Failed CEO or back-seat driver?** A non-exec works by influencing, not directing nor executing. You need to be sure that a new non-exec, particularly a first timer, will understand that the role is to be a critical friend, rather than do the executives job for them. Of course, there are circumstances when you may need a non-exec to become executive, perhaps a thought for recruiting a new chair when the executive team is weak, but generally it is best avoided. An experienced non-exec is likely to understand the difference between exec and non-exec, and references can be taken to verify this.

1. **Always take up references.** In particular, speak to the chair of a board that a candidate non-exec has served on recently, to explore how they work as part of the board team. Don't leave the head-hunter to do this if you want to make sure that you get a fully nuanced and balanced view of their capabilities.

2. **Give a candidate a list of your future board meetings** and ask them for any conflicts. The number of dates that they can't make is an indicator of how much effective spare capacity they have.

Board evaluation

"Annual evaluation of the board should consider its composition, diversity and how effectively members work together to achieve objectives. Individual evaluation should demonstrate whether each director continues to contribute effectively."[76]

This description of a 'board evaluation', from the Corporate Governance Code, is a bit of a misnomer, as evaluation means judging, or determining the significance, worth or quality. Most boards do not judge their own significance, worth or quality. They reflect and get some outside views on how they work together. The Code recommends individual evaluations of each director's contribution, implying a formal

[76] UK Corporate Governance Code, 2018

performance appraisal. This is straying into difficult territory. A non-exec director, for example, may not like having a less than glowing performance appraisal, and this is unlikely to generate more board harmony.

Most board '*evaluations*' are in fact the polling of directors' views about the board, by questionnaire or by interviews with the chair or an outside consultant. The latter may also sit in on board and committee meetings to see for themselves. A questionnaire will very rarely ask questions about each individual director's performance, although they may ask something more general, such as whether meetings are chaired well. An external consultant may privately ask individuals what they think of each other, and directors are then very reliant on the tact and discretion of that outsider to handle such information carefully.

You could argue that in the world of 360-degree feedback, board evaluations should indeed, as the Corporate Governance Code suggests, include individual appraisals of performance and contribution. However, especially with senior directors, this can be a very touchy subject. Some people like to receive feedback, but no-one enjoys getting negative feedback. Some don't want feedback, and for some, the older and more senior they get, the less they feel they need feedback. There are also those that say they like feedback, but in practice it's like strolling up to a big cat to feed it raw meat. The lion may well take the bait, but you would still be lucky to get away with both arms intact.

One of my CEOs used to proclaim to the Board that he loved feedback: "*It's the breakfast of champions*", he repeatedly said. I took him at his word once, and it didn't end well.

> **Tip**
>
> My experience is that performance feedback is best given to senior people in small doses (two pieces at most, at any one time) slipped into general conversations, almost as an afterthought or in passing. Whatever, you do, don't call it a performance review. Have a cup of tea with the director and cover a number of subjects, ask their opinion of others and drop in a few observations as you go. If this doesn't work, you either have to accept the individual as they are and not waste any more time, or move to dismiss them.

The worthy writers of the Governance Code failed to think through the practicalities of board life. A chair should constantly be monitoring how directors perform and should indeed have an open dialogue with individuals about their, and other directors', contributions. This is part of what should be a continuous process of self-reflection. This is more a conversation, not a formal evaluation, and so much less threatening. For example, the non-execs should meet regularly together and discuss how the business is doing. Part of this should be a discussion about how the executive directors are doing. The chair should meet with the CEO regularly as well, and naturally will discuss how the board, committees and individual directors are working. The non-execs are expected to meet at least once a year without the chairman to discuss his performance.

The annual board 'evaluation' should be more about how the board works, how it gathers information, debates business issues, and makes decisions. It should be a discussion about how directors all work together and how they can be more productive together. This must never be confused with an evaluation of an individual's performance.

If you don't believe me, try beginning your next domestic discussion about what groceries to buy, and who should clean the bathroom this week, by doing a performance evaluation of your partner.

The board *'evaluation'* is a very important item on the annual calendar. It does give the chair and directors a chance to stop and think about how they all work together. It should flush out issues that have perhaps remained unsaid for too long and also allows directors to let off steam about concerns. The involvement of an external consultant is very helpful here. A questionnaire is a very blunt instrument. Ask a closed question rating some aspect out of 5, and you get a straight answer, but there is no nuance to a numeric rating. Ask an open question on paper, and people don't generally respond with very helpful sentences. However, a questionnaire can point the chair, or an outside consultant, to the difficult areas that could usefully be explored in a subsequent interview. People are far more forthcoming verbally than in writing.

Obviously 'difficult' personal feedback needs to be delivered in private, so it often helps for general board feedback to be given to the board, and then individual meetings to be held with each director to discuss aspects that are more related to an individual, for example how they chair a meeting or whether they are contributing enough.

If the nomination committee wants an outside consultant, it is worth choosing carefully. There is significant resistance from investors to using head-hunters for this, as it is thought that they might use boardroom discontent to rustle up more business for them. This may be cynical, but committees may well feel that it is just not worth risking investor disapproval on this. The charges for this work vary significantly, and it is not necessarily the case that the more you pay, the better you get. The best board evaluation consultant[77] I ever used was actually the cheapest, because, ironically, she mainly worked in the public sector and was trying to break into plc work.

---

[77] Radojka Milijevic of Campbell Tickell, since you ask. Other very good consultants are available.

When directors have to leave involuntarily

This is a very tricky subject. The Corporate Governance Code envisages that directors:

a) Serve out their terms (normally 2 terms of 3 years, but up to 3 terms i.e. - 9 years - possible); and

b) Respond effectively to performance evaluation if there are any issues; but

c) May resign over major disagreements; or

d) May be voted out by shareholders at the AGM, as there is annual re-election.

There is no mention of how a board should remove an underperforming director who doesn't take the hint and go themselves. The nomination committee may decide that it is the best interests of both the board and the company if one of the executive or non-exec directors leaves. This decision-making process is normally led by the company chair, although it may be agitated for by others.

Dismissing the CEO. This is probably the most common dismissal from a board. It has to be led by the company chair, as the CEO's line manager. It is also where the short-term contingency succession plan really comes into its own. The removal of a CEO leaves a major power vacuum, which needs to be filled by an immediate interim or permanent replacement, another executive covering across or the chair stepping in. It may be that the succession plan had already indicated an issue and plans had been set in place sometime previously, to identify a successor. If the successor is an internal appointment (such as the CFO stepping up), the process can be smooth and immediate.

It is difficult to undertake a full external search (as opposed to a confidential review of the market) in advance of telling the CEO, as word tends to get round, but it has been done. The risk is very high however, as a leak is likely to cause a justifiably hostile reaction from the incumbent. If there is an interim solution, this can work well for a short period, but remember that an interim person lacks authority and can't easily take long-term decisions.

I once asked a CEO to agree to leave in six months, but to stay in post until then. That gave time to identify a successor and for the CEO to look for another job. If that is kept confidential, then the process can look amicable and the business not be disrupted. It is however dependent upon the maturity and goodwill of the departing CEO[78]. On the other hand, I have seen CEOs dismissed on the spot (always do this outside of the office to maintain confidentiality) and told not to return to the office.

---

[78] In this case, the individual played an exemplary role and made a huge difference to the successful and smooth handover.

Dismissing the CFO (or another executive director): This is more straightforward as it is likely to be led by the CEO, although, for a CFO, the chair of audit will have a big say as well. Again, the committee needs to be happy that succession and cover are managed appropriately by the CEO.

Dismissing a non-exec: This is not very common, but I have seen it happen (and done it myself). Generally, this should be led by the company chair, and usually arises if there is a general feeling that an individual is not putting the time in, is missing meetings or is disruptive. The chair would normally 'have a word' with the director. If the problem persists, then the chair will suggest that the non-exec does not seek re-election at the next AGM, which can make the move seem more part of natural succession. The departing non-exec may well seek confirmation that the other non-execs agree, so it is important that the chair has the other board members onside.

Dismissing the company chair: Undoubtedly this is the most difficult departure to orchestrate and handle. It needs to be led by the senior independent director. Handling an underperforming chair is a real moment of truth for the non-executives. Those seeking consensus and an easy life will tend not to want to remove a chair, until there is absolutely no alternative. A poor chair may well fail to lead the board, undermine board meetings by allowing too much or too little discussion, focussing on unimportant matters to the exclusion of key issues, and not standing up to the CEO. In short, the board can be destroyed as a functioning body by a poor chair, so this can be one of the most destructive problems you can face.

Some chairs will go gracefully, especially if they have been in the role for a number of years already. Others will resist until faced with board unanimity and resolution. Some won't forgive. One chairman, knowing that I had been an agent in his departure, told me that the proposed incoming chairman had made it a condition of their accepting the role that I stand down immediately as a non-exec. Needless to say this was found to be untrue when I simply went to speak to the new chair.

Removing the chair is one of the most unpleasant and difficult tasks that a board can have.

Diversity and inclusion

All male, white boards are often very effective. However, they always lack something - a female or ethnically diverse viewpoint. Given that these categories make up the majority of the population, that is a significant disadvantage. Personally, I've found that boards with a good mix of sexes tend to work better, with more different perspectives and a less macho, more cooperative culture. There is a real value in diversity.

There are plenty of pieces of research that claim that companies perform better when led by boards with more women. Sadly, every time I have reviewed the statistics, they have proven to be poorly done, and largely wish-fulfilment[79]. Companies are highly complex systems with thousands of variables interacting every day. It really would be surprising if one variable (the self-declared sex of certain board members) really were such a big driver that you could get statistically significant result on overall profitability. It is amazing what you can prove if you set out to get a result and then search only for confirmatory evidence. If sex were such a powerful overwhelmingly determining factor in performance, nomination committees' jobs would be easy. Just appoint two women to the board and profit will boom.

Forget the wish-fulfilment, statistical nonsense. A board with diverse experiences and viewpoints will be a better leader for a business in today's world. It's essential that females and ethnic minorities should be encouraged into senior business positions. When a nomination committee thinks about who next to recruit to the board, it should always regard diversity as an important factor.

It mustn't just be about the board. One key reason why females and ethnic minorities are underrepresented on boards is that they are underrepresented in senior management. The board therefore should be looking at how it can develop and grow women and ethnic minorities in its own executive management. In the long-term, this will be how we reduce inequality and realise opportunity.

The problem is that when you are the majority, the world just looks very different. An ethnic minority, female executive in one company explained to me recently the racial discrimination that she suffered daily in Britain. When you have never experienced discrimination yourself as a minority, it can be hard truly to envisage how harmful it is. It's like the self-confident, arrogant man who doesn't believe in bullying because he has never been bullied.

[79] See my blog at www.simonlaffin.com for some analysis of such statistics.

As the saying goes:

"Walk a mile in someone else's shoes, before you judge them"[80].

It was only when I joined a board in Asia, in which I was the only ethnic minority non-exec, did I begin to really understand. For example, you feel that you are being over-sensitive to events and comments, as no-one else seems to mind. This is also a key reason why the response to lack of diversity cannot be just one person on a board. Nowadays, I understand much better why, for example, boards with at least two women seem to work better and are more enjoyable.

Progress is being made on increasing female representation on boards, but even here it is more on the non-exec side, than the executive. Getting ethnic minority representation is even more challenging, as there are so few with the training and experience demanded to serve on boards. Boards must encourage their own ethnic minority managers and require head-hunters to put ethnic minority candidates on their long lists.

---

[80] Almost certainly derived from a Mary T. Lathrap poem "Judge Softly" published in 1895

Summary

In many ways, companies represent the merger of people and capital. However, capital is just an enabler: Only people make things happen. The nomination committee – is really nowadays the people committee – is a fundamental building block of the success of a company. It has tremendous power and responsibility, not just on recruiting new non-execs, but in guiding succession planning of senior executive and director roles and encouraging diversity throughout the organisation. The committee can help the board by managing an effective board review process, where an external consultant can help in getting beneath the skin of the board and following up on board issues. However, the individual performance appraisal of directors is generally best left out of the board evaluation, but with the chair constantly monitoring how individuals contribute to the board and feeding back to them informally when appropriate.

Succession planning should be reviewed regularly and treated with great respect. On one level it is risk-management, preparing for the inevitable, and sometimes sudden, change of personnel. On another level, it is about planning for the future and developing future leaders. It is also about consciously shaping the diversity of the future and working to make this happen.

The nomination committee is about far more than just nominating.

Chapter 10 - Owners, Managers and Shareholders

"We do not view the company itself as the ultimate owner of our business assets but instead view the company as a conduit through which our shareholders own assets."

- Warren Buffet

Shareholders own the company, whereas managers run it. Ideally, managers are also shareholders, so that they have common interests and experience with shareholders. Directors run companies on behalf of shareholders. They need to act in the interests of others, i.e. to act as agents for shareholders. The board needs to counter the risk that shareholders lose trust in the board by good communication with them.

Shareholders themselves come in all shapes and sizes from small private ones, families, wealthy individuals, large institutional holders, to private equity. Increasingly, institutional shareholders are being encouraged to become more active in board issues, even as retail (i.e. private individual) shareholders are becoming more disenfranchised. Because institutions have limited interest and stretched resources, they are increasingly farming out governance decisions and voting to proxy agencies.

Shareholders almost universally want to grow their financial investment - to get a shareholder return. Some particularly want to see that return as capital appreciation from a rising share-price, others focus on income from dividends, and others want a balance of the two. Boards need to be aware of what shareholders want, and to respond to that if they can.

Directors as agents

Executives naturally enough, are focused on developing their careers and maximising their remuneration and bonuses, but good remuneration schemes reward executives when shareholders earn a return. Executives should also own shares themselves, so that they have a good overlap between personal interests and those of shareholders. Among the executives, CFOs often regard looking after shareholder interests as part of their role, not least as they are usually responsible for investor relations.

Non-executives do not, in listed companies anyway, generally have incentive schemes and bonuses, just a fixed fee. Their interests are in the business doing well and shareholders being content. A non-exec trades on their reputation, so they are very aware of the need to avoid public criticism of either themselves or their board.

The board therefore, has a mix of different interests and motivations that should come together, to further the interests of shareholders and other stakeholders. Ideally, directors would think like shareholders, but it is also easy to get caught up in board discussions and politics and lose sight of shareholder interests. It's important to beware of 'motivated reasoning' – the unintentional bias introduced by emotion into thought processes and decision-making, in order to lead to a preferred outcome.

It affects us all.

The more pressure a director feels under, the more emotion is generated. Pressure and emotion are the enemies of rational decision-making.

> **Tips**
>
> 1. **Directors should always try to do the 'right thing'**, rather than necessarily the expedient option. When times are tough and emotions are running high, it is even more important to take a step back and ask yourself: 'What is the right thing to do?'
>
> 2. **Boards should also explicitly consider what shareholders would want** the board to do and what would, in the view of the board, be in the best interests of shareholders.

Bear in mind, however, that doing the right thing, and doing what shareholders would want, does not guarantee a perfect outcome. Nor does it guarantee that the board will be recognised for making the best decision, especially when there is confidential board information not seen by outsiders, not to mention critics who have the luxury of 20:20 hindsight. On a number of occasions, I have seen boards heavily criticised, but unable to defend themselves for fear of breaching confidentiality.

Main types of shareholders

Institutional shareholders: These can be active or passive, although the former will engage with a company far more than the latter. An active institution may well request two (or more) meetings a year with management to hear about the strategy and performance. A large institution may well run several different funds that may invest in a company, so a single investor may have a range of opinions and fund managers. However, institutions are almost always rational and sensible, and instinctively supportive to boards. If a major institution's fund managers start to express disquiet about a board or management, this needs to be taken very seriously. Institutions make up around 70% of all listed company shareholdings.

There is normally a separate corporate governance team in institutional investors, who worry about ESG matters. In larger institutions (like Legal & General and M&G) the corporate governance team will form their own opinions or even send out letters giving their policies on ESG. However, smaller institutions tend increasingly to outsource their ESG opinions to a voting or proxy agency.

Wealth managers: These are companies that invest on behalf of small retail shareholders. Examples include St James Place, Rathbones, and Vanguard. Some funds run by wealth managers are passive, i.e. they invest in companies simply in proportion to that companies' market capitalisation compared to an index, such as FTSE 250. Others are active, as they make stock selections based on investment theories and models.

These investment managers are rational investors but can be variable in quality. Company directors can get an unrivalled opportunity to see both sides of active wealth managers, investing their own savings in them, as well as seeing wealth managers as shareholders of companies. It can be a rather sobering experience for a director to be quizzed by the same people who look after their own savings. In fact, some directors have moved their own money from wealth funds based on seeing their fund managers in meetings with management.

Tip

Ask the executive directors if they have met your own wealth manager (if you have one). Ask which fund manager they saw and how was the meeting. You will learn quite a bit about the people who manage your money.

Private individuals: These constitute around 13% of all UK quoted stockholdings, held by some 18m people in the UK. They are usually called *'retail'* investors by the City. These days private individuals are likely to hold company shares through a nominee account. A nominee account is where banks, online operators or ISA providers hold the shares on behalf of clients. There are, for example, over 2m people in the UK who have an ISA account, which have to be nominee accounts.

Aside from ISAs, the decline of paper share certificates has pushed retail shareholders into nominee accounts. These are often cheap to use, but then the operators don't want the hassle of passing on information, annual reports or voting forms. They certainly don't want to bother voting the shares in nominee accounts. This means that private shareholders are becoming increasingly disenfranchised. It is somewhat ironic that a key driver of this is government policy in incentivising ISAs without giving investors protection of their rights. A company doesn't know who the beneficial owner of the shares is when owned through a nominee account. These shareholders will not in general get any communications from the company for the same reason, but can of course access information via the internet. The progressive disenfranchisement of private shareholders is a very poor reflection on modern governance, and should be addressed by regulators.

Private shareholders can be very focused on the dividend, especially if they are using dividend income as a pension.

Wealthy individuals and families: These are very high net worth people who can invest significant amounts, from tens of millions to billions, such as Bill Gates (wealth £85bn[81]) and Joe Lewis (wealth £4.4bn[82]). They may be activist investors (discussed on page 187), as they are able to take significant shareholdings in companies and try to

[81] Sunday Times Rich List 2019

[82] Forbes 2020

influence the board. My experience is that boards should be careful with these types of investors, as they are very wealthy people used to being able to get their own way, and may be intolerant of boards that don't comply with their wishes. They may be indifferent to corporate governance procedures and other shareholders' interests. If they really want to, they usually have enough money to sacrifice short term value in return for getting their own way.

On the other hand, having powerful shareholders on your share register can be very helpful. Bill Gates, for example, would be a handy name to be known as a shareholder and boards might be able to leverage the contacts and influence of wealthy persons.

Tip

Don't confuse *active* with *activist* shareholders:

An *active* shareholder buys stocks according to a methodology or model, as opposed to a passive shareholder who simply buys stocks according to market capitalisation as part of a basket or index.

An *activist* shareholder is someone who puts heavy pressure on a board to do what it wants, often by demanding a board seat, threatening to vote against the board or withholding support.

Private equity: Generally, a private equity (PE) firm will hold stock in private companies rather than publicly listed ones and will often take a public company private. Private Equity is usually an engaged shareholder, taking a very close interest in a company, nominating and controlling the board. The more troubled the company, the more private equity will intervene in management and the operation. But equally with a well-performing portfolio board and trusted management, a company may face little intervention from a private equity owner. PE is usually very rational and focused on the financial returns from an exit. Rational shareholders are often the easiest for any board to deal with, and private equity (slightly less encumbered by the listed-world's ESG agenda, for example) is pretty single-minded about financial performance. Bear in mind though that private equity managers are just very engaged fund managers. Their capital comes from investors who subscribe for perhaps 10 years or more in a very illiquid fund, in order to target high returns. Private equity therefore faces its own pressures to deliver absolute returns.

The charge that private equity investors are short-termist can be unfair. They will typically invest for three to five years, and their investment is generally very illiquid, as they need to sell a portfolio company to get their money out. In contrast, institutional shareholdings are usually highly liquid, and holdings are bought and sold, at least in part, regularly. The difference is that private equity makes money by exiting the business, so its focus is on absolute returns, based on an exit, i.e. one point in time. That exit must sell the promise of future success to any purchaser or new investor[83], so private equity has to in practice focus also on performance beyond its holding period.

Activist investors: These are institutional investors who like to target underperforming businesses and pressurise them to change to release value. Examples are Crystal Amber and Coast Capital. They may want a change in the board, or a higher dividend, or the sell-off of parts of the business. Activists may agitate for change with modest shareholdings. If they have just a small few percent of the stock, they may well still propose AGM motions, nominate directors they like, and try to encourage bigger shareholders to support them.

---

[83] Some investors insist that private equity retains a portion of its shares after the initial exit, precisely to make sure that it has an interest in future performance too.

Sovereign wealth funds: Act very much like institutional shareholders, but some may be stricter on ESG matters.

What shareholders want

There is a lot of governance and academic angst around directors having different interests to shareholders – the so-called *'agency problem'*. Shareholders are supposedly only interested in long-term shareholder return, whereas managers might take short-termist actions to get incentive pay-outs or take unnecessary risks with shareholder's money. This is a key reason why boards have non-executive directors, who should regard themselves as overseeing management, with a particular focus on looking after the long-term interests of all shareholders.

Income and growth: Income funds, like most retail shareholders, take a close interest in the dividend. Their model is to create a healthy, stable and growing dividend stream. However, even they must keep a careful eye on the share price, as their investors would not thank them for delivering a dividend income at the cost of a fall in the value of their investment. Growth funds, on the other hand, will look for companies that are undervalued or who are undergoing a turn around. They are less worried about dividend and more interested in capital growth from a rising share price.

Absolute and relative performance: Some retail and wealthy investors will be looking for absolute growth in total shareholder return (growth in share price plus dividends). There are also some 'absolute return' institutional investors (the clue will be in their title, e.g. 'Blackrock European Absolute Alpha Fund'). Most active institutional investors are however, looking at getting a return higher than their competitors (i.e. more relative alpha[84]). They will buy shares where they believe in both the company and management.

---

[84] See chapter 5

Shareholder perceptions and understanding: Shareholders are like other human beings. They want to know what's going on, know who they can trust, and they want to be listened to. Inevitably, companies spend most of their time with large shareholders, which usually means institutional holders.

They tend to judge a company by:

1. Their perception of the market and the company fundamentals and model.

2. Whether they like and rate the CEO and CFO (the two board members they meet most often).

3. The company track record of delivering on City expectations and the absence of surprises, especially bad ones.

It can be as much a problem if an analyst or shareholder overrates your company as much as if they underrate it. In the former case, they tend to set up high expectations for performance that the company may find difficult to match.

I remember an analyst who thought that a particular innovation that we had would transform our company's performance. We knew it wasn't that decisive, but we couldn't persuade him. When it eventually became clear that the innovation wasn't such a big deal, the embarrassed analyst turned hostile on the company and kept us on his sell list for years afterwards. Another time, a major shareholder was our No1 supporter and bought a very large stake. However, we began to realise that the fund manager had misunderstood the difference between gross cash and net cash (i.e. that gross cash excludes debt). The shareholder was demanding that we return cash to shareholders at exactly the time we were worried about running out of cash to run the business. By the time the fund manager realised his error, it was too late, and we were off his Christmas card list for life.

Tip

Enthusiastic, over-optimistic shareholders are often a bigger problem than pessimistic ones. The latter often just sell up and move on. The former stay and keep being disappointed.

Shareholder insights: Shareholders and analysts may sometimes see the business more clearly than directors. These informed outsiders come to the business with the impartiality of strangers, free of the baggage that insiders may carry. On several occasions, I have come out of a shareholder meeting and thought that they were right about some aspect of the company and that we hadn't seen it clearly enough. In fact, the whole exercise of preparing shareholder presentations can be cathartic. If you spend hours perfecting a presentation of your business model, and find that you've not quite convinced even yourself, then the board may need to think again. It's happened to me several times.

I remember the same analyst who got overexcited about the technical innovation, later got some market research that challenged how good our brand was with customers. We disputed it with him, but after we came away, we had to admit that he had highlighted something that we had been in denial about.

Shareholders tend to draw their opinion on the CEO and CFO naturally enough largely from their meetings with them (as well as the financial results of course). This explains how boards can be mystified by individual shareholder's views on the executive team. Shareholders can form very strong opinions, especially if they believe that individual directors haven't told them the whole story or didn't know a particular fact.

> **Tip**
>
> Ask the company brokers to give a report on shareholder feedback after each results announcement.

Don't take offence that shareholders rarely worry about who is on the board, apart from the CEO and CFO. A fund manager is unlikely to be able to name the other directors without looking it up. Generally, if a shareholder does take the trouble to look them up, it is bad news. If they are unhappy with the CEO, they may well turn to the chair and perhaps summon them to a meeting. It is good practice for a chair to be available to shareholders, although, unless something is wrong, most shareholders don't bother. However, if the shareholder's corporate governance team is unhappy, they may well look up the relevant committee chair, especially if it is about remuneration issues. If they are not satisfied with the chair, they could speak to the senior independent director.

Shareholders hate surprises: Like any boss, shareholders don't like surprises. They tend to place great store on companies delivering on their expectations. It is always best to under-promise and over-deliver, although under-promising often irritates shareholders too and they will probably just add something to their numbers to compensate.

Tips

1. Make sure that the CFO regularly produces a report on what profit expectations are by sell-side analysts (i.e. analysts employed by banks, rather than shareholders) so that you can check that the board's expectations are in line with those of the City.

2. Ask for each broker's forecasts, not just consensus (which tends to be a numerical average of them all), as any outlying forecasts may be an issue with shareholders who put particular weight on one individual analyst, especially if they are the house analyst (i.e. work for the company's broker).

Large shareholdings

You can get a great feeling of confidence and pride when a shareholder buys a big stake in your company. They clearly trust the board enough to put a lot of faith and money behind the company. But can you have too much of a good thing? Yes, you can.

If a non-institutional shareholder acquires 25% or more of your stock, there is a real possibility that it will start requesting a representative director, which may make life a lot more difficult for a board. Even an institutional shareholder may act more proprietorially if they have over 20% of a company's stock. They certainly expect to be treated especially well in terms of meetings and being listened to when they express a view. Of course, boards may be delighted to have a large buyer of the stock and a big, supportive shareholder can be a great friend to the board. Just remember that there are pros and cons to large shareholders.

If a shareholder reaches 30.0% of a company's stock, it will normally have to make an offer for the whole company (under UK takeover rules), so it is not uncommon for a shareholder to keep a 29.9% holding.

A shareholder could have a large stake below 30%, and have acquaintances[85] who may happen to agree with them on many issues. This potentially gives them influence beyond their strict shareholdings and could form a voting bloc in excess of 30% of stock. However, if they make formal agreements between themselves or start buying more

---

Tips

1. If you have any large shareholders (say over 15% of the stock), it pays to find out who they are friendly with and which other shareholder, analysts or bankers they talk to. Ask the company broker to research this, especially if they are not familiar with the shareholder.

2. It can even be useful to know whether a large shareholder or fund manager is friendly - or even related to - any journalist or sell-side analyst, as in difficult times, there is a good chance that they will use that contact. I got some really bad press once in a national newspaper when an unhappy fund manager had a close relative who was a City reporter.

---

[85] A blue-chip institutional shareholder would be very unlikely to do this, as its compliance department would be very strict to avoid being a possible concert party.

stock, then they risk being deemed a concert party, and this could trigger the requirement for a full offer[86]. However, simply voting in the same way does not of itself render them a concert party.

Be aware that large shareholders have put a lot of money into your company and they may not want to put more. This can be a major factor if you need more capital. If you preserve pre-emption rights (see later), then you need to offer large shareholders their pro-rata amount of new stock. If they decline to take this up, then you need to find other shareholders to invest disproportionately more to make good. This can make equity raising very tricky.

Proxy agencies

The proxy agencies, such as ISS and Glass Lewis, are increasingly powerful as institutional shareholders delegate responsibility for voting. Shareholders who argue strongly for companies to work hard on ESG, may themselves opt out of responsibility for voting their stock. An institutional investor could be investing in hundreds of companies, but if ESG is really important then taking responsibility for voting those shares should be a cost of holding them.

The proxy agencies appear to tend to take a read of the relevant sections of an annual report and then adopt a tick-box mentality to scoring the company. In my experience, they will not enter into any discussion with a company being assessed. They may well be willing to change any factual error that they make, but will not debate any nuance. I remember having problems when one agency made a big fuss that we didn't put EPS prominently enough in the annual report and remuneration schemes. The fact that we were a property company that targeted yield and net asset value was completely lost on the agency

---

[86] The UK Takeover Code runs to 425 pages, so this is just a small example and a board needs to consult their Rule 3 Advisor (a bank or other qualified adviser) to explain any Takeover Code issues.

executive, whose experience and knowledge of the property industry was somewhat lacking.

Having said all this, the agencies generally get their verdicts about right. However, if one of these self-appointed guardians gives your company a '*red top*' alert, you will receive many institutional votes against or abstentions. This is something to be avoided if you can, as it brings bad publicity and shareholder irritation.

Shareholder votes

Turnouts in public company general meeting votes are often around 80% or less. It depends on how many large shareholders there are, as they can vote large tranches of votes themselves, and how many retail holders there are, who are often disenfranchised by the nominee system. A good rule of thumb is that a shareholder with 20% of the stock is very powerful and you really want to do everything you can to get them to support a resolution.

If there is a shareholder, or group of shareholders, with 40% or more of the stock they will generally win *any* vote. With annual elections, they could vote out any directors they want to, and vote in any they choose[87]. Fortunately, the instances of this power being used are fairly rare, particularly as non-activist institutional shareholders generally shy away from such direct intervention.

Investor relations (IR) advisory companies

There are a number of IR advisory companies, of whom the most influential is Makinson Cowell, now part of Lazard. Many PR companies also have IR teams. These companies are useful conduits for information flow both ways and can give boards a better understanding of how shareholders are thinking. Companies will get this from their regular brokers, but it can be useful to have an alternative view, not least

[87] And this does happen, as I know from personal experience.

as brokers can have conflicts of interest. For example, brokers like corporate activity and fund-raises as they generate fees, but also may have other clients with different interests, such as hedge funds, that generate higher fees than most companies pay in brokers' fees. Brokers have to balance, at times, conflicting interests. Sometimes, also, I wonder about brokers' appetite to give bad news to management; after all, brokers in practice work for the executives.

Some IR advisory companies will do an audit of your shareholders to get their private and considered opinions on your company and management. These are much more comprehensive than broker feedback but can be expensive.

Tip

Broker feedback from shareholders is very helpful. However, especially in tricky times, an alternative source of feedback is also useful, either through talking to an IR adviser, doing a full IR audit, or the chair talking directly to major shareholders.

Dividends

A dividend is a form of shareholder distribution, i.e. company profit being distributed to shareholders. Most shareholders, especially of listed stocks, expect to receive a dividend. A typical company could pay out 50% of its earnings as dividends. This is known as the dividend pay-out ratio (the dividend per share expressed as a percentage of earn-ings per share). A Real Estate Investment Trust (REIT[88]) has to by law, pay out at least 90% of its property income as dividends.

The mathematical inverse of the pay-out ratio is the dividend cover, which is earnings per share divided by the dividend per share, ex-pressed as a ratio. A dividend pay-out ratio of 50% is the same as a dividend cover of 2.0x. Indeed, this cover of 2.0x (i.e. earnings are twice the dividend) is a good benchmark for most companies. A com-pany that is expanding fast and needs capital to invest may well pay lower dividends to help fund this, giving a dividend cover of 3, 4, 5x upwards. Shareholders value a stable and predictable dividend flow, so you should satisfy yourself that any level is sustainable. It is possible to have an uncovered dividend (i.e. the dividend is higher than the profit, a cover of less than 1.0) for some time, but it is very difficult to keep this going for long.

The other ratio to understand is the dividend yield. This is the dividend divided by the current share price, and so is a rate of (income) return for a shareholder. The average dividend yield across the market is usu-ally around 3 or 4%. If your company's dividend yield is much higher than this, say 6 or 7%, then this may be an indicator that the market thinks that your dividend is unsustainable and likely to fall. For exam-ple, say profit has fallen, but you maintain the dividend and so your dividend cover falls. Your share price may fall, in response to your lower profit, so your dividend yield goes up. The market will fear that eventually you will have to cut your dividend to reflect your lower profit. On the other hand, if your dividend yield falls below 3 or 4 %,

---

[88] A REIT is a property company that in return for always paying out at least 90% of property income (profit) gets certain tax advantages.

this may be a symptom that the market thinks that you are going to raise the dividend.

Tip

Start asking questions of management and the company brokers if dividend yield rises much above 4%. It may be a sign of trouble, or at least that the market thinks there is trouble ahead.

Boards are tasked with setting a dividend. The first question that you need to ask is whether any shareholder distribution would be legal.

Is a distribution legal?

A company can distribute only *profits* to shareholders, so there must be sufficient accumulated profit in the top company's balance sheet. The accumulated profit built up that is available for distribution to shareholders, is shown as the distributable reserves. If you look at the bottom of the balance sheet, you will see a number of reserve accounts listed, some of which are distributable and others not. The accounting bodies have conspired to make this highly complex, so I won't go into the details here. However, an alert director will ask the CFO or audit partner to list out the distributable reserves to show that they exceed the shareholder distribution being proposed.

Be careful that dividends are tested against the parent company's reserves, *not* the consolidated group reserves. Often the parent company accounts are in a forgotten section at the end of a set of group results in an annual report.

1. Any shareholder distribution is made out of the parent company accounts, not the group consolidated ones. This may be the only time you look at the 'company' accounts, usually buried right at the back of an Annual Report.

2. Be aware that it has to be the last filed accounts that show sufficient reserves. Management accounts don't count, nor does any profit earned after the last set of accounts filed with Companies House.

It is illegal for UK companies to pay a shareholder distribution that does not meet these conditions. If you subsequently find that an illegal distribution has been made, you will have to either claim it back from shareholders (not a great idea) or pass a retrospective EGM resolution to absolve shareholders from any claim from the company to get the money back. Best not get yourself into this position, although it does happen (and, yes, I speak from experience), especially since the law was tightened.

Do shareholders like dividends?

There's not much point in paying a dividend unless shareholders want one, but it's pretty rare for them to be unpopular. Dividends do three things:

1. Pass some of the profits onto the owners of the business (i.e. shareholders)
2. Reduce cash balances or increase net debt for the company
3. Signal confidence in the future to the market

Do dividends matter?

Theoretically dividends shouldn't matter. It's all shareholders' money whether its distributed (paid as dividends) or kept in the business (and so reflected in the share price). Shareholders should worry only about total shareholder return (TSR), which is share price appreciation plus dividends paid. A higher or lower dividend theoretically should not affect TSR.

However, there are a number of issues to bear in mind when setting a dividend:

1. **Is it sustainable and affordable?** A dividend cover near 1.0 does not give much spare for investment or any profit decline.

2. **Is the company sitting on or generating a lot of cash** that is not delivering a return? In that case it would be better for that cash to be in shareholders' hands.

3. **A rising dividend sends the market a sign about management confidence** and this may be reflected in a higher share price. Alternatively, a cut in the dividend suggests that management is foreseeing more difficult times ahead.

4. **Shareholder distribution may be part of the company moving to a different capital structure**, such as increasing debt and leverage. This alters the risk profile of the company and may move the valuation of the stock.

Some shareholders might have tax advantages in receiving capital gains from a rising share price, as opposed to income from dividends.

Other forms of dividend

Dividend in kind: Some companies offer investors dividends in shares, rather than cash, either through a scrip issue of new shares or a 'DRIP' scheme (whereby the company purchases its own shares in the market to give to investors). The advantages to shareholders are that, if they don't need the cash, they can reinvest the dividend in additional shares with no dealing costs. The advantage of a scrip issue to the company is that it preserves its cash, issuing new equity instead of buying shares to fund it. The DRIP uses cash, but slightly reduces the shares in issue, with some benefit to earnings per share. In the UK, there is no tax difference in taking a cash dividend versus shares.

Tip

If a new scrip or DRIP scheme is being launched, a director should ask what level of take-up is expected in order to justify the modest additional costs for the company.

Special dividend: Sometimes a company will declare a special dividend. The description '*special*' simply implies one-off. It is typically where the company wishes to pass on the proceeds of a sale of a major asset or division, or where it wishes to increase significantly its gearing or reduce its spare cash. In other respects, it's no different to an ordinary dividend.

Share buybacks

Companies can purchase their own shares, using cash that otherwise could have been used to pay a dividend. This is a form of shareholder distribution. It requires shareholder permission, and it is common for an AGM resolution to be put annually to give boards the power to undertake a certain amount of share buybacks, often as a matter of routine rather than expecting it to be used. The company also has to comply with the same rules about having distributable reserves as when paying a dividend.

Why do a share buyback?

If a company buys back its own shares, this will reduce the issued share capital. In the first instance this shouldn't have any effect on the share price, as the company reduces its cash, and thus value, proportionate to the reduction in the number of shares. However, any further gain thereafter in the value of the company would be spread over fewer shares, boosting future earnings per share or net asset value per share.

The buyback, like any distribution, also signals management confidence in the future, which may boost the company valuation and thus share price. This is particularly true if the buy back is part of an established ongoing programme of repurchases. A buy back may also be initiated as a one-off, if for example a significant part of the business has been sold off or the company gets a one-off receipt of cash. In this case, the benefit is likely to be one-off as well.

Share buybacks or dividends?

Share buy-backs offer capital gains in place of dividend income. Some shareholders (such as growth funds) may prefer capital gains and others (such as private shareholders or income funds) may favour income. Most tax authorities levy lower rates of tax on capital gains than income, so there may be tax advantages to buy backs over dividends. Buy backs also enable shareholders to defer their tax bill as tax is charged only when shares are subsequently sold.

On the other hand, some shareholders may favour cash in hand, so they may prefer dividends to buy backs.

Dividends tend to be 'sticky'. Shareholders don't like the dividend being cut, so boards are reluctant to reduce the rate of pay out unless there is a lasting downturn in profit expected. Buy backs, on the other hand, can be more flexible, as there isn't necessarily the expectation that they will be repeated at the same level.

Share buybacks are more likely to benefit earnings per share. This is because, although the company loses interest from the cash it used to buy the shares, the buyback offsets this by reducing the number of shares in issue. Management may be incentivised to grow EPS in their long-term incentive plans, and so may benefit more from buybacks.

Is there evidence that favours either buybacks or dividends?

Any evidence is difficult to assess as it's a bit circular. If a company is doing well, it is more likely to pay higher distributions. Separating out the underlying cash flow performance from the impact of the subsequent distribution is difficult. The best data comes from the US, where buy backs are fairly common.

Shareholder distributions are a large factor in total shareholder return (TSR). Over the last 80 years, 44% of the TSR of Standard & Poors 500 companies came from shareholder distributions. Buybacks have become a more popular form of distribution in recent years. Until the early '80s, less than 10% of shareholder distributions in the US were buybacks, but nowadays they are 50-60%[89].

McKinsey[90] found that there was no significant relationship between growth in TSR and whether the company paid out distributions, be they dividends or bought back shares. Their conclusion however was

---

[89] CFA magazine

[90] http://www.mckinsey.com/business-functions/strategy-and-corporate-finance/our-insights/paying-back-your-shareholders

that companies that frequently engaged in buy backs did best. This seems self-fulfilling: Only very successful, cash generative companies can afford to do frequent buy backs and they are likely to be companies whose share price is likely to reflect that performance!

Some argue that companies should buy back shares when the board feels that the company is undervalued. However, this would suggest that the board has a better understanding of market value than the market. McKinsey concluded that they have 'rarely seen companies with a good track record of repurchasing shares when they were undervalued; more often than not, we see companies repurchasing shares when prices are high.'

The theory is that, unless shareholders put a significant weight on their own tax benefits of buybacks, they should be indifferent to share repurchases compared to dividends. The statistics, such as they are, back this. The form of distribution has no significant impact of shareholder returns.

The underlying financial performance, plus the decision to pass some of the success on in shareholder distributions, in whatever form, are the key drivers of shareholder return. It is strong financial returns plus the determination of the board to reward shareholders that delivers total shareholder return.

Rights issues, open offers and placings

The other end of the spectrum from shareholder distributions are capital raises, when companies go to the market and try to raise more capital by issuing more shares.

Rights issue: All shareholders are offered new shares in proportion to their holdings, usually at a significant discount to the prevailing share price. A 1 for 2 rights issue would simply mean that all shareholders are offered 1 share for every 2 shares they currently hold. This delivers perfect pre-emption (see later), and so, is the more popular mechanism for most shareholders.

A shareholder who doesn't take up their rights may be able to receive some of the discount value without investing more cash, as their allocated shares may be sold on the market and the price difference remitted back to them. For example, if shares are issued at a 30% discount to the current share price, existing shareholders will be motivated to take up the shares. If they instead sell their rights, they may receive broadly the difference between the discounted price and the market price after the shares have been issued[91]. For these reasons, the rights issue is generally the default mechanism for boards when they consider raising equity.

Open offer: This is similar to a Rights Issue, but any shareholders who do not participate won't receive any value for any allocated shares that they do not take up. It therefore adds more incentive to existing shareholders to participate, as shareholders' existing holdings are being diluted by new shares being offered at a discount. Only if they take up their pro-rata allocation of shares will they avoid being diluted. Open Offers retain full pre-emption rights.

Firm placing: This offers no pre-emption. The company will have presold the shares to one or more new investors, likely at a discount. This means that other shareholders will not be able to access any of the discount and may feel aggrieved. However, it enables a company to bring in new investors to the equity issue, which is important if it believes that existing shareholders would not be prepared to provide all the extra capital requested. A firm placing however, annoys shareholders who are not offered any of the stock at a discount. This particularly affects retail (private) shareholders. A firm placing is therefore, best kept for a small raise, or an emergency situation, in which the company needs guaranteed funds quickly.

---

[91] If, for example, a company offers a 1:1 rights at 30% discount the theoretical ex-rights price will fall by 15%, suggesting that the rights are worth 15% of the starting price.

Placing and open offer: This retains partial pre-emption but also enables a company to bring in new investors as well. Existing shareholders are offered a proportion of the new shares in the open offer (pro rata to their holdings) but can also apply for more shares. If demand from existing shareholders exceeds the total allocated in the open offer, then the company may claw back some of the shares allocated to the placing. This therefore gives full pre-emption in the open offer, and partial pre-emption in the placing.

There are other mechanisms, and these can become much more complex, so won't be covered here.

Pre-emption rights

The board is contemplating an equity raise. The brokers and CFO talk in respectful terms about preserving pre-emption rights and what this means for how they raise the new capital. But all directors should understand these issues, particularly as shareholders take this very seriously, and may well hold the whole board to account on this.

Pre-emption is simply the right for existing shareholders to buy new shares before others can[92]. For a private company, this would ensure that the board couldn't issue a large tranche of shares to another party and so dilute an existing shareholder's holding and voting rights without the latter's approval.

For a liquid publicly listed stock, shareholders will expect pre-emption rights for any significant share issue. Usually, the focus is on any price discount being offered on the new shares. Take an example: A company with a share price of 400p places a 1 for 2 share issue at 300p (a 25% discount), without first offering it to existing shareholders. On a pro-forma basis, the existing shareholders would lose 8% of the value

---

[92] In the UK, the Pre-Emption Group (representing listed companies, investors and intermediaries) clarified its principles in March 2015. https://sway.office.com/HHPgz98MJB2jfEqM?loc=swsp

of the holdings as the price moves to the blended average price of £3.67. Meanwhile the new shareholders get an immediate gain of 22%. You can see why the existing shareholders would be pretty cross about it.

Pre-emption rights mean that any significant new share issue for cash should be offered first to existing shareholders in proportion to their current holdings. This means that if they take up these rights, they would not be disadvantaged, as they would get their fair share of any discounts offered.

A new share issue might also be launched in order to provide equity (as opposed to cash) to pay for an acquisition, with the new shares being offered to the target company shareholders. In this case pre-emption would be impractical, so the issue is likely to be whether the price effectively being paid is a reasonable one.

A company will often put a resolution to the AGM for a general authority to disapply (i.e. ignore) pre-emption. You can probably get away with using this if it is no more than 5% of the total share capital, or for up to 10%, if anything over 5% is for a specific acquisition or capital investment, which is fully disclosed at the time.

Companies are expected, if possible, to inform shareholders and to discuss with them, any intention to initiate a cash raise, particularly if it is to be non-pre-emptive.

Shareholders will expect a strong business case for the raise, covering alternative sources of finance, consideration of the cash raising mechanism, requirement for avoiding pre-emption, and demonstration of good corporate governance and value enhancement.

Some shareholders adopt a very purist line on pre-emption. Their corporate governance team may vote their shares against *any* capital raise which is not almost completely pre-emptive. This can be despite the fund manager being supportive of the capital raise, having understood the need to get new shareholders and to ensure the issue is a success.

They may well still buy the shares, even in a non-pre-emptive element. A vote against therefore may be largely symbolic, but given that this would be a special resolution, requiring 75% majority, it wouldn't take many symbolic votes to threaten the issue.

Tip

Take pre-emption rights very seriously and think hard about how different classes of shareholders may be affected. Do not be surprised how cross shareholders can get about not getting their rights looked after. Ask questions of the brokers or financial advisers to satisfy yourself that any disregarding of pre-emption is absolutely necessary, not just convenient.

How does a board decide which mechanism to use?

The key issue is generally whether the board is sure that existing shareholders will buy all, or nearly all, of the new shares. A board needs to take account of pre-emption, but is even more focused on making the share issue a success. It is not in shareholders' interests for an equity issue to fail, with all the question marks that this would raise about the company.

Companies usually get an equity issue underwritten, so they are sure of receiving the cash. However, by definition, underwriters will only support an issue if they think it will be almost fully subscribed. It is an insurance policy not a subsidy! The underwriters may also force an even bigger discount in the offer/rights share price in order to reduce their risk.

There are also different sorts of underwrite – for example 'soft' and 'hard'. The underwrite may simply guarantee a company the proceeds if a shareholder agrees to take up its rights but then reneges on it. This is very different to an underwrite that guarantees the proceeds even if they can't find shareholders to buy the new stock.

Be aware that your large shareholders may want to do some or all of the underwriting themselves (and receive the commission for doing so). By definition, they believe in your company. They also know that a successful share issue is a boost, but an unsuccessful one can be disastrous.

If a company feels that it needs to bring new shareholders in to make the issue a success, then it is likely to move towards some variant of a placing, possibly combined with an open offer to provide some pre-emption. The board has to reconcile the desires of some shareholders, who insist on preserving pre-emption, with its need for certainty that the shares will be pretty much fully subscribed.

> **Tip**
>
> Make sure that the Board discusses whether to approach existing shareholders for possible underwriting. An individual shareholder may not want to be 'brought over the wall', i.e. briefed about such a price-sensitive matter in advance so they can't trade the stock. However, others will be happy to for a short period and may get very cross if you don't offer them part of the underwrite (and the fees arising from this).

93

---

93 This is a complex area, so I can't attempt to cover all the issues arising. It is always difficult to talk to a shareholder about a confidential project that is price-sensitive. It requires them to commit not to buy, sell or lend stock while they hold this information. Many shareholders will refuse to be made an 'insider' in this way, as they fear losing the ability to trade your stock. These issues need to be worked through carefully with your financial adviser/bank. The latter may well be keen to talk through vast spreadsheets of different outcomes, but stop them and ask them about these issues first.

Summary

The relationship between boards and shareholders is a long and complex subject. It is about personal dealings between people on both sides of corporate associations between companies who invest and companies who trade and financial relationships in shareholder returns and capital raises. The most important factor is trust between both sides. The board wants to trust that shareholders will understand the business and be there when the company needs help, especially in raising capital. Shareholders want to believe that the board and management are looking after their money and interests, creating long-term sustainable and predicable value. They also want to be listened to and taken seriously when they have something to say. All directors have a big role in making sure that this mutual trust is sustained.

Chapter 11 - Buying: Corporate Acquisitions

You may serve your entire board career never having to worry about corporate activity, never trying to launch a bid for another company and never being worried about being bid for. But the chances are that you will face the possibility – or at least the threat. Usually, a board that is going to launch a bid will have plenty of notice. A strategy review may reveal the need for greater scale or the desire to enter a new market or acquire new capabilities. Management and bankers will review possible targets and come up with a 'game-changing' opportunity. This process may take months, or quite likely years, to take from first idea to deal completion, and may well take years more to successful integration.

On the other hand, someone else can bid for you with no notice at all. It can happen as a nasty shock that ruins your afternoon. A board can be plunged immediately into a sudden existential crisis.

Directors need to know the outlines of what might happen, and things to watch for. In the event that something happens, you will have advisers and bankers who will help, but it's enormously valuable to understand in advance what the risks and potential pitfalls can be. You may not have much time and may need to move fast. This chapter gives the basics of what a board should look out for in acquiring other companies and the next chapter looks at the difficult situation of being bid for. The two chapters should be read together as they are two perspectives on the same issue. A bidder will develop a much better strategy if it understands the motivation and tactics of the target company, and vice-versa.

Most of the lessons from acquisitions can be applied to all large projects of any type, so these are explored in some detail.

First of all, however, we need a word about advisers. These people are absolutely crucial in corporate activity and you will be dealing with them extensively.

Advisers

Every board has advisers; financial, accountants, tax, remuneration, HR, IT, ESG, PR, and IR, to name but a few. However, boards must never forget that although such advisers have specialist knowledge, they usually don't have actual board experience. In the area of corporate activity, even above all others in this book, do not rely solely on advisers for your decisions.

Advisers can explain the law, the various City codes, their own experience, custom and practice, even give you advice on how they think it best to handle a situation. However, they may not necessarily understand your business and the position it is in. They may not have served on any board and may have their own agendas. If things go wrong and the board is made to look stupid, most of your advisers will be nowhere to be seen. When it comes to it, the board is on its own.

One of my least favourite politicians[94], Margaret Thatcher, is quoted as saying:

"Advisers advise, but Ministers decide". This is even more true for boards and should be Rule No.1 in any situation.

---

[94] The list is admittedly quite long

One of the most important tips in this book

Advisers advise, but directors decide.

One of my companies, a property one, was bid for out of the blue. We turned to our Rule 3 adviser[95] and asked them for their own valuation of our company and of the bid. They did pages and pages of analysis, that basically said that the offer was a good one and we would have difficulty turning it down. Their reasoning was that it was at a material premium[96] to our share price and to net asset value. However, the board believed that net asset value was not the key metric, and the current share price was undervaluing the company.

We had begun a turnaround that was delivering results, but the City had yet to fully buy into our story. Moreover, we thought that we were an income stock, where most shareholders bought us for our dividend, and our dividend yield was significantly higher than the market (implying possible upside to the share price). We felt that the real value of our company was derived from that dividend yield, which was well underpinned by earnings, secure and growing steadily. We felt that the advisers didn't fully understand our property world and the investment

---

[95] A Rule 3 adviser is an independent adviser, usually an investment bank or firm of accountants, appointed under Rule 3.1 of the Takeover Code, who advise the board of the target company as to whether the financial terms of any offer are fair and reasonable and whose advice must be disclosed to shareholders in the offer document.

[96] Real estate companies may be sold at a premium that is much lower than other companies, as there tend to be fewer synergies (usually cost savings) from combining two companies that could fund a higher premium.

proposition of our company. We persevered, stuck to our valuation and fought off the bid[97].

One of the most important success factors in a deal is the quality of the advisers on the *other* side. I always check anxiously who the other side are using, as it can make a big difference. Morrisons had a rather clever, difficult banker in their deal with Safeway. Given that this was a very amicable takeover, his attitude was counterproductive. Some advisers thrive on setting up conflict from which they can then claim victory to their client. In this case, this attitude simply fed Sir Ken Morrison's paranoia that Safeway might be deceiving him in some way. This cost Morrison money, as he was so worried that Safeway was trying to sell itself to another party behind his back, that arguably he paid a higher price than he perhaps had to.

Choose carefully the quality and culture of your banking advisers. Safeway had a mix of two very good affable, clubbable bankers and a harder hitting sharp younger, more tactical one. It enabled a mix and match approach to the other side. On the other hand, having three lead bankers is too many and this caused some conflict. It's a good idea to talk to people on other boards and ask for recommendations on good advisers and don't have too many advisers.

---

[97] This was a good decision as we had carefully assessed the evidence and the risks. It also turned out to be the best choice for shareholders and other stakeholders, as the share price subsequently rose strongly, and the business has since flourished.

Tips

1. Think hard about whether you want aggressive or collegiate advisers. You can mix them, but pay careful attention to who you field in negotiations with the other side. The other side will take their cue as to what sort of people you are from your advisers.

2. Bankers like to negotiate with other bankers, like stags locking horns at dawn. So, they sometimes dislike principals (i.e. their clients) talking directly to each other. Bankers talking to each other can be very useful and helpful, as they have deal-making experience and can be more dispassionate, but if you want to make real progress in a difficult deal, principal to principal (usually chair to chair) discussions can succeed.

You should also be very careful about incentives for advisers. On a bid for a company, most advisers would typically get paid only on successful completion. This gives them an enormous incentive to get the deal done. Their reward is much more likely to be driven by the deal happening, rather than on you paying the lowest price. The only realistic protection here is to put in a fee that ratchets down the more you end up paying for the target company. On defence work, when you are bid for, advisers may well get a fee whether it happens or not, but are likely to get a ratchet if the price is higher. Some advisers expect astronomic fees for corporate deals[98]. This is justified by them on the basis that they often work for free on abortive deals (which they generally do).

---

[98] Frankly, they usually ask for and often get huge fees on other corporate activity, such as equity raises, too.

Tips

1. Take a hard look at adviser incentives, so that you understand how their fee is generated and calculated. Most advisers are talented, upright and honest people, but they are all human and have budgets and targets to deliver.

2. Get independent advice on fee levels and look at how much other deals have generated in fees. Do not assume that you have to pay what they ask or what others have paid. Look at other transactions and fees that have been paid, not just the precedents that your advisers show you. Try to negotiate, especially if you have the luxury of a choice of advisers.

Corporate acquisitions – are they a good idea?

Whether acquisitions add value or not is a favourite subject for commentators, who love to conclude that they don't. The Cass Business School looked at this topic and concluded that, most deals don't add value to share price performance in the three-year period after they are announced, but that successful deals create more value than unsuccessful ones destroy[99]. In a way, this sort of analysis is similar to the economic modelling looking at whether advertising works or not. The reality is that neither advertising nor acquisitions create value by themselves. Both work well in the hands of skilful practitioners making thoughtful decisions at an opportune time. However, acquiring companies has many more risks than launching a new marketing campaign. In advertising, the most you are likely to lose is the production and media cost. If corporate acquisitions go wrong, it can go wrong pretty

---

[99] Cass Business School, M&A Research centre,

2011 quoted in cfo.com https://www.cfo.com/ma/2012/06/do-mergers-add-value-after-all/

disastrously, even possibly threatening the survival of the acquiring company.

For example, Hewlett-Packard bought Autonomy for $11bn in 2011 and a year later wrote its value down by $8.8bn, with allegations of 'serious accounting improprieties' by Hewlett Packard while former Autonomy management claimed the other side had had 'serious cold feet' and never really tried to integrate the business.[100]

It's like using a chain saw. In the right hands, at the right time, with the right motivation, they are fantastic tools to do a great job. In the wrong hands, at the wrong time, or with the wrong motivation and you end up with a lot of blood on the floor.

Leo Apotheker, the CEO of Hewlett Packard was fired by HP's board just weeks after the Autonomy deal was announced[101]. Botched acquisitions can be seriously detrimental to a director's career.

Reasons to acquire another company

There are many reasons to look at buying another company. The principal ones are;

1. Gaining greater scale.

2. Geographic expansion.

3. Vertical integration (buying a supplier or customer).

4. Acquiring new knowledge, skills or techniques.

5. Removing a competitor.

---

[100] Reuters, 'HP had 'buyer's remorse' over ill-fated Autonomy deal, court hears' 6 January 2020 https://www.reuters.com/article/us-autonomy-hp-lynch-idUSKBN1Z51VC

[101] Reuters 'Ex-CEO Whitman says was happy to throw HP predecessor 'under the bus' over Autonomy deal' 5 June 2019 https://www.reuters.com/article/autonomy-hp-lynch/update-1-ex-ceo-whitman-says-was-happy-to-throw-hp-predecessor-under-the-bus-over-autonomy-deal-idUSL8N23C5V9

Diversification (geographic and product).

This isn't a book about corporate strategy and is not about how to evaluate acquisitions. It is about how boards should challenge acquisition proposals and think through the reasoning and the risks.

The board needs to ask many, many questions, particularly around the risks of an acquisition.

Below are two tales of acquisitions, one successful and one less so, that I witnessed at first hand, both of them involving the Safeway grocery chain, initially by Argyll Group and then by Morrisons. It is not a business school case study. I was there and saw them first-hand. They highlight many issues that arise from acquisitions and questions that boards should ask.

One success story and one cautionary tale

(a) Success story: Argyll Group buys Safeway in 1987

Argyll in 1987, was the UK's No.5 grocery retailer. That year, Safeway Inc, recently purchased by KKR in a private equity buy-out, decided to sell its British arm, the sixth largest UK player, to raise cash. Argyll saw the opportunity to acquire it and grow to be No.4, which it did for £681m[102]. What followed was arguably one of the most successful retail mergers in the UK[103], although it left some legacies that helped to derail the later Morrisons merger.

Argyll was led by Sir Alastair Grant and David Webster. They had a very clear plan, which admired Safeway's powerful, modern American-style customer proposition (wide range, an emphasis on fresh food, good quality products, and strong service culture), but also recognised

---

[102] The Safeway deal happened three years before I joined Argyll in 1990.

[103] See 'The grocers – the rise and fall of the supermarket chains' by Andrew Seth and Geoffrey Randall

that Safeway's backroom functions and financial acumen were less good. In contrast, Argyll's main fascia, Presto, had a less distinctive customer proposition that appealed to its slightly downmarket customer base, but the business was run on a very canny 'northern' basis with a tight cost-base and efficient backroom processes. However by the time that the integration of Safeway was completed in 1993, the Presto brand had been ditched completely, and the group had even renamed itself Safeway plc. To the outside world, it looked as if Safeway had taken over Argyll, not the other way round.

The lessons from a successful acquisition

1. Customer needs drive company integration

Safeway had a 55% higher sales per square foot than Presto and 76% better profit. Safeway was a better customer proposition, and so Argyll started converting Presto stores into Safeway, with impressive early results. Extensive consumer research was done to identify which parts of the Safeway proposition were most attractive to different demographics.

This in turn drove the overall Safeway proposition development and the pace and targeting of the conversion programme.

> **Tip**
>
> An integration that gives benefit to customers is likely to be much more successful than one that just offers cost savings.

2. The integration is phased in and adapted, rather than imposed as dogma

Like many projects, the initial results of the tests were very successful, benefiting from strong management interest and motivation. Argyll however didn't force itself to an ambitious target to convert all the stores in a short time period. In fact, the conversion programme lasted six years until 2003. The roll-out and the conversions themselves were however, adapted to build in new learning as they went. By 1991, the uplift from converting the remaining Presto to Safeway was diminishing, and the conversion programme halted. It was restarted in 1993, after improvements to the core Safeway proposition meant that better uplifts were being achieved, and also because the business needed the simplicity of having only one fascia.

> **Tip**
>
> The process of trial, roll-out, review, amend and roll-out is just as important in an acquisition as any other major project. This may take time that will be well-spent.

3. A merger of businesses should use the best of both

The integration was treated as a merger of the operating businesses, not a takeover by Presto. Argyll's aim was to have post-integration management made up of 1/3 ex-Argyll, 1/3 ex-Safeway and 1/3 new outside recruits. When I arrived in 1990 (as one of the outsiders), you could still tell who was ex-Presto and who ex-Safeway. However, this was breaking down and it was clear that best man for the job was broadly being applied. By 1994, the group had one distinctive Safeway culture; a mixture of Presto, Safeway and outsiders.

> **Tip**
>
> Best person for the job, best process and best system should be the mantra. Integrators need to avoid the natural preference for managers to prefer the *'familiar that always works for us'* in place of the *'best one for the new business'*.

4. Profit increases after a successful acquisition

As a result of the successful merger, group profit before tax rose strongly to £417m in 1993 and the newly renamed Safeway plc entered the FTSE 100. In the end, an acquisition will be judged by the financial return.

5. But even a successful integration won't solve all the problems

Once the sales uplift from integration and the synergy gains were achieved, Safeway struggled to grow profit further after 1993. Despite being No.4 in the sector, the group still suffered from a scale disadvantage against the bigger three (Tesco, Sainsbury's and Asda), its stores were still physically smaller than rivals, and the portfolio was even more diverse, causing substantial complexity.

Eventually, the board decided that it needed greater scale and so, following abortive attempts to merge with Asda, a takeover deal was agreed with Morrisons in 2003.

(b) Cautionary tale: Morrisons buys Safeway in 2004

Not all acquisitions are so successful because acquisitions are difficult
and complex. If the integration is misconceived and poorly executed
from the start, it can take a long time for the underlying strategic benefit of the merger to come through.

Sir Ken Morrison, chairman and chief executive of the eponymous
chain, had built his chain up from a market stall to No.5 in the UK
grocery market. He did that through his outstanding leadership and
drive. It is well-known that he despised bankers, consultants, analysts
and non-executive directors in equal measure, but he knew every one
of his 100 store managers, how his business ran and, above all, what
his customers wanted.

The Morrison success story was built on standardisation and simplicity. We all 'know' that businesses benefit from simplicity. Morrisons
was a chain of near-identical stores built largely in downmarket demo-
graphic areas in the midlands and northern England. Sir Ken loved
simplicity and standardisation, wanting all stores to be almost identical.

Morrisons offered great 'everyday value' with low base prices and
around 1,000 promotions, largely multi-buys, with many service counters offering variety and a 'good honest quality'. Little went to waste,
as food near its sell by date would be used in the customer and staff

restaurants or repackaged in a service counter (e.g. excess prime meat was converted into mince).

Sir Ken didn't believe in complex systems. He told me once that he designed their ordering system one day in a store canteen. He described what he meant. I said *"But that's just a stock & order card."* *"Yes,"* he agreed: *"And that's all the system is."* *"But how does this do forward ordering?"* I asked. *"Ah,"* he replied: *"We are just now trialling a system to automate some of our forward orders"*. This was in 2003, some 10 years after all the other majors, including Safeway, had fully automated re-ordering.

Safeway had struggled as No.4 in the UK grocery market, and had tried a number of strategies without any lasting success. Eventually, the board concluded that scale was the major issue. A couple of attempts to merge with Asda failed, and it was considered highly unlikely that the competition authorities would allow such a merger of No.3 and No.4 anyway. But Sir Ken was tempted by the prospect of growing faster and coveted the Safeway superstores and hypermarkets. He was initially very cautious, not wanting to threaten what he had created so far and took many months to agree to explore the idea. Sir Ken told us, at the time, that it was his fellow executive directors that were more ambitious. It was they who were urging him to go for a takeover and who were so confident of making it a success. Notably, Morrisons had no non-executive directors and no independent voice in the boardroom.

The acquisition was a nightmare for the first few years. Safeway stores lost both customers and revenue and profit crashed. The idea of putting the businesses together to achieve greater scale was a good one, but the implementation was disastrous. So why did the £600m combined profits of Safeway and Morrisons, not to mention another £300m of synergies, dissolve into a £300m loss two years later?

The lessons from a flawed integration

1. Only buy what you understand

Acquiring a company in a sector of which you have no experience is inherently very risky. As authors are told to write only about what they know, so corporate acquirers should only buy what they understand. On the face of it, the Safeway deal met this criterion. It was a fairly straightforward combination of two supermarkets[104] to give greater scale, efficiency and buying power.

However, the Morrisons team was experienced only in running a simple, standardised, largely manually-controlled business. They just had no experience, or understanding, of running an excessively complex, heterogeneous, systematised business.

> **Rule No.1 of acquisitions is to understand what you are buying.**

2. A good idea is just an idea till it's executed well

The acquirer knew the grocery business well and was a great operator. There was neither international expansion nor diversification. On paper, this was a slam dunk just to gain scale synergies from putting two rivals together. But there is a difference between having a good idea and actually delivering it. I have had bankers come to board meetings with great ideas for companies to buy, and sometimes you have to tell them: "Great idea, but we are not ready at the moment. We couldn't risk handling the integration."

---

[104] A description is given in 'Trolley Wars. The Battle of the Supermarkets' by Judi Bevan

> **Tip**
>
> Good ideas are not enough. They have to be executed well, which requires management with the capacity and experience to handle major change programmes, possibly with reluctant employees in the acquired company.

3. Simplicity has its own challenges

Morrisons was a simple business run in an efficient, uncomplicated way. Reordering was manual. Ranges were near identical in all stores, each with very similar layouts. Sir Ken made almost all the decisions in a Thursday morning weekly meeting in his office, which suited their dominant 'command and control' culture. He didn't need complex processes. New store developments were evaluated by 'counting chimney pots', i.e. driving around neighbourhoods, when other supermarket companies were using sophisticated geographical databases. He spent a lot of time visiting stores and fixing problems there and then. This is fine for 100 stores, but it isn't scalable, and failed when Morrisons suddenly had over 600 stores. Simplicity based on small size will inevitably come apart when you acquire another business to get much bigger scale.

Sir Ken didn't believe in sophisticated management. He had confidence in his own judgement on decisions. He didn't need strong management around him. He needed people who would do what they were told. As a result, his colleagues on the board were not the strongest, and there was very little middle management. This made for a simple lean structure, but also contained the seeds of future problems. It was not a structure that could cope easily with complexity or a heterogeneous store portfolio and customer base.

4. **Complexity is very challenging – you can't just impose simplicity**

Morrisons acquired a difficult situation when it bought Safeway. Safeway was a much bigger business than Morrisons, with 500 stores and a turnover of nearly £9bn, against 120 stores with less than half the turnover. It was much more heterogenous, with multi-formats (hypermarkets, superstores, supermarkets, convenience stores and BP petrol stations), where Morrisons had one. It had a very diverse customer base with slightly upmarket demographics, whereas Morrisons had a more homogeneous, downmarket customer base. Finally, it had complex network logistics and IT systems, while Morrisons had experience only of relatively simple IT and two hub and spoke regional distribution depots.

Safeway had struggled partly *because* of its excess complexity, which had only been made worse by its integration with Argyll. This became evident in the mid 1990s, when not even the advice of McKinsey, which ironically also played a lead role in the contemporaneous turnaround of Asda[105], seemed able to identify a strategy to turnaround Safeway's stagnating profit. Later a new CEO, the charismatic Argentinian, Carlos Criado-Perez, similarly struggled, adding significant complexity, with a major promotional strategy, designed to be so fiendishly complex that Tesco couldn't, for once, copy it.

In the end, the complexities of store portfolio and promotional strategy proved too difficult for the Morrisons team, brought up on simplicity.

Tip

You can't simply impose simplicity on a complex business. Actually, trying to simplify a complex business is itself a very complicated thing to do. As Leonardo Da Vinci said: '*Simplicity is the ultimate sophistication*'.

---

5. Customers are the ultimate arbiters of success

Safeway, in the run up to the takeover, did some research that showed that in areas where there were both Safeway and Morrisons stores, Safeway customers tended consciously to reject Morrisons, preferring even Tesco and Sainsbury's. Morrisons dismissed this evidence, but it would come back to haunt them.

---

[105] Mckinsey had already deployed it's prime retail team to Asda by the time that Safeway came calling. As a result, Mckinsey provided a team less experienced in retail to Safeway. The former team later turned up at Sainsbury's helping with Justin King's turnaround. It's a small world.

Almost all grocery customers have a choice of where to shop. Safeway customers liked strong, largely price-led (i.e. not multi-buy) promotions and a wide range with upmarket lines.

This is why Safeway customers were choosing to go there, rather than to Morrisons.

It was therefore a brave decision by the incoming Morrisons management to stop price promotions and replace them with multibuys. They then reduced Safeway's range, especially on fresh lines, and put in a more generic cheaper, downmarket product range.

Safeway's customers responded by moving to Tesco and Sainsbury's, and this loss was offset only marginally by an influx of very price-sensitive customers seeking the lower 'everyday' prices of the (less profitable) new range.

Tip

Acquisitions cannot take customers for granted. Even a deal that gives synergy and saves millions of pounds in costs won't look such a good idea if customers go elsewhere. Remember that most acquisitions throw up large amounts of goodwill. And goodwill is easily lost.

[106] Goodwill is the difference between what someone pays for a company and the value of the assets and liabilities that are bought.

6. Rejecting best person/system/process for the job will not give you the best result

There was to be no merger of management. Initially Morrisons agreed to 'best man for the job', but the reality was different. Safeway's head office, west of London, was closed progressively and employees could either take redundancy or apply for a job in Morrisons head office in Bradford, sometimes at a lower grade. Few took the latter, fearing for their long-term future. As a result, Morrison lost the people who knew how to manage the complex Safeway business.

Morrison simplified the supply chain by disposing of the automated replenishment system, explaining to store managers that they would have to go back to writing their own forecasts again. The core multi-million-pound ERP (i.e. business-wide integrated) system that Safeway had just finished installing at great cost was peremptorily cancelled[107].

Morrisons rejected Safeway's promotional strategy. Rightly, they disliked supplier funding for promotions coming in as lump sum monies at the year-end (with other volume and activity-related rebates). This year-end sum had grown over the previous years to £600m, twice the annual profit, so their concern was absolutely fair. Controlling such an accrual was a very tricky task for the finance team (and had given me countless sleepless nights). However, Morrisons management said that they didn't believe the sums were real, despite the fact that they had been externally audited, and that furthermore, they didn't approve of collecting them. And they were men and women of their word. They stopped trying to collect these monies, and then fired all the finance

---

[107] A consultant later told me that he loved Morrisons. Why, I asked. Because, he said, it was the only company that had, as Safeway, paid him to install an ERP system, then paid him to remove it after the takeover and then paid him a third time to reinstall it later when they realised their mistake.

team and the buyers who knew where the money was[108]. Morrisons management lost control of the funding sums, and lost the people who could have retrieved the situation when they realised their error. They then did the only thing they could do, and blamed Safeway's accounting systems.

Tip

A good strategic decision will only work if the implementation is done well. That implementation will almost certainly require the co-operation and expertise of incumbent management. Winning over and exploiting the talent in a business is not a luxury, it is how the implementation plan will need to work. Poor integration will destroy the value that should have flowed from a good acquisition idea.

---

7. Simplicity plus complexity results in more complexity

Morrisons had built a brilliant model; a simple, homogeneous business with a thin management structure under clear single-person management. However, this also limited its scale. Morrisons didn't want to develop new stores that were significantly smaller or in different demographics. There was a limit to how many stores Morrisons could run with this model, not least as Sir Ken couldn't know and visit each

---

[108] In fact, one supplier told me that all his Christmases had come at once. Morrisons had 'apparently forgotten' that he owed them a couple of million pounds and he was able to reverse his accrual to the direct benefit of his bonus. He was not alone.

one regularly. There was a limit to its scalability, perhaps a key lesson for all founder-led businesses.

Safeway had been complex partly because it struggled with a diverse store portfolio. It wasn't possible to simplify the combined business just by imposing the Morrisons model. In so far as this happened, the result was then not popular with Safeway customers, especially in range and promotions.

Tip

1. Simplicity won't help much if the customer doesn't like the result.

2. When simplicity meets complexity, it is complexity that wins. You can't just impose it. It is a very complex and risky process to eliminate complexity.

---

8. **Some companies have strategic problems that are not solved by being acquired**

We can analyse the Safeway acquisition with 20:20 hindsight, but maybe this was a business that was too difficult for anyone to manage successfully. Two successive CEOs at Safeway struggled and Morrisons then laboured. Grocery retailing is a tough business and scale takes a toll on the smaller players.

Tip

Boards must not be tempted into thinking that acquisitions solve all business problems. They may well make some of them worse.

---

9. Post-acquisition integration is really difficult and shows up any failures in management and its decision-making

After the extent of the integration problems became visible, Morrisons recruited independent non-execs to their board and professionalised their management. Performance recovered.

As Richard Pennycook, the new Morrisons CFO at the time, said: *"The group could no longer be controlled by a small top team that acted on instinct. The new Morrisons ...needed new experience and thinking, and more analysis." (Guardian 24 March 2006)*

Issues for a board to consider on an acquisition

1. Pricing and returns

You may well find that more time is spent debating the price to pay and the tactics, than ever is devoted to debating whether the board really should be buying a particular company. Be absolutely sure that the target is a company that is right to acquire. As soon as the debate becomes; *'Well it would be nice to have if we can get it cheap'*, alarm bells should ring. Warren Buffet, who knows a thing or two about buying companies, said;

"It's far better to buy a wonderful company at a fair price than a fair company at a wonderful price."

Advisers typically produce pages of presentation and spreadsheets of comparisons and scenarios. Ensure that the comparisons are really valid. In their search for comparatives, advisers will sometimes stretch the point, including deals such as a small take-private deal for a niche player, for example, that are not good comparatives for a multi-billion-pound contested take-over. The inevitable conclusion from these pricing benchmarks will be that there is a wide range of values for the target company, that stretches from the current share price (or even lower), probably upwards to 50% or more, higher.

A good starting benchmark is a 30% premium to the recent share price for a public company. This is the control premium, the extra a company is often expected to pay to get control of another. However, the ultimate price paid will be the result of supply and demand. How much does your board want this particular target company? Does the target board want, or is it under pressure, to sell?

Every advisers' valuation will include a net present value (NPV) valuation, which takes the expected post-acquisition cash flow and discounts it back to how much it is worth in today's money. This will usually be the highest price suggested for the purchase, as it doesn't fully take account of the risks in integrating an acquisition. It is the value today if everything goes exactly to plan. And, as the Prussian Chief of Staff[109] said, "*no plan survives contact with the enemy*".

Tip

Ignore the net present value valuation for an acquisition. It's almost always too high and allows for no setbacks.

2. **Post-deal integration is not a nice thing to have. It *is* the value generator or destroyer.**

Deals do not create value. Successfully executed integrations create value. Morrisons got a great deal in buying Safeway, paying £4bn for assets valued at £6bn. But as discussed above, profit subsequently fell dramatically due to its integration problems, so it didn't end up looking like such a great transaction (though performance recovered under different management). Morrisons did not do a risk analysis of the takeover and so had not thought through the issues and risks[110].

Advisers love deals and will toast a board that pulls off a great deal. But remember that the day after, the board will be all alone with its hangover. Your share price may well have shot up already to incorporate all the synergies that you promised. The problem is that you now have to go and deliver these benefits and avoid any hiccups. The work

---

[109] Field Marshal Helmuth Karl Bernhard Graf von Moltke (1800-1891), Chief of Staff of the Prussian General Staff from 1857 to 1871, Great General Staff (GGS) from 1871 to 1888.

[110] Morrisons did employ a major consulting firm to help with integration planning. However, Sir Ken was irritated by them, as they started raising difficult issues. The consultants didn't last long.

on how the new company will be integrated must start well before the deal is even signed.

A good acquisition idea has to be executed with very fine margins for error before it will be a success.

Tip

Ask for the plan for the first hundred days of integration of the new acquisition *before* the board agrees to make a final offer. Don't take assurances that there is plenty of time for this later. There isn't. You need to think about execution before you set the final price.

---

3. Identify inconvenient disadvantages

Acquiring a company can be exciting and fun. Who wants to be a party pooper and talk about the possible disadvantages? Of course, a board should ask very carefully about disadvantages. If the target company is doing badly, is it really because management is useless, or maybe the company has structural competitive disadvantages? I have seen a number of acquiring companies (like the consortium that bought Flybe when I was chairman) apparently assume that they will improve target company performance because, as corporate conquerors, they are obviously better managers. However, even if acquirer managers are better (a big 'if'), that still doesn't guarantee that they will run the target company much more successfully.

What generally happens is that the new managers gradually realise that the target company has more problems than they realised. This is generally the point at which the acquirer announces that it was misled by previous management about the true state of the company. What they actually mean is that they hadn't realised how many problems the incumbent management team was facing.

Tips

1. Do not accept a business case for an acquisition that hinges on the view that your management will do a better job than the incumbent. Insist that the business case features concrete strategies, tactics and policies that your company will do that is different.

2. Ensure that a paper is tabled about the disadvantages that the target company suffers from, and how these will be removed by your acquisition.

4. The customer doesn't care about your integration plans

Most acquisitions force companies to become inward-looking. There are so many things to sort out; management and people, integrating processes and systems, locations and legal requirements as well as delivering promised synergies. The tendency is therefore to put all your effort into the running of your business and forget about the customer. Morrisons knew that its range was successful, so why shouldn't Safeway shoppers like it too? They did no market research (Sir Ken believed in his own insight, not that of consultants) and when Safeway did its own research, prior to the completion of the deal, Sir Ken refused to listen to the warnings. Telling customers who want X that this doesn't matter, because you are offering Y cheaper, might work, but if you haven't tested this beforehand, it is just a leap in the dark.

The great success of the Argyll purchase of Safeway, was that it realised that the acquired Safeway was the better customer proposition, and, in brand terms, this became a reverse takeover. In the end, it is the customer who decides if an acquisition will be a success, not the bankers nor consultants, and not management wearing blinkers.

Don't take your customers for granted after an acquisition. If you change the proposition, without testing and ensuring that they prefer the new version, don't be surprised if your customers leave. Never lose sight of the needs of customers. If you redesign a supply chain to save lots of money, but it results in running out of stock, customers are unlikely to be sympathetic.

Tip

Always ask 'what's in it for our customers?' in any discussion about an acquisition. You will be surprised how many acquirers forget about them. Your complexity is not the customers' problem.

---

5. Speed isn't everything

Any integration plan must have clear timetables. There should be a hundred-day plan (i.e. a series of activities and objectives for the first three months). This is because you are most likely to get things done in the initial period and if there are tough decisions, they are easier to take, put behind you and then move on. However, there is value in testing some of your assumptions in the early weeks and months, to make sure that what you thought as an outsider still seems right once you are inside.

Prototype, test and only then roll-out: This is an important rule for all projects, not just acquisitions. In the ubiquitous *'make it happen'* cul-

ture, there is a tendency to rush straight from idea or preliminary prototype to roll-out. An enthusiastic executive presents to the board a
great idea that she has developed in one product-line, one store, or one
factory and translates these early results into massive gains if you roll
it out quickly. But developing a prototype is not a test as to whether it
will succeed. The Hawthorne effect[111] is well-known. Put a lot of focus
on a project and it is quite likely to succeed.

That's great, but you should then test it in the cold light of day (or as
footballers would ask, would it work on a cold Monday night in
Stoke?). Even then, after a successful test, roll it out, rather than immediately go national. This enables you to adjust your approach as you
learn more. This is as true for any roll-out of new products, marketing,
process or system.

A board would be very brave to roll out an integration or massive
change programme without prototyping it and testing it first[112]. But
some do, partly because everyone feels in such a hurry to deliver. There
are times when taking your time pays handsome dividends. The integration of Argyll/Presto took six years and was a better outcome for
that. When it comes to over-hurrying projects, Warren Buffet, as ever,
had a pithy epithet:

"You can't produce a baby in one month by getting nine women pregnant."

As a rule of thumb, implement a fast programme for change that you
consider inevitable (such as checking your plans against the reality of
running the new business, identifying duplicated functions and offices,

---

[111] The Hawthorne effect notes that just observing people will itself affect their behaviour. In business,
a cherished new project with lots of management support and attention is almost guaranteed to work
better than when that same project is a business-as-usual roll out. Some academics dispute the effect exists,
but I've seen it in business more than once.

[112] But sadly this is exactly what governments and regulators tend to do! See chapter 15.

and management changes) over the first 100 days, but don't rush major change programmes (such as a roll-out of a new format or product, especially ones that impact on customers).

Tip

Look hard at the integration timetable (usually a Gantt chart in an appendix). Ask:

- Are some projects being planned to happen too quickly or rushed?

- What are the decision-points on projects?

- What do we need to know by then to make a decision?

- How will we know if a project isn't working?

- What will we do if it isn't working?

---

6. Don't think that an acquisition will solve all your problems

Corporate acquisitions can bring scale, new techniques, new markets, and new geographies, but they won't solve other issues a business has. An acquisition is not a case of *'with one bound, our hero was free'*. If your company has a problem, such as tough competitors, a weak supply chain or poor financial control, an acquisition is likely to make this worse, not better, at least in the short-term. Management will be distracted by integration, with executives wanting to get involved in the shiny new toy.

Change itself causes risk and integrating a new company causes lots of change.

7. Friendly or hostile?

It is important for a bidding board to consider what stance it wants to take with a target board. There may be macho advisers, and even directors, who are dismissive of the target board and advocate a hardline. They will urge you make an offer and accompany it with threats to get the deal done. However, in my experience, on both sides of deals, you are almost always better off keeping it friendly and respectful. You will get far more information from a target company if you show that you are thoughtful and considerate, as opposed to slamming an offer on the table.

When Medicx bid for Assura (where I was chairman) in 2013, it put a price on the table, saying that this was agreed with a majority of Assura's shareholders (via irrevocables[113]) and that it was just a matter of Assura giving them due diligence information disclosure to finalise details. I suspect that this was the result of a combination of naivety on their board and aggressive advisers (one of whom had history - as I said, beware the motivations of advisers). Actually, merging the two

---

[113] See chapter 12 for a discussion of 'irrevocables'

businesses together wasn't a mad idea, but the price for Assura was way too low, and all the value upside would have gone to Medicx shareholders. Their board would have been much better starting with a cup of tea between the two chairmen to explore what would work. As it was, Assura repelled the bid, and Medicx wasted reputation, time and money for no gain[114].

The best deals tend to start with a personal relationship being established between a board member (usually the chair) on both sides, often commencing with that 'cup of tea'. Sometimes, deals need to take time and develop a joint understanding of mutual interest. One of my companies got a bit impatient – after cups of tea had dragged on over many months - and gave a target company a formal Offer Letter during an informal discussion. The temperature in the room instantly dropped several degrees and the informal chat closed in a tense and formal froideur. We'd made a mistake. They may not have been serious in looking at a deal with us, but trying to push it along by becoming formal halted any prospect of a friendly deal. Given that we didn't want to become hostile, the deal was then doomed.

Corporate deals do not generally benefit from macho tactics, unless you are very sure that you can win without any help from target management, and the latter has no alternative to doing a deal with you. If you upset the target board, don't be surprised if the target does everything it can to thwart the deal. And it can make life very difficult for you! I have been on the receiving end of a few bids, where a little humility and respect would have led to a much better outcome for the offeror.

This is as true for private equity deals as listed company ones. CVC Capital Partners, with whom I worked for a decade, has a model to work with incumbent management and never to go hostile. In many

---

[114] Medicx, the No.3 in the sector, later successfully merged with the No.2, PHP, in 2019 to form a rival of similar size to Assura.

cases, we approached target companies and were rebuffed by management, which was the end of the matter. Although the media portray private equity as marauding capitalists laying siege to target companies, the reality is often very different. Private equity knows well that information is gold dust to any bidder and people will tell you more and be more prepared to work with you, if they at least respect you. There is no value to be gained by irritating target boards to put barriers in your way.

Lone Star's 2015 take private of Quintain Estates and Development plc was a textbook example of a friendly private equity approach culminating in an offer price high enough that the board decided that it had to be put to shareholders with a recommendation to accept.

Tip

1. Don't upset the target board or management, unless you really have to (whatever your advisers say).

2. Don't act in a hostile fashion if you can possibly avoid it.

3. Think about early contact between the respective chairs, preferably starting before you have decided to make a bid. A personal relationship of trust is almost always extremely valuable in getting agreements and smoothing the whole process.

---

8. An acquisition is not a conquest

This is a very common error. Acquiree company managers at all levels tend to regard themselves as the superior team and they try to impose everything from management, processes, systems to product line on the acquired company. It is good practice for an acquirer to make an honest impartial assessment before completion of what the target company does well and who are the key people to retain. This may seem rather simple, but it's rarely done fully.

9. Cash or shares

You can offer shares or cash or a combination of the two for the target company. Boards need to remember that if you offer your shares, the value of that offer goes up and down with your share price. This may limit how much you can offer for a target. If the market thinks that your company is paying too much for an acquisition or that the purchase is a mistake, it will mark your share price down to compensate, reducing the value of your offer. If you increase the value of your offer to restore the value to the target company, your share price is likely to fall further, negating the increase. This is not a good place to be in when trying to close a deal.

Tip

Do ask your bankers what they think the share price reaction will be to the deal, especially if offering shares. If there is a chance that the shares will go down, think very hard.

---

10. Investor support is necessary

It is crucial that a board sells the deal to its shareholders (and frankly the media too), speaking directly to large shareholders individually. Of course, you may not be able to brief investors until late in the process, as it involves giving them price-sensitive information and therefore making them insiders unable to trade your stock. Shareholders who happen to own stock in both the bidder and the target may be more receptive to the deal than others, so look for common shareholders. Institutional shareholders are generally, with good reason, wary of bankers hawking deals around, and are often sceptical that acquisitions are the answer.

Hammerson, for example, had to abandon its 2018 purchase of Intu, following a shareholder revolt, and given the subsequent financial problems at Intu, the shareholders seem to have been justified. Institutional shareholders' first instinct is usually to support management, but they will still need to be convinced.

Tip

Know your shareholders as much as you can and talk to the large ones as early as you can.

---

11. An independent view is essential

Executives proposing an acquisition are likely to be very enthusiastic about it. Similarly, advisers, working for the executives and anxious for fees, are also probably going to be keen. Much weight therefore falls on the chair and the non-exec directors to be a counterweight, to ask difficult questions and challenge risks. Morrisons had no non-execs or independent chairman when they took over Safeway, so they didn't have any independent challenging decision-making. Non-execs must risk making themselves unpopular with the executives by asking the sort of questions listed here.

12. Leaks happen

Many deals leak, and there are a multitude of motivations for leaks. Takeovers move share prices, so there is a strong incentive for some traders to get hold of early information and trade the stock to make profits. The media loves reporting on takeover battles as it makes for great copy and prominent scoops. Some parties think that a well-timed leak will put pressure on the other side in a deal. Others leak to make sure that the first report on the deal is favourable to their side. Information can leak accidentally as someone sees papers left around an office, overhears a conversation or sees a prominent business leader entering or leaving another company's office.

Leaks are generally damaging to an acquisition. They lead to the target's share price rising fast, encourage hedge funds to buy the target looking to make a fast profit, attract media interest and speculation, and can create political interference. Importantly, it is just much more difficult to conduct negotiations when they are in the public eye.

The board therefore must maintain extraordinarily tight security on any proposed corporate deal. The regulations are also now very clear, and a company must keep a register of who knows unpublished price-sensitive information. Boards must ensure that such information is kept to as few people as possible. You should assume that when it comes to juicy information, everybody tells at least one other person.

I remember one very sensitive deal many years ago, the details of which were discovered by a competitor. This was shortly after it was briefed to the government. It was claimed that a senior executive may have had a partner who was a high-ranking civil servant. In another deal, a very senior banker mentioned a deal, for which he was providing financing, to another businessman, as 'he thought he might want to get involved'.

The businessman certainly did, and he quickly bought a large tranche of shares in the target company, which he used (unsuccessfully) to demand a share in the deal.

A proposed deal between Safeway and Asda in 1998 was splashed on the front page of the Mirror newspaper[115].

The leak had the (perhaps intended) result of putting a halt to the discussions, whilst providing a spin that set the narrative of ('top team', 'supergroup', 'lifesaver') Asda saving ('embattled', 'struggling') Safeway.

Safeway never managed to recover from this initial spin. Some practitioners of the dark arts, argue that if something is going to leak, do it yourself first so that you set the narrative in the media.

It is illegal to leak price-sensitive information. What's more, I'm not convinced that it is a clever strategy. Things have a habit of coming back to bite you later.

---

[115] The front page of the Mirror was an unlikely spot for a business story, but it did share the page with a photograph of Liz Hurley revealing sparkly underwear (The Mirror 11 May 1998). This was the highpoint of the Mirror's City coverage from the entertaining City Slickers (James Hipwell and Anil Bhoyrul), who were later convicted of a share tipping scam (BBC News 7 December 2005), unrelated to this deal.

> **Tips**
>
> 1. **Instruct your advisers,** especially bankers and PR companies, **not to leak** under any circumstances and keep repeating this.
>
> 2. **Don't leak yourself.** It's illegal and you will not necessarily remain in control of the aftermath. You may ask why you have to instruct advisers to obey the law. Most of course, absolutely follow the law already, and especially now as rules are tighter. However, let's just say that it does no harm to make this crystal-clear.

Journalists love a scoop, but don't like being used[116]. Once a story is out – even if you set the initial spin – you may lose control of it. Others brief against you and new information gets out. Deals are much better done in the shadows than in the light of a feverish media frenzy.

Mergers

Some corporate acquisitions are called mergers, because it sounds better and leaves some pride in the target. However, sometimes there are real mergers where two businesses come together and try to share the

---

[116] As part of the Safeway leak, the City Slickers published a personal attack on me. Later, when they then wrote a general letter to all FTSE100 CFOs asking to meet, I was the only one to respond and I subsequently bought them both lunch. They were grateful to be taken seriously, and so then published a number of (ever so slightly tongue-in-cheek) complimentary articles about Safeway and me as well. I was also able to find out who leaked the original story on the Asda merger. The moral is that you have to ride the punches from the media, and you have to work with them whatever they write. Moreover, if someone does leak something, others usually get to know about it.

management and the benefit. This chapter focuses on take-overs, because they are the most common form. However, the same lessons listed apply to mergers.

Many of the learning and tips from acquisitions are equally applicable to all sorts of large projects, so they are well worth reviewing when a board considers such activities.

Summary

Corporate acquisitions are a tool that can be as helpful - or as lethal - as a chainsaw. It is not a matter of whether they are a good enough tool, it's a matter of whether they are in the hands of appropriately skilled people and used for the right purposes. It may be a good idea to cut a tree down, but if you botch the execution, it can turn very messy very quickly.

Boards need to adopt a sceptical mindset to counter the natural enthusiasm and desire to gloss over possible problems from executives and advisers. A great strategic idea executed cleanly can transform a company's growth, scale or profitability. This chapter has used examples, especially on deals that I have seen first hand, to identify questions that directors (and not just non-exec ones) should be asking to make sure that this happens for your company.

Chapter 12 - Selling: Corporate Defence

'G4S is Not for Sale – At Least at this Price' - **Ashley Almanza, CEO of G4S**[117]

I was having a good day, sitting in my office at home sorting a few things out. Then, late afternoon, the phone rang. It was the chairman of a smaller competitor. I hadn't spoken to him before, but he went straight to the point. He was calling me to tell me that they were making a bid for my company.

As a board member, the first you may hear of an approach like this is likely to be when an urgent board meeting is called. There will probably be bankers and lawyers at this meeting advising the board on its responsibilities. However, as discussed in the last chapter, the board can feel very alone in this process, as advisers are extremely important, but in the end the board takes the decisions and it alone faces the consequences.

This chapter highlights key things that a board needs to know about handling the situation when you have to respond, and mount a defence, to being bid for. It is not a summary of the Takeover Code nor of the complex law involved, but gives an overview of the sort of issues that arise in responding.

---

[117] Quoted, Sunday Times 1 November 2020

An unsolicited approach

An unsolicited approach means that the target board has not sought talks with the potential acquirer before being bid for.

The target board may have had some inkling that something might happen, or it may come completely out of the blue, as in my case. An unsolicited offer need not be hostile. It may not even be unwelcome to the target board, especially if the price looks generous.

Most approaches will initially come in a private approach to the chair, CEO or perhaps to your bankers. This gives the board time to consult with advisers and consider the matter out of the glare and pressure of publicity. The approach may come with a formal Offer Letter, with a price stated, or it may be just a verbal approach to open discussions. The offeror may give a deadline for a board response, threatening implicitly or explicitly to go public. This is an aggressive tactic applied by a party that thinks this may go hostile. The offeror may threaten to withdraw if its offer is not accepted in a certain timeframe. This is likely to work only if the price offered is a very full one.

In general, the initial offer will probably not come with threats, so the board is not required to make an immediate response. However, the board may be advised to have a response ready within a week or so to avoid the impression that it is not taking it seriously.

The first task is to assess whether the approach is genuine. This may seem strange, but fake takeover bids are made. In 2015 a small unheard-of company launched a takeover offer for cosmetic giant, Avon, but this subsequently appeared to have been merely an attempt to manipulate the share price[118].

If the first you hear about an Offer is when it is on a Press Release or stock exchange announcement, or leaked in the media, then it will be

---

[118] Reuters Breaking News 4 June 2015

difficult to avoid it being hostile. However, in the end, the only party who determines if an offer is hostile is the target board. If the board believes that an offer (however delivered) is reasonable, or not far from being at a recommendable price, and worth discussion, the approach would not be considered hostile.

Approaches and offers

An approach is contact from a possible acquirer that is fairly specific. It may not include a price, but must have some specific details. A casual chat about hypothetical options would not generally be an approach. An approach may come with an Offer Letter.

An Offer Letter will be highly conditional, subject usually to getting confidential due diligence information, possibly board approvals (from both sides) and competition clearance. The media often talk about an Offer Letter being tabled as if it were a formal bid with a firm price. However, a price subject to due diligence is just a marker. Some private equity firms, for example, are notorious for putting in a high initial indicative price to engage interest from a board, knowing that they will find a reason in the due diligence process to reduce it later.

An Offer is more formal than an approach, requiring a formal Offer letter, but will still be conditional on a number of fronts, such as due diligence and competition authority clearance. Importantly, an Offer is not a commitment to bid, it is just a statement of terms that might be satisfactory to the bidder.

There are a number of categories of offer:

1. The 'knock-out' offer

This is an offer that you think is so good, that you and your advisers want to accept it without much ado. You will want to be sure that the offer is 'real', i.e. that the offeror will carry through on it and has the means to do so. Assuming that you are happy with this, you can proceed onto the next stage, due diligence. Beware, of course that the bidder may be planning to use the information gained in due diligence to justify reducing their offer, in the same way that house buyers sometime use structural surveys to negotiate a lower price.

2. The 'interesting, but not enough' offer

This is a very common type of offer. It isn't high enough, but it's enough that you can't dismiss it out of hand. Typically, every first offer is rejected as inadequate and very rarely do bidders put their final offer in first. Your advisers might describe this offer as 'well judged'. It is high enough to show they are serious, and, since everyone assumes they would be prepared to go higher, it may be difficult for the target board not to engage with them.

3. The 'insult' offer

There are several reasons why a board might receive an offer so low that it regards it as insulting. The bidder might be playing a public relations game, prior to going hostile. The bid price might mysteriously leak into the market, hitting the target's share price. It can be accompanied by negative comments about the target company, its products or management. Alternatively, the bidder may just be trying it on, just to see how strong the target board is. If the target engages, the offer may yet be lifted to an acceptable level in time. Although the offer may feel insulting, the target company is best advised to react coolly and professionally, making great efforts to ascertain the real motivation of the bidder.

However dubious the bidder's methods, institutional shareholders rarely applaud a public fight about them.

4. The 'spurious' offer

This is an offer where the target doesn't believe that the objective is to succeed. The most obvious would be where a competitor bids, perhaps with the objective of getting confidential information from the process. In this case, the target board may either refuse to engage, or decide that it is prepared to entertain an offer, but won't provide confidential due diligence information. The bidder, if it is serious, will then have to bid with either publicly available information only or heavily redacted private information. I have seen a number of spurious offers over the years, and offeree boards need to be careful as the UK Takeover Panel seems to favour possible bidders in terms of requiring information disclosure.

5. The 'I want to join the party' offer

This is where an offer has been made by someone else, and others then also knock on your door. They may do so in order to gain information, especially if they are competitors or private equity just interested in the sector. They may also do so if there is a regulatory inquiry. When Morrisons announced its bid for Safeway in 2003, Sainsbury's, Tesco and Wal-Mart (amongst others) all announced their intentions to make an offer. This had the effect of ensuring that the original offer, together with the new ones, would get referred to the Competition Commission, and possibly blocked or at least delayed (ultimately by 14 months). It also meant that the competitors had a seat at the table with the Competition Commission. The Safeway board refused to give those competitors any sensitive due diligence information, as it did not believe that the 'indicative offers' tabled had a genuine chance of being delivered.

Rule 3 advisers

The board will need to get advice from its independent advisers ("Rule 3 advisers"), usually a bank. Rule 3 of the Takeover Code requires that the target board must obtain independent advice from a competent financial adviser on any offer and disclose that advice to its shareholders. They should give you independent advice on how to proceed. Importantly they will give you a view on the 'value' of your company and therefore if any offer is worth serious consideration (*"recommendable"*).

Tip

It is wise for all publicly listed companies to have a 'Rule 3' adviser always lined-up, with a broad understanding of your business, in case of an approach. You need to move quickly after most approaches, so it is not a time to be casting around to find someone to take you on. The adviser could be your company broker, although many companies prefer a different corporate adviser.

How do they value your company?

The advisers will bring packs full of spreadsheets and numbers. There are two basic ways of measuring: comparables and absolute. The comparables will be using measures such as PE ratios, EV (value of shares plus net debt)/Ebitda, and market cap/net asset value against other companies, based on trading multiples or comparable takeover or merger offers. All of these are useful.

Absolute measures will include net present value (NPV) or net asset value (NAV). The NAV will be most useful if the company is a property company, where an acquirer is most interested in just getting its hands on the assets. As discussed in the last chapter, the NPV is generally pretty useless for acquisitions, because it will tend to be based on your own management's forecasts[119] of profit and cash, discounted at an estimate of the company's weighted cost of capital. This takes no proper account of risk, so it's the value if everything goes to plan. Not surprisingly, it tends to show a value much higher than other metrics.

The control premium

You expect an acquirer to offer a price above the current share price. The question the board will face is how much higher it should be to be recommendable - the '*control premium*'. The starting point for discussion is generally a premium of 30% above the current share price. This is just a custom and practice benchmark, but nevertheless an important one. In some sectors, such as property, 30% may be rather high as the bidder may be looking largely just to acquire assets. Advisers will show the board comparables of similar deal premia as context.

The current share price is usually taken as the price at the close on the day before the Offer is received or announced (the '*undisturbed*' price). However, this can still be misleading if the short-term share price has been volatile, or the market had started to get wind of a deal and your share price had started to rise immediately beforehand. It may be better to look at the 3-month average, before any speculation, in that case.

---

[119] You can't base an NPV valuation on analyst expectations, rather than management forecasts, as analysts tend to forecast only two or three years out, and an NPV is mathematically dominated by forecasts for years well beyond this.

Initial board responses

The target board can respond in a number of ways:

1. *'No, thanks'* and a refusal to engage.

This could be because the indicated price is much too low, and the offeror has said that it will not raise it. Alternatively, the target board may believe that the offeror is not credible, hasn't the funds or is not a suitable owner for their company. Safeway had a number of approaches over the years from diverse businesses as a DIY chain and Philip Green[120]. None of these were thought (rightly) to be credible. You may be surprised how many letters boards get from various companies and 'private equity' firms that you have never heard of who assure you that they are assembling a consortium and already have funds lined up[121].

This flat no response can be confusing for the bidder, as it wants to know whether the board is refusing to engage at any price, or whether it is just waiting for a higher price. Almost certainly there will be adviser-to-adviser contact as the bidder tries to understand this. Faced with a brick wall 'No', the bidder has a number of options; to move to a *'knock out'* offer; to go away, at least temporarily; or to appeal directly to the target's shareholders.

---

[120] Philip Green told journalists: "What do I know about food? Well, I eat it. And it cannot be more difficult than textiles, where you have all those shapes and sizes and colours. An apple is just an apple." The laughter was heard in food retail boardrooms across the country as he destroyed his credibility as a bidder. Quoted in Guardian 21 January 2003

[121] There are many possible motivations for people making such ghost approaches, from seeking publicity to getting confidential due diligence information.

2. 'No, not at that price'

This is a 'come-on', suggesting that the offer is close, but not high enough. The bidder may then seek guidance from the target's advisers as to what price would be acceptable. The target board's advisers may, or may not, provide such guidance. It doesn't really matter as this is now a negotiation. This situation is quite common and most 'agreed' mergers will have gone through a few private rounds of offers, refusals and improved offers.

3. 'Not at the moment'

There may be a non-price reason why the target board doesn't want to talk at that moment, and the message may be that the time isn't right. This could typically be when a new CEO has just joined, and the board wants to understand what the new person thinks they can achieve. Alternatively, the target board may be aware of a new development, that it is not known yet by the market, which it thinks will boost the share price, such as a new product launch or new contract.

4. 'Interesting, but there's more you need to know'

The target board may believe that outsiders don't fully appreciate its value, due to price-sensitive information not yet in the public domain (such as an exciting new product being developed). It offers to provide additional information about its company (such as management accounts or new product details) to tempt the bidder to make a higher offer. The target offers due diligence access to financials and/or commercially sensitive data on the clear condition that it won't accept the original offer, but is prepared to help the bidder come to a higher value. This would be a common situation, particularly for a private or specialist company.

> **Tip**
>
> A board will often respond with a "No, not at that price" response (typified by the G4S quote at the start of this chapter). Unless the approach is incredible, stupid or badly motivated, shareholders, broadly speaking, expect a board to take seriously any approach that is at a significant premium to the current share price.

Defence strategy

It is good practice for every board to have a defence strategy prepared, not least as bids can come at unexpected times, from surprising quarters and at zero notice. It is therefore basic risk management to have given some thought in advance to how the board would respond to an approach. Defence should be understood in its widest sense. The response can vary from a fight at all costs to repel the approach (perhaps you think it spurious or wouldn't get competition approval), to a response to negotiate the best value for shareholders and to protect stakeholders.

The defence strategy might comprise arguments that:

1. The current share price undervalues the company
2. The company has brighter prospects than the market thinks
3. The offeror may not be able to complete the transaction (e.g. it may be unable to get the financing, or competition regulation may not allow it)
4. The offeror's share price may be overvalued, so any offer in shares may not be as good as it appears
5. Shareholders would do better if the target were bought by, or merged with, another company (the *'white knight'* defence)

The basic defence arguments are similar whether a deal is friendly or hostile. However, they may be expressed in a more aggressive tone in a hostile deal, and the target board may refuse to give a hostile bidder additional due diligence information. However, if the bid is at a significant premium to the undisturbed share price, boards are likely to come under pressure from shareholders to engage with, and consider carefully, a bid, even if the board considers it hostile.

The final board decision

As in the last chapter, *"Advisers advise, but directors decide."* Advisers are likely to opine, if pushed, whether an Offer is "capable of being recommended", i.e.;

1. The price and structuring are likely to be acceptable to shareholders;

2. The offeror has the funding to pay for the deal;

3. The offer does not have excessive conditionality; and

4. The deal has a reasonable chance of passing competition and other regulatory approval

The board will then have to decide whether it will recommend it. It will want to discuss its own private views of the company's prospects. Some directors may not believe management's forecasts are achievable or others may think them too conservative. Some may believe that the company is still undervalued because they see strategic developments that could increase value in the future, while others may believe that there will be trends that will put pressure on value in the future.

The board should always be putting the interests of their shareholders as a whole at the forefront. There may be some shareholders however, who would prefer a deal for other reasons, such as their desire to be bought out. The board should be aware of these individual interests but keep referring back to the overwhelming interests of all shareholders.

The board also has to consider the interests of other stakeholders (i.e. consider the Companies Act, Section 172). This is very tricky. Most acquisitions will result in job losses, so are they in the interests of employees? It is easier to think about how the long-term interests of the company would be best safeguarded. For example, if there are a number of job losses in the short-term, but that this would enable the business to grow under new ownership this might be the best way to safeguard jobs long term. A similar argument might apply to customers and suppliers.

The Flybe board in 2019 recommended an offer at only 1p per share. The board believed, and was advised by its Rule 3 advisers, that this was the highest offer that it could expect in the circumstances that was deliverable in the timescales needed. This deal would keep Flybe operating, to the benefit of its employees, customers and suppliers. The Board had to weigh up the chances that another higher deliverable offer would come along later against the risk that credit facilities would be withdrawn, especially from the credit card companies, threatening the immediate viability of the company. This was a very difficult and tense decision that was debated through a long night in the boardroom.

One stakeholder that cannot be taken into consideration is the board itself, although it wouldn't be human to expect any director not to think about their own position. An acquired board is likely to be dismantled and non-executives, and perhaps executives too, will be made redundant. It is one of the few occasions that turkeys have to vote for Christmas. Directors must ignore their personal interests; however difficult this may be.

What are irrevocable commitments?

To the man in the street, an irrevocable commitment is one that you cannot get out of. So, an 'irrevocable' is a commitment that a shareholder will act in a certain way, for example that it will vote in favour of a takeover bid. However, in the streets of the City, nothing is ever that simple. An irrevocable is a very useful instrument to a bidder as it should give some certainty about how a shareholder of the target company will react to a bid.

The key point is that an irrevocable commitment can have conditions attached to it, i.e. it can actually be revocable. The UK Takeover Panel, which tends to take a legalistic approach, may allow a potentially *revocable* agreement to be called '*irrevocable*' in public announcements.

For example, one of the '*irrevocables*' signed by a shareholder in the Medicx/Assura bid was conditional on the target Assura board actually recommending the offer. This was only revealed when Assura managed to get a copy of the original irrevocable agreement itself. It then became clear to the board that this was not therefore a true ultimatum. It was able to reject the offer and cause the irrevocable to fall away. Of course, a board would be wise not to do this without some tacit approval from the relevant shareholder.

Tip

It is imperative that the target board gets hold of either the actual irrevocable document or an independently produced summary. You cannot necessarily rely on a summary produced by the offeror or its advisers.

Summary

There are few moments more stressful for a board than dealing with an unsolicited approach. Some deals ultimately run smoothly, with goodwill on both sides and a fair price that delivers value to both parties is agreed.

However, some approaches are characterised by mistrust, pressure, leaks, media-briefing and threats. A target board has to act in an exemplary fashion, seeking and listening to its advisers. It then has to take its decision against this background based on trying to balance the interests of different stakeholders. The toughest backdrop to this is when the board is also concerned about its company's short-term liquidity, not least as directors' decisions can be reviewed later for wrongful trading, as well as knowing that a leak itself could dramatically affect the company's credit position.

And after all this, the board will know that its decision will later be evaluated purely with 20:20 hindsight of what happens later. Unsolicited approaches are indeed the land of sleepless nights.

Chapter 13 - So You Want A Chair?

At some point in a non-exec's career, she or he may feel ready to step up to be a chair. Being a chair is not for everyone and the career path from non-exec to chair is a much less well-defined one than the executive route to CEO. In this chapter, we will look at how being a chair is different to being a non-exec, the chair's role in the company, the different ways you can get to be a chair and how a chair can interact with both executives and non-executives.

The chair of what?

The chair is often described as the company chair but is really chair of the board. The key role of the chair is to lead and manage the top decision-making body of a company. The CEO leads the company, and the chair leads the board.

This distinction is important as the CEO must feel that they are running operations and leading the strategy. The CEO must also be seen by the outside world as the boss of the company. The CEO should be in the spotlight and take the credit for good performance. The chair can bask only in reflected glory.

The chair's role is to ensure that the top executives, particularly the CEO, are the right people for the job, and that the board supports the executive team with the right guidance, counsel, supervision and incentive arrangements.

When the sun is out, the chair should be in the shade, enjoying the reflected warmth.

> **Tip**
>
> A good chair is barely visible when times are good, but highly visible when times are tough. Be wary of a chair who maintains a high-profile when the company is doing well (i.e. achieving or bettering City expectations). Good chairs should not use their company's performance to boost their egos. Leave that to the CEOs.

The chair's role is much more difficult when performance falters, City expectations are not met, or when corporate activity is happening, especially when being bid for. This is when he or she may well need to step into the limelight, and shoulder both the responsibility, and suffer the public brickbats.

Executive or non-executive chair

Most listed companies will have non-executive chairs. They may well spend a day or two per week[122] on company business, largely reading paperwork and liaising with board colleagues. An executive chair would be more like three, four or even five (or more) days a week, with meetings with company executives at levels below the board, and even possibly chairing the executive committee or executive board. Assuming that there is a CEO in place, the main difference is simply the amount of time the chair puts in and the greater involvement in day-

---

[122] In a company crisis, especially a takeover battle, even a non-exec chair may well become effectively full-time for a period.

to-day decisions. However, if there is no CEO, then the Executive Chair could effectively be an interim CEO.

An executive chair can seem like a contradiction in terms and certainly the scope for overlap and conflict between the CEO and executive chair is very real. There is a distinct benefit in having a chair at one removed from management, so executive chairs seem to be appropriate only when there is no CEO, or if the latter is struggling with the breadth of their role and need very active support.

I have been executive chair four times for three different companies, always because we had no CEO at the time. It is strange, but your attitude does change as you move from non-executive to executive.

Suddenly those tough questions, that you used to ask as a non-exec, become an irritating intervention in you running the business. You feel ownership of management and operations, which is pretty tricky to reconcile with impartial oversight. At the board and committees, you feel that you are neither fish nor fowl, conflicted by feeling you want to ask challenging questions, yet knowing that you are the one to answer those self-same difficult queries. This is why chairs are best left non-executive.

Tip

Be wary of joining a board with an executive chair, unless you can see strong reasons for it.

The independence of the chair

In Governance Code land, there isn't such a thing as an independent chair. This is because they are a bridge between the non-executives and the executives. You can't have a free-standing bridge. The Code however requires a chair to be independent at the time of appointment.

Good governance therefore rules out the CEO, for example, or a representative of a major shareholder, becoming the chair. It would be very difficult for an executive to have a mindset independent of management if they have worked closely in the business. It is also not good for a new CEO to have a chair who used to do their job. A chair who was a representative director would also struggle to convince other shareholders of their independence from their nominating shareholder.

The buck really does stop here. A chair is not just a busier non-exec director.

It does feel different to be a chair, compared to a non-exec director. It is the one job in the company that has no boss. There is no-one higher in the hierarchy. You can argue that everyone in the end has a boss, being their customers, but this conflates economic pressure with management. However, large shareholders are the ultimate kingmakers, and a chair who ignores the views of such shareholders whilst overseeing less than stellar financial performance, does indeed risk shareholders exercising their influence, if not actual votes.

In practice, chairs are very aware that they are the ultimate authority within the company. They have that final responsibility with, in practice, little power as non-exec. The chair can be a very lonely place.

The key roles[123] of a chair are to:

Lead the board: The chair should lead the board, as well as chair meetings. Boards look to their chair to set the agenda – both literally and metaphorically. If the executive team is too dominant, the CEO can set the board up to discuss what they want and avoid difficult subjects. The chair needs to put issues on to the agenda that they or other non-execs are concerned about. If, for example, the chair believes that

---

[123] These are the behavioural and leadership roles. There are also of course governance tasks that a chair has to fulfil (see the Corporate Governance Code or any typical chair job description).

internal culture is an issue, they should be putting it on the agenda and forcing discussions on the subject.

Set the culture of the board: Some boards are high performing teams, but others are just periodic meetings of individuals. Some boards are warm and friendly, others can be either supportive or antagonistic, and some are formal and others relaxed. The mood however is largely set by the chair, by the way they lead the meetings, how they consult members, how they encourage or discourage debate, and how they use, or discourage, humour. The culture of the board has also a tendency to trickle down to senior management. If the chair is aggressive in style in board meetings, don't be surprised if the CEO adopts a similar attitude in his executive team.

Tip

The culture of the board will reflect the chair's personality, and this is why a new director would do well to look hard at the chair before joining a board.

Lead discussion about board composition and performance review of directors: This tends to happen either in the nomination committee (see chapter 9) or at a non-executive directors' meeting. Whilst the chair should seek every director's view, they will expect the chair to have a view and to lead the debate. Especially if there is a difficult decision, the chair is crucial in transferring a sense of discontent into a decision to take action. If the chair is half-hearted about a change, it is unlikely to happen.

Seek a board consensus: When there is a decision to be made, some chairs will give their view at the outset. This provides leadership to the other directors, but does require the chair to listen to subsequent views and change their mind if appropriate. If the chair doesn't listen and take account of others' views, the board will become resentful and dysfunctional. Other chairs will go round the table and hold their opinions to themselves, until everyone has their say. This is very participative, but if the chair is known to have strong views, it can leave directors out on a limb giving their view, which might be shot down later by the chair or leave them isolated. I generally tried to let the debate develop before giving my view as chair, but to be honest, often forgot myself out of impatience or excitement to express an opinion earlier in the discussion. In truth, there is no one right strategy, other than to hear all the different views and seek to get consensus.

Tips

1. A chair should seek consensus on decisions, but there may be times when this is impossible. It is worth the chair going round the table to each director to get their view on big decisions. They will not want to let a director later say that he didn't really agree.

2. If consensus isn't possible, the need for the odd vote and majority decision is not the end of the world. It would be a problem, however, if a vote were needed more than very occasionally.

Take responsibility: The buck stops at the chair. They must stand up for board decisions both inside and outside the boardroom, supporting the CEO in implementing board decisions and standing by them. When shareholders or the media attack board decisions, the chair must be prepared to stand up and justify them. This is especially important these days as the rising expectations of boards and companies mean that more non-financial and ESG issues are becoming controversial.

The speed of social media means that a small issue can become toxic before you can even fix a date for a board meeting to discuss it.

Be proactive: The chair cannot afford to sit back and await the next board meeting. They need to be worrying about what might happen next, what shareholders are thinking, what new regulations are coming in, is the board working well, is the succession plan good enough, should we be discussing this new development in the board, and so on. You can get away with being fairly reactive as a non-exec, as issues are usually brought to you, but a chair needs to be identifying those issues and bringing them to the board.

Tips

1. A chair role is not for someone to retire to. A board needs an active, engaged chair not least as, when there are challenges, the chair needs to spot looming trouble, step up and take a lead. A nomination committee needs to think carefully about this when appointing a new chair.

2. When appointing a new chair, always sit back and consider whether they could realistically act as an executive chair/interim CEO. Do they have the time, skills and knowledge to do this? You are not asking whether they could be permanent CEO, but could they cover this role for six months to a year?

A chair should be phoning fellow directors individually from time to time. If they aren't, then they won't be picking up on early warning signs and murmurings about issues. A chair needs not only to spot issues, but also actively to seek them out.

Keep a check on the CEO: CEOs live in executive teams that generally says yes to the boss. Not many careers are built on saying no to your superiors. With the best will in the world, many CEOs begin to believe their own PR. As Baron Acton said: '*Power tends to corrupt, and absolute power corrupts absolutely*'. One of the most important roles for a chair is to keep a CEO's feet firmly on the ground and to restrain them from rash acts or getting carried away.

One CEO wanted to give their bonus to charity as a public gesture. Great idea, I thought, until I realised that the charity he had chosen was linked in several newspaper reports to a terrorist organisation.

How to become chair

There are no set rules for chair progression, other than a daft regulatory prohibition on a chair being on the board for more than nine years[124]. Nine years is an arbitrary time period, after which, in the Corporate Governance Code, a director's independence disappears. Personally, I agree that nine years is not a bad limit for the upper length of any non-exec's tenure, but it's not so much about independence. Most people get a bit stale and set in their ways after nine years in any job. In fact, I would encourage any non-exec to consider their position after six years on the board. But being chair is a very different role from being a non-executive director.

If you were considering chair succession from a blank piece of paper, you would perhaps decide that appointing an existing non-exec would give a balance of already-earned experience and a new insight. You might plan a new non-exec to join the board, then graduate to chair a committee, perhaps even become the senior independent director. They would then be in a great position to step up to chair when the incumbent retires. However, the Corporate Governance Code makes this rather difficult, as a really experienced non-exec, with perhaps five

[124] Corporate Governance Code, paragraph 19

or six-years' experience on the board could serve as chair for only three years at most.

The Code is confused. If nine years is the outer limit benchmark for independence, why is this applied to a chair who is not considered independent anyway?

The tendency is therefore to look to bring an outsider in to be chair, rather than succession plan to develop a non-executive director. An outsider does bring in new ideas, but does also throw away hard-earned experience. The average tenure of a CEO is around five years, but a non-executive serves typically six to nine years. In particular, I've noticed that a chair who has served longer than the CEO does tend to have a bit more of a longer-term perspective.

A recently appointed CEO expressed concern to me, that her executives were complaining that she had tightened controls too much, and that this was squeezing out their entrepreneurship. I explained that this complaint has been made pretty much every year of the ten in which I had been involved with the company, including at times when the controls had been pretty loose[125]. Perspective comes with experience.

The nomination committee can still decide to appoint an existing non-exec as chair, if they haven't served too long already on the board. There is no requirement for a search or benchmark against external candidates. The nomination committee may however decide to launch a search and identify a short list of external candidates, possibly with

---

[125] This complaint of controls squeezing out entrepreneurship, by the way, is a common one, but having read the chapter on risk, I trust that you will see that business without good controls is not entrepreneurship, it's a ship without a rudder or charts.

an existing non-exec also on the list. This, however, can be awkward as a non-exec will be being assessed by their colleagues[126].

The chair and the CEO – two egos can be too much.

The CEO is the most important[127] person in the company.

The chair is the most important person in the boardroom. Therefore, the relationship between the CEO and chair is the most important one for the company. It can also be the most difficult, as they are both leaders and they have to share power. The CEO needs a strong ego, as they have to lead a diverse group of people, perhaps many thousands, and keep faith in their own abilities and strategy. The chair does not *need* a strong ego. Their job is to lead consensual decision-making in a small group of fairly homogeneous businesspeople. In fact, a chair with a strong ego is likely to struggle with a strong ego-ed CEO. There may not be a boardroom big enough for two powerful egos. Chairs need to leave their ego outside the boardroom door. They do however need confidence to lead the board and stand up to the executives.

To be successful, both the CEO and chair need to work hard at their relationship. This means talking to each other. The most basic requirement is a monthly one-to-one talk, but in difficult times it may need to be much more frequent. I have had periods when the CEO and I used to have several calls a day.

---

[126] This situation happened to me once, and the nomination committee chose an outside candidate over me. Another director – a rather hostile shareholder-representative one – somewhat gleefully then explained to me that I would now have to resign from the board as the board had rejected me. I noted that they had preferred another candidate for chair, which gave me no reason to resign as a non-exec, as we were all adults and the rest of the board wanted me to stay on. In fact, the external candidate turned the role down, and I ended up as chair a month later, much to the anguish of the hostile director.

[127] 'Important' is shorthand for why the CEO is the leader and boss of the company. If the term 'important' offends the reader, perhaps think of influential instead.

The Chair and the CEO – too comfortable is no good either

I had a chair once who was a very affable chap and friendly with the CEO, probably the two key reasons why he was appointed, as he had little business experience. However, the CEO liked both a drink and the opposite sex perhaps too much (with no suggestion of sexual harassment), but the chair would not deal with it. He was just too nice. The CEO dominated board meetings and proved very difficult to pin down on any of the issues of the day. It was clear both would have to go eventually, and despite the reluctance of the non-execs to take the tough decisions, a new properly-professional chair was eventually found. It did not take the new chair long to remove the CEO, much to the relief of the rest of the board.

The CEO has to respect the chair, who has to keep a distance from the CEO. In the end, if there is a problem with the CEO, it is the chair who has to deal with it.

Responsibility with little actual power. The chair role is not for everyone.

One of the joys of being a non-exec is that there is no career path you are expected to follow. Non-execs should not feel that they have to seek board advancement. There is of course a path for those that want it; committee chair, SID, to chair, although these roles may have to be on different boards. The chair is a major step up in responsibility and time commitment from a non-exec role. It is also a major step up in visibility if things go wrong.

The chair is a role primarily as a facilitator of both the board and the executive team. It has little direct power, other than the lead role in removing the CEO. In the good times, it's one of the best jobs in the world. In the bad times, it can be one of the worst, as you have limited power, but total, and very public, responsibility. Worried nights can come swiftly, and painfully, to a chair.

Chapter 14 - Relationships, Resignations and Regulation

This chapter looks at informal contact and highlights the many benefits of communication between directors, even if it is these days by video. It talks about trust and personal relationships, even sexual ones, discussing where trust can be lost if information is not accurate or shared. There is a short reflection on what happens when it's time to leave the board and consider resignation. It then discusses board regulation, and highlights the lack of evidence-based regulation, as well as regulators' over focus on governance rules and formal requirements. The chapter contrasts the importance of relationships with the dry governance rules that live in a world seemingly devoid of the practical reality of humans working together.

The importance of life outside the board meeting and informal contact

Director education always puts most of its focus on board meetings, but actually it isn't board meetings themselves that determine whether boards succeed or fail. The test of a successful board is in the informal contact and relationships that are built up. It is a good sign whenever a director feels that they would benefit from informally discussing an issue with another director. Conversely, it is not a positive indicator when directors feel that they can't, or won't, discuss things outside a formal board meeting.

Informal discussions outside, and ahead, of board meetings are very important;

1. **Some discussions are best held one to one**, such as performance or personal ones.

2. **Some directors want more information than others**. For example, a director with a background in IT may want to understand the technical details of an IT project or one with a finance background may want to satisfy themselves about the accounting involved. It can be frustrating and time-consuming for all directors to listen to such technical debates in a board meeting, when briefings could have been held separately in advance.

3. **Most reasonably complex projects require quite a lot of background and explanation**. Briefing directors individually in advance enables them to ask more questions and come to the board well-informed. This is especially important when the proposal is not in their specialist background.

4. **Board meetings tend to be formal** and the bigger the board, the less airtime each director has. If the CEO and chair want to bring directors with them, the informal chats are much more likely to allow directors to speak freely and register concerns.

5. **It is helpful for the presenters, CEO and chair to know if there is concern** about, or opposition to, any particular board matters. These issues can therefore be addressed in advance of the meeting or more time allocated to controversial parts of the agenda.

Of course, the larger the board the more difficult it is to have informal one-to-one conversations with everyone. This is a very important argument for smaller boards.

There are two other main sources of informal contact; non-exec meetings and board dinners. Both of these are invaluable. Separate non-exec meetings give the non-execs a chance to raise sensitive matters and 'let off steam' about issues. In doing so, they also alert the chair to tensions and concerns. They benefit from having an agenda, provided that the chair has taken soundings in advance to include all the things the non-execs want to raise.

Some executive directors, especially CEOs, resent non-exec meetings, especially when they are held after the board meetings. This drove one of my CEOs mad, as he thought we were all sitting around talking about him and trying to become a '*shadow board*' (i.e. an inner cabinet making all the big decisions). He always wanted me to tell him how the non-execs thought the board had gone, but he couldn't see that getting the non-execs together actually enabled me to answer this! A certain paranoia amongst CEOs about non-exec meetings is actually fairly common, even though, on the other side, executive directors tend to discuss things amongst themselves after a board.

Maintaining relationships with videoconferencing

Throughout the book, I have talked about calls and meetings.

Increasingly, these are being held by videoconference as travel gets more expensive and the impact of the COVID-19 pandemic is felt. Videoconferencing has itself replaced many phone calls, as well as meetings. The value of seeing another human face in any interaction actually seemed to become more important in the pandemic as in-person contact reduced.

Videoconferencing meetings came into its own through the pandemic. It also came of age as the dreadful setup of camera and big screen, with little figures just visible, at the end of a meeting room table became obsolete.

The new setup of individual head and shoulder images of each participant on Zoom or Teams (to name but two) became the norm, giving much better interactivity.

Mind you, I have spent many hours on multilingual video calls, where the combination of masks being worn and hearing only a translator's voice, means that you have to play the 'who's speaking now?' game. Technology has come a long way, and there is still far to go.

However, the increasing ability to interact with other humans without long periods of costly travel, let alone infection risk, means that many future meetings will continue to have a significant virtual element.

The end of the pandemic will not mean the end of the *'you're on mute'* problem.

Tips

1. Try to have every participant in a videoconference with their own device giving a head and shoulders view of them. A camera at the end of a table is generally pretty useless.

2. Stop presenters projecting slides on videoconferences. It is better to have everyone's faces on screen, so you can judge reactions. The material should have been circulated in advance so everyone should have it in hard copy or on their own screen. If this requires directors to buy another device, the cost would be easily paid back by savings on travel iny using videoconferencing.

3. Embrace the advantages of videoconferencing, as you can bring in participants or presenters anywhere in the world at no extra cost.

4. Videoconferencing works for formal discussions, but you do lose the informal 'water-cooler' chats. This makes one to one or small informal discussions outside of the board and committee meetings even more essential. There is no excuse for not doing these, not least as so much time is being saved in not having to travel.

Hybrid meetings, with some element of videoconferencing, are likely to become much more common, post-pandemic. Extra effort needs to be made for those not physically present as they miss out on the chat before and after the meetings, find it more difficult to pick up non-verbal cues and tend to feel separated.

They need to be asked their opinion more frequently as it can be difficult to interject fast enough on a video line.

Trust: The importance of the truth, the whole truth and nothing else

I was working with one company that was in financial difficulties, as changing market conditions had seriously exposed the misplaced strategy. There was however no suggestion that anything improper had gone on. The external auditors were high quality, and there was a competent internal audit team with appropriate risk models. The financials were going the wrong way, but there were one or two areas that were not getting worse, as you would have expected. Something didn't feel right. Eventually, management admitted that they had changed an accounting policy, without telling the audit committee, to capitalise losses, making the profit look better as those losses were being put into the balance sheet. The figures that the board had been looking at, and relying on, were at best misleading. This had not been spotted, or at least not reported, by either internal or external auditors. In these circumstances, it is very difficult for an audit committee to spot the issue.

That is a real example, but fortunately, outright distortion of data for a board is very unusual. However, a board can only work successfully if it knows all the relevant information. A board cannot know everything that matters. It just doesn't have the time. With luck, executive management will know most of what really matters. They will then brief the board on what it thinks the board needs to know. This will be supplemented by knowledge that non-executives glean from other roles and sources.

The prime source of information for non-execs is what the executives choose to pass onto the board. Non-execs can of course ask further questions, and this will elicit further information. Unfortunately, in my experience, non-execs do need to spend time trying to crosscheck information, and while the information they get is usually accurate and comprehensive, there may be times when this is not so. A director may be surprised at how often a KPI appears to contradict what management is saying. It is worth challenging this, as the explanation is usually illuminating. It may well be that the KPI is being distorted by a one-off factor. Sometimes, this provokes a useful discussion as the distorting or one-off factor may be being forgotten. It may be that the question is followed by an awkward silence as the CFO starts flicking through his packs to find a reason.

Management is likely to present information in a way that fits with its view of the world. This is perfectly natural. However, one of the roles of non-executives is to be independently minded, and even to apply a little 'devil's advocacy'. In my example, I should have spotted the discrepancy and challenged it. I was a bit naïve in my early days, and it hadn't occurred to me that someone could have been effectively manipulating the number.

However, also often forgotten, is that it is an important role for executive directors also to challenge numbers or information presented to make sure that they are accurate and comprehensive. Executives should not leave it to the non-execs, or remain silent, when it appears that colleagues are sharing potentially misleading information.

If someone in management does decide to distort (or, let's say, 'misrepresent') the data, it would be very difficult for a non-exec to detect. In the example above, neither internal nor external audit appear to have spotted a change in an accounting policy, let alone reviewed if it was the right thing to do. Directors should not rely on auditors to spot such problems. They may do so, if it's material enough, or you get lucky. They may well see such an event so early that it is corrected before the board even hears about it (by the way, a good reason for audit committees to be wary of 'corrected differences' in an audit report). But the auditors currently feel no responsibility for internal management performance data (even if, as here, the data was subsequently published). Internal auditors will only take responsibility if they are directed to *audit* the performance measure itself.

Tips

1. An audit committee must require any material change in accounting policies to be approved by it. This is an important check and balance for non-execs.

2. It is also however, worth asking whether any changes in accounting policies, treatments or estimates might have had an effect on important KPI's.

3. If you spot a possible issue, or strange trend, or apparent inconsistency, through advance reading of the board papers, ask about it before the meeting. If the answer is easy, then it can be dealt with quickly. If the response suggests to you that there is a real issue, it gives you a chance to raise this in the subsequent board meeting, at which management have had notice of the point you will raise and so will not feel ambushed.

If something doesn't feel right, especially if the management narrative doesn't seem to fit with some of the numbers or the KPI's, it is always worth asking questions. You may need to start out by asking apparently dumb questions. You will be surprised at how often an apparently stupid basic question elicits a very revealing reply. You may well find that one question leads to another and so on. It is worth persisting until you have an answer that satisfies you. Of course, it may be better to ask these questions outside of a board meeting. Your colleagues may thank you for saying that you will take the issue up after the meeting and report back if anything material arises, rather than elongate a board discussion. It may also be more comfortable for management to research the answers rather than to be put on the spot in the meeting.

> **Tips**
>
> 1. **Try to cross-refer information with financials and KPI's**. If there are discrepancies, or things just don't feel right, ask about them.
>
> 2. **Keep asking questions** to drill down to get the answer you want, but not necessarily at a board meeting itself.
>
> 3. **Look for help from auditors**, but do not rely on them. If unsure, ask the internal auditors to do a specific project on the area concerned.

Use the time between meetings to gain information and establish if there is an issue, but feel free to raise the issue at the meeting for discussion and to alert everyone to the point.

Relationships can get a little too close: Sex in the boardroom

People are only human. They develop close feelings for other people, sometimes very close. Ideally, the other person works elsewhere, but sometimes the two people work in the same place.

Many executives will have come across co-workers who are in a relationship. This knowledge can vary from being a matter of mild interest, to one of real discomfort. I had a boss once who was having an affair with his deputy in our small team. It was very uncomfortable for the rest of us, but there was also a degree of black humour, as they tried to hide what everyone already knew. Most companies these days will have policies against relationships with subordinates, particularly as they could nowadays be construed as sexual harassment (although there was no suggestion of that in this case).

However, rules don't guarantee compliance, especially in matters of the heart. So, what do you do if you discover that there is a liaison at a company at board level or involving a board member?

Firstly, look up the rules to establish the legal and corporate positions. Is there a company rule that forbids or defines parameters for such relationships? The rules may well be different for affairs between co-workers, as opposed to those between boss and subordinate.

The easiest thing is to ignore the situation. You may feel that you should 'do something', but if it doesn't seem to be interfering with work and you don't feel that it is exploitative, there may be plenty of other more important matters to worry about. Just keep an eye on it. If you don't feel comfortable with this, the next step is to quietly mention it to the chair, and leave the 'hot potato' steaming nicely in their lap.

The most problematic relationship is often one between a CEO and a senior executive. I have seen this a few times, and it is rarely a good thing. Inevitably other executives know about it, resent the special bond, and fear the pillow talk. This shouldn't be ignored. A non-exec would be wise to discuss it privately with the chair, and if they decline to engage on it, raise it at a non-exec meeting. An executive director should also raise it privately with the chair, and with a sympathetic non-exec if the chairman does nothing. The very least you should aim for is that all the non-execs are aware of the issue and can take it into account when they participate in board discussions and decisions.

You could of course raise it directly with the couple involved, but this depends entirely on your relationship with that individual. It is high risk, but if you feel that you can, this may be the most discrete and effective way of handling the situation.

If you feel that the relationship is exploitative, then you must raise it at board level. If the board declines to take any action, then you must decide whether to live with it or resign. If the relationship is not exploitative, any director has to apply their own discretion and judgement. How dysfunctional is the relationship to the company and its board? How concerned are the other directors? How much fuss do you want to make? There is no right answer here, but you should try to work out, all things considered, what is in the best long-term interests of the company?

A final word on your due diligence when you join a board. A few years ago, the chairman asked me to lunch shortly after I joined the board. Always happy to chat over some food, I assumed that he was being welcoming and that we could get to know each other a little better. In fact, he wanted to tell me that there was a 'relationship' that I needed to know about between the CEO and a senior executive. How kind of him to tell me a week after I had signed on.

Tip

In your final due diligence before joining a board, ask the chair a direct question as to whether there is anything you should know about personal relationships in the senior management and the board. If you get an astonished denial, you can rest more easily. That's what due diligence is for. But you might just find out something that could save you a lot of trouble later on.

Is it time to go?

For most non-execs, the right time to leave a board is between six years (usually two terms of office) and nine years. There are always exceptions of course. Maybe the rest of the board has changed for some reason, and the value of historic knowledge and continuity outweigh the danger of staleness. It is helpful for a non-exec to discuss this with the chair at least a year in advance, which gives six months to find a replacement and six months to dual run.

I retired from the Northern Rock Board at the end of my initial term of 15 months. I had joined the Board to help stabilise, and possibly sell, the business when it was reeling from the 2007 run on the bank. Although I became chair of the audit committee when the bank was nationalised, I never felt that I knew enough about banking to do as good a job as I would have liked to. After a year, the bank had been stabilised, nationalised and funding secured. I felt that my job was done and stood down.

There may come a time when directors feel that they can't stay on the board for other reasons. They may be unhappy with the strategy, the execution or their colleagues. There have been several times when I have questioned remaining on a board. Do you stay and fight, or have you fought and lost and can no longer in all conscience be a part of the board?

Individual director resignations from disagreements are still fairly rare. Richard Cousins resigned, as senior independent director, from the Tesco board in 2017 over the proposed acquisition of Booker, with which he disagreed. This example of a principled stance, which was made public, is laudable, but unusual. More common is that a director stands down and goes quietly, perhaps to spend more time with their family.

Non-execs have a particular problem when they are thinking of standing down over a board issue. It will tend to mark them as a potentially difficult person for future head-hunters and nomination committees if they want new non-exec roles in the future[128]. It therefore takes some bravery to follow Richard Cousin's example.

Better regulation, not more rules

Regulation is one of the banes of every board's life. There was a time when the regulators worried about too much change coming too quickly. Not now, however. Why do we have so much new regulation? There's increased media focus, both social and traditional, political pressure, and regulators feeling a need to 'do something'. Behind a lot of this is the great lie: *'The answer to failing regulation is more regulation'*. It isn't. The answer is better regulation, not more.

I am not against regulation. We clearly need it as the untrammelled free market is a pretty wild, amoral place. It's just that regulation should have some basis that goes beyond a newspaper headline or politician's soundbite. Here are the eight principles for good regulation from the Financial Conduct Authority[129]:

1. Efficiency and economy

2. Proportionality

3. Sustainable growth

4. Consumer responsibility

5. Senior management responsibility

6. Recognising the differences in the businesses carried on by different regulated persons

7. Openness & disclosure

8. Transparency

---

[128] Richard Cousins remained as CEO of Compass until his untimely death in 2017.

[129] https://www.fca.org.uk/about/principles-good-regulation

These are all good and worthy, but isn't something missing? There is nothing about making sure that the regulation actually *works*, that it is evidence-based and that its ultimate impact is judged against its intended. It's a bit like the pharmaceutical industry having a code of practice that doesn't include making sure that it's drugs actually work[130]!

Evidence-based medicine is a well-established movement in health care. Even the UK Government published a White Paper back in 1999 ("Modernising Government"), admitting that it *"must produce policies that really deal with problems, that are forward-looking and shaped by evidence rather than a response to short-term pressures; that tackle causes not symptoms"*. Sadly, this went the way of many well-meaning political initiatives.

The UK Corporate Governance Code starts; *'The purpose of corporate governance is to facilitate effective, entrepreneurial and prudent management that can deliver the long-term success of the company.'* Fine words, but how do we know that it actually does this?

Corporate Governance regulators have not as yet woken up to the needs of evidence, analysis and proof. There was yet another outcry about executive pay a few years ago. They reacted by asking the great and the good as to what should be disclosed, and then mandating it. The result is 30 pages at least in every annual report listing every last detail of directors' remuneration. Where is the evidence that this has remedied the problem of excessive pay and payment for failure? I can see that investor interest and therefore pressure on boards has had an effect on boards, but such pressure was in fact the driver, not the result, of additional regulation.

Listed company directors have to put themselves up for re-election every year now. This was because people thought it would be a good

---

[130] And here it is: "Information, claims and comparisons must be accurate, balanced, fair, objective and unambiguous and must be based on an up-to-date evaluation of all the evidence and reflect that evidence clearly." Clause 7.2 of the Code of Practice for the Pharmaceutical Industry 2019.

idea. Where is the evidence that this would help and where is the post implementation review that shows it was effective in what it set out to do?

Would it be so hard to develop evidence-based regulation? This is what it should look like:

1. The original events that led to the 'need for regulation' are **thoroughly analysed**, and their **causes identified**

2. **The theory is tested** as to why the regulation will be effective against those causes, and what the **possible impacts** of the regulation might be

3. **The counterfactual** is tested: what would be likely to occur if the policy were not implemented

4. **The impact** of the new regulation is measured

5. Both the **direct and indirect effects** of the regulation are identified

6. **The uncertainties** and other influences outside of the regulation that might have an effect on the outcome are identified

7. The analysis is capable of being **tested and replicated** by a third party.

8. **The regulation is tested** to identify if it ever becomes unnecessary or develops unforeseen consequences.

This is a manifesto for good regulation. None of the current corporate governance rules would satisfy this standard. Yet, given the costs of implementing the governance rules, is it unreasonable for regulators to justify themselves with a bit of evidence?

Put simply, governance regulation should start with an analysis of what has gone wrong in companies, identify regulation to stop this recurring elsewhere, and then check that this is being successful. The analysis into what goes wrong at companies should be far-reaching and insightful, going beyond condemning individual directors and failures of risk management. It needs to look at culture and accept human fallibility.

The answer to failing regulation is not more, but better, regulation. However, inevitably when boards fail, the cry goes out for heads to roll, more rules and more power for the regulators. And you don't solve anything by just rebranding the regulator again[131]!

We all need rules, but the regulators are perpetuating a lie in suggesting that rules improve performance. Football teams couldn't play a match without a common set of rules. But you won't improve Crystal Palace's performance by adding new rules. Teams of people improve with better tactics, advice, and encouragement, not more rules.

This should be the regulators' toughest challenge yet. How can they go beyond rules and compulsion; to encouragement, best practice and helping boards? They need to accept the discipline of evidence, the limitations of rules, and open their eyes to the importance of culture and how to foster the right one. And that probably requires culture change at the regulators themselves.

[131] This happens so often. The FRC is planned to be replaced by the ARGA in 2023.

Summary

This chapter has made a plea for boards to put more focus and more effort into informal contact. It is crucial to directors understanding issues better, gaining consensus and developing better relationships and trust. The best step forward in board governance is not more governance rules. It is informal communication. Humans simply work better together when they communicate more, understand each other and develop trust. That doesn't preclude greater challenge. It just means that information giving, lobbying and challenge is best in smaller, informal discussions.

Regulators can't cope with this because they trade in rules not good practice, procedures not people, preaching not promotion. If they spent more time researching how boards and companies get things wrong, evaluating processes rather than trying to pin-point 'guilty' directors, and working with board directors, we would see less, but better regulation, more education and more ideas to help boards work better.

Chapter 15 - Some Closing Thoughts

The key to boards performing better is able, informed, experienced people working together within a common, basic framework. That framework in the UK is the Corporate Governance Code, (together with various legal requirements). Many commentators and regulators implicitly appear to believe that governance rules are more important than those core requirements of ability, information and experience. That is why there is so much external focus on regulating boards, rather than on helping directors to perform better[132].

Board regulation is increasingly driven by those with little knowledge or experience of boardroom life. Ever growing disclosure requirements have led to vast, repetitive executive remuneration reports, pages and pages of complex environmental disclosure, accounting disclosures, meaningless risk schedules, and never-ending tables of derivatives. There is a benefit in mandating disclosure of key information, but that doesn't mean pages of repetitive or complex data, together with requirements to repeat every year the same basic governance information. The Financial Reporting Council bemoans such 'boiler plate' reporting, but how many ways can we say the same thing that they ask us to say every year?

---

[132] It is true that the Code encourages board evaluations, which are welcome, but this is neither explored nor developed into any notions of director development or best practice.

Regulation too needs to be driven by able, informed and experienced people. I hope that some of them might read this book, and understand more about board life. It would also benefit many other commentators, and others who work with boards, to understand the stress, the balancing acts and the decision-making.

It is clear that directors cannot rely just on regulations to guide the board to do its job, in the same way that you can't plan a holiday using just an airline timetable. A board cannot tick off its compliance with the Corporate Governance Code and think that it is doing all it needs to. Boards should put continuous effort into communicating more, working better together, and therefore taking better decisions.

Priority one for boards should be to recruit and retain able people of whatever ethnic, religion or sex. If you listen to many investor groups, government and media, the *only thing* that appears to matter is diversity, but a board's function is to do a very difficult job overseeing very complex, dynamic, risky enterprises. Gaining greater diversity is a complex and ambiguous area, especially for an elderly white male to write about. Being a board director is a complex and professional job. If you were about to have a heart operation, would you insist that the team of surgeons operating on you included an ethnic minority and 30% women? No, but you would want the best medical team, irrespective of race and sex. You would want a team of the best people, who have good understanding and knowledge of the medicine involved, who have diverse and varied experience and work well together. My point is that targeting diversity is not about hitting quotas, it is about assembling the best team. And the best teams are ones with high quality people from diverse backgrounds and experiences.

Ability is equally distributed across race and sex. When boards, like other groups of people, end up with one sex dominating and the underrepresentation of some ethnic groups, then clearly boards are not, in fact, even getting the truly most able people. You can't get the best people if large parts of the population are disadvantaged. The lack of diversity at senior levels in all types of organisation is moreover a moral scar on us all. The problem for boards may be nomination committees discriminating in favour of people like themselves (let's be honest, here; pale, male, and perhaps stale), and maybe there is insufficient diversity in candidates with the knowledge and experience demanded. In my experience head-hunters and the vast majority of nomination committees are really trying to overcome conscious and unconscious bias. Pressure for greater diversity is helping to pull up more female candidates, especially non-execs. Ethnic diversity is much harder as it seems to be routed in deeper problems in society generally, but we must try harder.

Priorities two and three for boards are having directors who are experienced and well-informed. Experience doesn't have to be in being a director. It can be in being a business customer (for example, a marketing agency choosing a director with fast moving consumer goods experience) or specialist technical background. Diversity of experience is also important, and that is a key reason why boards need more females and different ethnicities. To get that diversity, realistically at present, a board may well need to be less dogmatic on the level of senior business experience for some candidates. Apparent positive discrimination is needed in comparing the different business experiences of female and ethnic minority candidates, but in reality, it's simply a trade-off between *different* experiences.

The need for more informed directors is always rising, as the demands on boards grow. We need more help for inexperienced directors and more development for those who think they are experienced. There is a corpus of basic knowledge of ways things happen and tips on how to make things better that is missing from most board education. This is especially important for aspirant directors who don't have prior public board experience. I very much hope that this book can contribute especially to those who need to get up to speed with board life to face such challenges.

Boardrooms need to open up more to the outside world generally. Being a board director is a closed door to executives below board level, politicians, and even many regulators. Opening up the boardroom, so that more people understand what happens there, is incredibly important for society, it offers the opportunity to understand what boards can and can't do. Business has historically been terrible at doing this. Directors are too busy coping with their own businesses to campaign for better public understanding of boards and business. They often struggle with the new regulatory requirements, let alone responding to yet another government or FRC consultation on new rules. Those that do are likely to be self-selecting in being larger companies; those coasting, rather than struggling.

That's not good enough. Directors should do more to talk about what they do. It would certainly be great to see, for example, more schools and universities inviting board directors in to talk about what it is like to work at the top of business. If that would encourage more females and more people from ethnic communities into business, and into dreaming of joining a board, that would be a major win. Greater diversity in business must start in young adults by spreading greater self-belief, and interest in business, around people from all sorts of backgrounds.

Broader lessons

There are also some wider lessons, I think, that come out from these pages, because serving on a board has many characteristics in common with other areas of life and cooperating in groups.

Make evidence-based decisions: Making good decisions isn't about always getting the best outcome as judged by 20:20 hindsight. That's just not possible. It is about using the *information* that you have at the time to make a rational decision. This includes identifying when you need more information to make a decision, as exemplified by the need, emphasised in this book for directors to keep asking questions, so that they never approve something they don't fully understand. Sadly, corporate governance regulation repeatedly fails this test, with little or no actual evidence basis being used for new rules.

Take risk-based decisions: This book stresses that risk is not a tick box governance activity, it is the heart of all good decision-making. Every action – or indeed inaction – has risks, and these must be considered for a good decision to be made. We need to think through what might happen, how we can lessen the chances of that event occurring, and how can we reduce the undesirable effects if it did. This requires us always to think through the worst-case outcome; how might this come about, how would we respond, and can we tolerate that event?

Don't leap unless you have to: Speed of decision and action has its place. If you fall into a pool of crocodiles, speed is pretty important. Otherwise, if you can avoid rushing decisions and actions, you may well deliver a better outcome. This doesn't mean prevarication or analysis paralysis. But if you can delay a decision to get more information or to reconsider the risk, and you can do so with little cost, you should try to do so.

Prototype, test and only then roll-out: This is a case of taking your time in implementing an action. If you are faced with building six flat-pack chairs, you would do well to build one completely first and test that it's okay, before starting the other five. It's not a great idea to be already rolling out an idea – or mandating it nationally - when you discover a fundamental problem and have to start all over again. Don't be fooled by enthusiasts who argue that you have no time and something that works in theory must be rolled out immediately.

It's not just boards that can fall into this error. Corporate governance legislators don't even bother prototyping, let alone testing, but go straight from consulting the 'great and the good' to mandating it. The very people who lecture boards about taking good decisions, castigate those who make ones that deliver poor outcomes, and insist that we conduct risk reviews, are precisely the ones who legislate without seeking evidence, without conducting good decision-making processes, don't conduct risk reviews and don't test for outcomes.

Always give yourself wiggle room: The world is an unpredictable place; the unexpected always happens and people change their minds. Always, if you possibly can, give yourself discretion to change your mind or your decision. I've lost count of the times that I have encouraged boards to give ourselves some wiggle room, and I've lost count of the times that we've been glad of it. Whether this is giving discretion to remuneration committees, delaying a final sign off on a decision to the last minute, or not telling others too much about future plans (which might change), this is just a form of risk management.

Always try to do the right thing: Most people have advisers, friends and family whispering in their ears about decisions. Some will have ulterior motives, some will have different incentives and objectives, and others will be well-meaning and be perhaps right and perhaps wrong. In the end, we should try to do what *we* think is right. If it is our decision, we have to take responsibility, listen to others but in the end, apply our own judgement. If in doubt about your decision, think how it would look on Twitter, or the front page of the Daily Mail or Financial Times.

A final word on being a board director

This book has opened the door a little into the boardroom. It has explained how to get on to a board, how to get on with decisions in the boardroom and how to make a difference with those decisions while you're there. There is a lot to learn and experience to equip someone to enter the boardroom, and there is even more to learn once they sit down at the table. The boardroom is a microcosm of life. There is a great deal of specialist knowledge required to sit there, but on top of this, boardrooms reflect many aspects of life.

It is not beyond anyone with ability, who is keen to learn and can gain good, useful experience to enter the boardroom. And the boardroom is a licence to learn more about business, power and people, and then to use that knowledge to make a better society. What could be more exciting?

Appendix

A Case Study of The Wielding of Large Shareholder Power

The Mitchells & Butlers shareholder dispute, as described by the company at the time in a letter to all shareholders

17 December 2009

Letter to Shareholders from the Board of Directors

The following letter has been posted to shareholders today:

Dear Shareholder

We thought it would be helpful if we detailed some of the events which have happened since the publication of the 2009 Annual report and accounts of the Company (the 'Accounts').

In this letter we explain the background to the appointment and recent removal from the Board of four Non-Executive Directors, the appointment of Simon Laffin as the chairman of the Company and, most importantly, ask for your support at the Annual General Meeting for resolutions proposed by the Board, especially in re-electing both Antony Bates and Simon Laffin as Directors.

Appointment of the Four Directors

Since October 2008, the Company's two largest shareholders have been Piedmont Inc, an investment vehicle whose ultimate owner is Joe Lewis, which currently holds 22.8% of the equity of this Company, and Elpida Group Ltd ('Elpida'), owned by John Magnier and JP McManus, which holds 17.6%.

In April 2009, Leo Fund, owning at the time 5.6% of our shares, requested that the Board appoint Denis Jackson and Ray MacSharry as new independent Directors. Leo Fund subsequently informed the Board on various occasions that unless the Board agreed to its request it would requisition a shareholders' meeting. On 24 June 2009 Leo Fund told the Company it had prepared a requisition to convene an EGM to propose a resolution to appoint Mr Jackson and Mr Mac-Sharry as Directors. Representatives of Leo Fund said they believed that Elpida and Piedmont Inc, who together with Leo Fund held over 40% of the Company's shares at the time, would vote in favour of that resolution. The Board therefore felt that it had little choice but to appoint them as Directors, but required Mr Jackson and Mr MacSharry to confirm their independence in writing, which they subsequently did. They were therefore appointed to the Board on 28 August 2009.

After Leo Fund's request, Piedmont Inc implemented its right to appoint up to two representative non independent Directors to the Board and therefore on 16 July 2009, Richard McGuire was appointed and on 18 November 2009 Douglas E McMahon was also so appointed. (This was because, at Piedmont Inc's request, the Company had previously agreed in principle in October 2008, that it should have the right to appoint up to two non-independent representative Directors for so long as it retained its shareholding in the Company.)

Why the Four Directors Were Removed

The Board believes that it is imperative that both collectively and individually Directors should represent and protect the interest of all shareholders. However, during November a number of concerning events took place:-

1. 15 November 2009 - chairman Appointment

Mr McGuire, a Director nominated by Piedmont Inc, informed the Board on 15 November 2009 at the final stage of the recruitment process, despite having been involved from the outset, that Piedmont Inc would not support the appointment of any of the three high quality independent candidates short listed.

2. 17 November - Position of the Senior Independent Director

On 17 November, Mr McGuire informed Mr Laffin, the then Senior Independent Director that "a small number of large shareholders" would vote against his re-election at the AGM. Mr McGuire said that he thought it better in fact if Mr Laffin did not stand at all. This conversation was subsequently confirmed in a telephone call that same day between Mr McGuire and the then chairman, Drummond Hall. At that point, the majority of the Board felt that the role of the Senior Independent Director was being improperly influenced by Piedmont Inc and its representative on the Board.

3. Conduct on the Evening of 25 November 2009

Whilst during their appointment it was notable that the four Directors appeared to have a consistent view on a variety of business issues and that these views differed from that of the rest of the Board, it is not unusual, in the normal business of a Board, to have differences of opinion between Directors on matters being reviewed.

However, on 25 November (the day before the Final Results were to be published), Mr McGuire decided to withdraw his responsibility statement (effectively a letter to the Auditors from each Director confirming that all known facts had been disclosed in respect of matters in the Accounts), despite very clear advice from the Company's Auditors and other advisers on the Accounts.

This was followed by Mr Jackson withdrawing his responsibility statement, stating that if Mr McGuire did not reinstate his responsibility statement then neither would he.

Mr MacSharry then also stated that unless agreement could be reached with Mr McGuire then he would also withdraw his responsibility statement.

Finally, Mr McMahon, who had not at that point signed a responsibility statement, also made it clear that he would not be signing it until Mr McGuire had reinstated his.

Shortly before midnight Mr McGuire reinstated his responsibility statement, an action that was then followed by Mr Jackson and Mr MacSharry and Mr McMahon signed his. The Accounts were duly published without any reservations or qualification.

4. Discussion on 27 November 2009

On 27 November, your Board made a further attempt to find an accommodation with the Company's largest shareholder. Adam Fowle spoke directly to Joe Lewis at some length that afternoon. It became clear during this phone call that agreement could not be reached with Mr Lewis over the appointment of an independent chairman.

Response by your Board

Following increasing press speculation and market rumour, your Board therefore felt that it had no alternative, and was strongly advised by all its advisers, that it had to draw shareholders' attention as soon as practicable to the increasingly difficult relationship between the Board and Piedmont Inc's representative, as set out in the announcement made by the Company on 30 November 2009.

Whilst the Board welcomes all constructive input into its decision-making process, it was felt by a majority of the Board that the actions of these four individual Directors indicated that they appeared not to be exercising judgment independently of each other, in the interests of all shareholders. Therefore, it was concluded that it was becoming extremely difficult for the Board to operate in the interests of all shareholders and that furthermore, the Executive Directors were being distracted from focusing on driving the operational outperformance of the Company for the best prospects of success of the Company.

The Executive Directors and the other Non-Executive Directors also considered that it was important to maintain a Board with a majority of independent Directors, who could ensure that the business was run efficiently for the benefit of all shareholders.

It was known to the Board (but possibly not Mr McMahon) that Sara Weller was intending to retire at the January 2010 AGM, that Mr Hall was also shortly stepping down from the Board, and that Mr Laffin had been threatened with being voted off at the AGM. In addition, Mr Bates will also be standing for re-election at the same meeting. It has not been practical to recruit and appoint replacement new Non-Executive Directors in the last few months, particularly as Piedmont Inc's representative had been reluctant to allow progress on this. This could have left the Board post the AGM with only two independent Directors (Sir Tim Lankester and Antony Bates), two Executive Directors and the other four Directors.

The Board therefore decided, in its duty to have a fully functioning independent Board for all shareholders, that it had to remove the four Directors as set out above. It also decided to ask Mr Laffin to become chairman as he had the skills and experience to lead the Board through this difficult time.

Since these events, your Board is back working effectively, leading and supporting executive management in their core job which they do best; that of running pubs efficiently and effectively, serving our millions of customers.

Why We Need Your Support

With over 40% of the equity in the hands of Piedmont Inc and Elpida, these two shareholders could together have a sufficient number of votes to defeat any resolutions put by your Board on behalf of all shareholders at the AGM on 28 January 2010. In situations such as these, every single vote counts.

Therefore, we would ask you to support all resolutions being put to the meeting and recommended to you by your Board. In particular, the Board feels that it is essential to retain a majority of strong independent Directors and so urges you to vote for the re-election of both Mr Bates and Mr Laffin. We sincerely trust that we can count on your support.

Yours sincerely

The Board of Mitchells & Butlers plc

Subsequent Events

In fact, Piedmont and Elpida successfully used their voting strength to remove me as chairman as well as the other independent directors, installing their own slate, in January 2010, led by John Lovering as chairman. Lovering lasted a year. He was replaced as chairman by Simon Burke, in February 2011, followed by the resignation, the following month, of the highly talented CEO, Adam Fowle. Simon Burke himself then resigned six months later in July 2011.

Who says that boards are boring?

Useful Resources

Books, Reports & Articles:

Animal Farm by George Orwell

Brand You: Turn Your Unique Talents into a Winning Formula by John Purkis

Corporate Fraud by Geraldine Lawlor of KPMG Forensic: October 2020

Guidance on Risk Management, Internal Control and Related Financial and Business by the **Financial Reporting Council**

How to Decide by Annie Duke

Meltdown: Why Our Systems Fail and What We Can Do About It by Chris Clearfield and Andra Tilcsik

Mistakes Were Made, But Not By Me by Carol Tavris and Elliot Aronson

Normal Accidents by Charles Perrow

The Grocers – the rise and rise of the supermarket chains by Andrew Seth and Geoffrey Randall

The Prince by Niccolo Machiavelli

The Run on the Rock, House of Commons Treasury Select Committee 2008

The Signal and the Noise: The Art and Science of Prediction by Nate Silver

The Signs Were There: The clues for investors that a company is heading for a fall by Tim Steer

The Snowball. Warren Buffet and the Business of Life by Alice Schroeder

The Stranger by Georg Simmel, Soziologie, 1908

The Trusted Advisor by Maister, Green and Galford

Thinking, Fast and Slow by Daniel Kahneman

Trolley Wars. The Battle of the Supermarkets by Judi Bevan

UK Corporate Governance Code

Websites:

CAA website on risk and safety management:

www.caa.co.uk/Safety-initiatives-and-resources/Working-with-industry/Safety-management-systems/Safety-management-systems/

Financial Reporting Council:

www.frc.org.uk/document-library/corporate-governance/2014/guidance-on-risk-management,-internal-control-and

McKinsey:

www.mckinsey.com/business-functions/strategy-and-corporate-finance/our-insights

Principles of the Pre-Emption Group:

www.sway.office.com/HHPgz98MJB2jfEqM?loc=swsp

Simon Laffin: www.simonlaffin.com

Index